BLOOM



# Olympiad ACE

## A Comprehensive Practice Book

for School Olympiads & Talent Search Exams

# MATHS

## Class 9

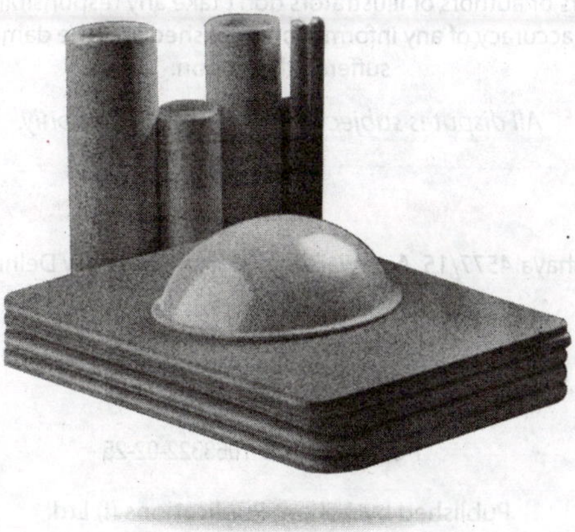

by

Amit Rastogi

Olympiad ACE

BLOOM

Bloom Cap Edu Ventures Pvt. Ltd.




卐 **Administrative & Production Office**

'Ramchhaya' 4577/15, Agarwal Road, Darya Ganj, New Delhi -110002

Tele: 011- 47630600, 43518550

卐 **PRICE:** ₹125.00

卐 PO No. : TXT-59-T063322-02-25

Published by Arihant Publications (I) Ltd.

For further information about the books log on to
www.bloomcap.org

Follow us on

# Preface

*"Future belongs to those Who prepares for it today"*

School Olympiads are National & International level competitions conducted by different Government, Non-Government & Educational Organisations with the purpose of making the children ready to face competitive exams. The challenging Questions asked in Olympiads motivate them to learn more & more and bring out the best result with improved academic performance. The Awards & Scholarship offered in Olympiads motivate children to aspire & strive for doing better and emerge out to be the best.

## Maths Olympiads

Mathematics is an integral part of all competitive exams be it Aptitude or Commerce or Science. Maths Olympiads are meant to develop Mathematical aptitude in school students. They provide students with an opportunity to master their concepts and comprehend tricky questions effortlessly. Challenging Questions of Maths Olympiads encourage students to develop a logical approach to solve Mathematical Problems.

**'Bloom Mathematics Olympiad Study Book Class 9'** is a perfect resource to Study & Practice for Olympiad Exams and other National & State Level Talent Search Exams & Other Competitions.

**Some Special Features of Bloom Maths Olympiad Study Books are;**

- Chapterwise Exercises having different types of Objective Questions at par with the Olympiad Level.
- Detailed Explanation for each question.
- Olympiad Pattern Practice Sets at the end.

This book is prepared by Expert Panel with the utmost care, still if you have any suggestions regarding its improvement, then feel free to contact us at support@bloomcap.org. We will try to inculcate your suggestions in the further editions.

# Contents


| | | |
|---|---|---|
| 01. | Number Systems | 1-3 |
| 02. | Polynomials | 4-6 |
| 03. | Linear Equations in Two Variables | 7-10 |
| 04. | Coordinate Geometry | 11-13 |
| 05. | Lines and Angles | 14-18 |
| 06. | Triangles | 19-24 |
| 07. | Quadrilaterals | 25-29 |
| 08. | Circle | 30-34 |
| 09. | Surface Area of Solid Figures | 35-39 |
| 10. | Statistics | 40-43 |
| • | Practice Set 1 | 44-50 |
| • | Practice Set 2 | 51-56 |
| • | Hints & Solutions | 57-91 |

Chapter 01

# Number Systems

## 1 Mark Questions

1. The sum of two irrational numbers always produces an irrational number.
(a) True (b) False
(c) Can't say (d) None of these

2. The sum of a rational number and an irrational number is a/an
(a) rational number (b) irrational number
(c) Not defined (d) None of the above

3. Which of the following option is correct?
(a) 0 is a positive integer
(b) 0 is a negative integer
(c) Every natural number is a whole number
(d) $\sqrt{2}$ is a rational number

4. The product of a rational number and its reciprocal is
(a) 0 (b) 1
(c) –1 (d) None of these

5. If $\frac{(2-\sqrt{5})+(3+2\sqrt{5})-(4+\sqrt{5})}{4} = p+q\sqrt{5}$, then the values of $p$ and $q$ are
(a) $\frac{1}{4}$ and 2 (b) $-\frac{1}{4}$ and $-\frac{2}{4}$
(c) $\frac{1}{4}$ and 0 (d) $-\frac{1}{4}$ and 0

6. The rational form $\left(\frac{p}{q}\right)$ of mixed recurring decimal number $1.\overline{37}$ is
(a) $\frac{136}{99}$ (b) $\frac{135}{99}$ (c) $\frac{137}{100}$ (d) $\frac{137}{99}$

7. If the number $x = 1.242424\ldots$ can be expressed in the form of $x = \frac{p}{q}$, where $p$ and $q$ are positive integers having no common factor. Then, the value of $(p+q)$ is
(a) 72 (b) 74
(c) 53 (d) 41

8. An irrational number between $\frac{3}{7}$ and $\frac{5}{7}$ is ______.
(a) $\frac{15}{7}$ (b) $\frac{\sqrt{15}}{7}$
(c) $\frac{15}{49}$ (d) $\frac{4}{7}$

9. Rational number $\frac{-23}{2}$ lies between consecutive integers is ______.
(a) –2 and –3 (b) –7 and –12
(c) –7 and –9 (d) –8 and –15

10. If $\sqrt{32-x\sqrt{15}}=\sqrt{27}+\sqrt{5}$, then what is the value of $x$?

(a) −5 (b) −6
(c) −4 (d) −2

11. After simplification, the value of $\frac{3}{5-\sqrt{3}}+\frac{2}{5+\sqrt{3}}$ is

(a) $\frac{\sqrt{28}}{22}$ (b) $\frac{\sqrt{28}}{28}$
(c) $\frac{25+\sqrt{3}}{22}$ (d) $\frac{\sqrt{25}+\sqrt{3}}{22}$

12. If $x=\sqrt{6}+\sqrt{5}$, then the value of $x^2+\frac{1}{x^2}-2$ is

(a) $2\sqrt{6}$ (b) $2\sqrt{5}$
(c) 24 (d) 20

13. If $a+\frac{1}{a}=\frac{1}{\sqrt{3}-1}$, then the value of $a^2+\frac{1}{a^2}$ is

(a) 3 (b) $-1+\frac{\sqrt{3}}{2}$
(c) $2\sqrt{3}$ (d) $4\sqrt{3}$

14. If $m$ and $n$ are positive integers, then for a positive number $a$, $\{\sqrt[m]{(\sqrt[n]{a})}\}^{mn}$ is

(a) $a^{mn}$ (b) $a$ (c) $a^{m/n}$ (d) 1

15. If $25^{x-1}=5^{2x-1}-100$, then the value of $x$ is

(a) 3 (b) 2
(c) 4 (d) 1

16. If $\sqrt{2^n}=1024$, then the value of $3^{2\left(\frac{n}{4}-4\right)}$ is

(a) 3 (b) 9
(c) 27 (d) 81

17. The rationalising factor of $\sqrt[7]{a^4b^3c^5}$ is

(a) $\sqrt[7]{a^3b^3c^2}$ (b) $\sqrt[7]{a^3b^4c^2}$
(c) $\sqrt[7]{a^2b^3c^3}$ (d) $\sqrt[7]{a^2b^4c^3}$

18. If $\sqrt[3]{x^2}-5\sqrt[3]{x}+6=0$, then the values of $x$ are

(a) 3 and 8 (b) 8 and 4
(c) 8 and 27 (d) 27 and 5

19. $(\sqrt[6]{15-2\sqrt{56}})(\sqrt[3]{\sqrt{7}+2\sqrt{2}})$ is equal to

(a) 0 (b) 1
(c) 2 (d) None of these

20. The value of $\left(\frac{x^a}{x^b}\right)^{a+b}\cdot\left(\frac{x^b}{x^c}\right)^{b+c}\cdot\left(\frac{x^c}{x^a}\right)^{c+a}$ is

(a) 0 (b) 1
(c) $x$ (d) None of these

21. If $a^x=c^q=b$ and $c^y=a^z=d$, then which one of the following is correct?

(a) $xy=qz$ (b) $\frac{x}{y}=\frac{q}{z}$
(c) $x+y=q+z$ (d) $x-y=q-z$

22. Which one is greatest out of $\sqrt{2}$, $\sqrt[6]{3}$, $\sqrt[3]{4}$ and $\sqrt[4]{5}$?

(a) $\sqrt[3]{4}$ (b) $\sqrt[4]{5}$
(c) $\sqrt{2}$ (d) $\sqrt[6]{3}$

## 2 Marks Questions

23. If $x = \frac{\sqrt{5}+\sqrt{3}}{\sqrt{5}-\sqrt{3}}$ and $y = \frac{\sqrt{5}-\sqrt{3}}{\sqrt{5}+\sqrt{3}}$, then the value of $x^2 + y^2 + xy$ is

(a) 48 (b) 57
(c) 67 (d) 63

24. $\frac{\sqrt{15+4\sqrt{11}}}{\sqrt{31+8\sqrt{15}}} \times \frac{1}{8+4\sqrt{11}-\sqrt{165}-2\sqrt{15}}$ is

(a) 0 (b) 1
(c) 2 (d) $\sqrt{15}+\sqrt{11}$

25. Match the following:

| | List I | | List II |
|---|---|---|---|
| A. | $\left\{\sqrt[m]{\sqrt[n]{\frac{1}{a}}}\right\}^{mn}$ is | i. | $\frac{3}{10} \times \frac{3}{10} \times \frac{3}{10}$ |
| B. | If $\frac{2^{m+n}}{2^{n-m}} = 16$, then $m$ is | ii. | $\frac{xy}{x+y}$ |
| C. | $\left(\frac{100}{9}\right)^{-3/2}$ is | iii. | $\frac{1}{a}$ |
| D. | $(x^{-1}+y^{-1})^{-1}$ is | iv. | 2 |

**Codes**

| | A | B | C | D |
|---|---|---|---|---|
| (a) | (i) | (ii) | (iii) | (iv) |
| (b) | (iii) | (iv) | (i) | (ii) |
| (c) | (iv) | (iii) | (i) | (ii) |
| (d) | (iii) | (ii) | (iv) | (i) |

26. Which of the following is not correct?

(a) The product of $\sqrt[3]{2}$ and $\sqrt[4]{3}$ is $(432)^{1/12}$.

(b) The rational factor of $(\sqrt{a}+\sqrt{b})$ is $-(\sqrt{a}+\sqrt{b})$.

(c) $(5+\sqrt{5})(5-\sqrt{5})$ is equal to 20.

(d) $\sqrt{10} \times \sqrt{15}$ is equal to $5\sqrt{6}$.

27. Match the following:

| | List I | | List II |
|---|---|---|---|
| A. | $\frac{2}{\sqrt{7}} = \frac{a\sqrt{7}}{7}, a = ?$ | i. | $\sqrt[3]{2}$ |
| B. | $\left(\sqrt[6]{27} - \sqrt{6\frac{3}{4}}\right)^2 = ?$ | ii. | 2 |
| C. | The rationalising factor of $\frac{\sqrt{3}+1}{2-\sqrt{3}}$ is | iii. | $\frac{3}{4}$ |
| D. | The greatest among $\sqrt[9]{4}, \sqrt[6]{3}$ and $\sqrt[3]{2}$ is | iv. | $5-3\sqrt{3}$ |

**Codes**

| | A | B | C | D |
|---|---|---|---|---|
| (a) | (i) | (ii) | (iii) | (iv) |
| (b) | (ii) | (iii) | (iv) | (i) |
| (c) | (iii) | (ii) | (iv) | (i) |
| (d) | (i) | (iii) | (ii) | (iv) |

28. The value of the expression $\frac{1}{1+\sqrt{2}} + \frac{1}{\sqrt{2}+\sqrt{3}} + \frac{1}{\sqrt{3}+\sqrt{4}} + \ldots + \frac{1}{\sqrt{8}+\sqrt{9}}$ is

(a) 0 (b) 1 (c) 2 (d) 4

29. If $x = 2-\sqrt{3}$, then the value of $x^2 - \frac{1}{x^2}$ and $x^2 + \frac{1}{x^2}$ respectively are

(a) $8\sqrt{3}, 14$ (b) 8, 14
(c) $-8\sqrt{3}, 14$ (d) $7\sqrt{3}, 15$

30. If $\frac{3+2\sqrt{5}}{3-2\sqrt{5}} = (p+q\sqrt{5})$, then the value of $22(p-q)$ is

(a) 34 (b) 35
(c) $-34$ (d) 37

Chapter 02

# Polynomials

## 1 Mark Questions

**1.** The degree of expression, when $x - y$ is subtracted from $x^3 - y^3$, will be

(a) 0 (b) 3

(c) 2 (d) 1

**2.** If $x = \frac{5}{2}$ is a zero of the polynomial $2x^2 + 2kx - 12$, then the value of $k$ is

(a) $\frac{1}{10}$ (b) $-\frac{1}{10}$

(c) $\frac{3}{10}$ (d) $\frac{7}{10}$

**3.** If $p(x) = x^2 - 2\sqrt{2}x + 1$, then the value of $p(2\sqrt{2})$ is

(a) 1 (b) $-1$

(c) 3 (d) 4

**4.** If $p(x) = x^3 - x^2 + x + 1$, then the value of $\frac{p(1) + p(-1)}{2}$ is

(a) 5 (b) 2

(c) 0 (d) $-2$

**5.** If $x = 3$ and $x = 0$ are zeroes of the polynomial $2x^3 - 8x^2 + ax + b$, then the value of $(a + b)$ is

(a) 5 (b) 4

(c) 6 (d) 3

**6.** What will be the values of $a$ and $b$, so that the polynomial $x^3 + 10x^2 + ax + b$ is exactly divisible by $x - 1$ as well as $x - 2$?

(a) 37 and 26 (b) $-37$ and 26

(c) 37 and $-26$ (d) $-37$ and $-26$

**7.** The value of $k$ for which $(x + 2)$ is a factor of $(x + 1)^7 + (3x + k)^3$ is

(a) $-7$ (b) 7

(c) $-1$ (d) $-6 - 3^{7/3}$

**8.** If $(x + 1)$ is a factor of $ax^4 + bx^3 + cx^2 + dx + e$, then the relation among $a$, $b$, $c$, $d$ and $e$ is

(a) $a + c + e = b + d$ (b) $b + d > a + c + e$

(c) $a + c + e > b + d$ (d) None of these

**9.** If 2 is a zero of $x^3 - 7x + 6$, then other zeroes are

(a) $-1$ and 3 (b) 1 and $-3$

(c) 1 and $-2$ (d) $-1$ and $-2$

**10.** If $(x + a)$ is a common factor of $(x^2 + px + q)$ and $(x^2 + lx + m)$, then the value of $a$ is

(a) $m - q$ (b) $m + q$

(c) $\frac{m + q}{l - p}$ (d) $\frac{m - q}{l - p}$

**11.** $x^3 + y^3 + z^3 = 3xyz$, if and only if

(a) $x = y = z$ (b) $x + y = z$
(c) $x + y = -z$ (d) None of these

**12.** The factors of $6x^2 + 17x + 5$ are

(a) $(3x-1)(2x-5)$ (b) $(3x+1)(2x-5)$
(c) $(2x+5)(3x-1)$ (d) $(3x+1)(2x+5)$

**13.** If $(x-3)$ is one factor of $x^2 + ax - 4 = 0$ and $x^2 - 4x + b = 0$, then $2a - b$ is equal to

(a) $\frac{13}{3}$ (b) $\frac{-19}{3}$ (c) 6 (d) $-4$

**14.** Factorize $a^5b - ab^5$

(a) $ab(a-b)(a^2+b^2)$
(b) $ab(a-b)(a+b)(a^2+b^2)$
(c) $(a-b)^2(a+b)(a^2+b^2)$
(d) None of the above

**15.** If $(a+b+c) = 9$ and $ab + bc + ca = 23$, then the value of $a^3 + b^3 + c^3 - 3abc$ is

(a) 108 (b) 207 (c) 669 (d) 729

**16.** $(p-q)^6 - 27r^3$ is equal to

(a) $\{(p-q)^3 + 3r\}\{(p-q)^3 - 3r^2\}$
(b) $\{(p-q)^2 - 3r\}\{(p-q)^4 + 9r^2 + (p-q)^2 3r\}$
(c) Both (a) and (b)
(d) None of the above

**17.** $xya^2 = (x-y)^2(a+1)$, then the value of $1 + \frac{4}{a} + \frac{4}{a^2}$ is

(a) $\frac{(x-y)^2}{(x+y)^2}$ (b) $\left(\frac{x+y}{x-y}\right)^2$

(c) $\left(\frac{x}{x+y}\right)^2$ (d) $\left(\frac{y-x}{y}\right)$

**18.** If $a - b = 6$ and $a^2 - b^2 = 222$, then value of $a^3 - b^3$ is .........

(a) 1890 (b) 6895
(c) 6214 (d) 1885

**19.** Which of the following is a possible expression for the length and breadth of the rectangle, whose area is given by $4a^2 + 4a - 3$?

(a) $(2a+1)$ and $(2a+3)$
(b) $(2a-1)$ and $(2a+3)$
(c) $(a+1)$ and $(2a+3)$
(d) None of the above

**20.** $(x+y)(x-y)(x^2+xy+y^2)(x^2-xy+y^2)$ is equal to

(a) $x^6 + y^6$ (b) $x^6 - y^6$
(c) $x^3 - y^3$ (d) $(x+y)^6$

**21.** The value of $P$, if

$$\frac{a^2 - 19a - 25}{a-7} = a - 12 + \frac{P}{a-7}, \text{ is}$$

(a) $-109$ (b) 110 (c) 109 (d) 110

**22.** Length, breadth and height of a cuboidal tank are $(2x-y)$ m, $(2x+y)$ m and $(4x^2+y^2)$ m respectively, Find the volume of the tank.

(a) $(4x^3 + 12xy + y^3)\ \text{m}^3$
(b) $(4x^4 + 12x^2y^2 + y^4)\ \text{m}^3$
(c) $(16x^4 - y^4)\ \text{m}^3$
(d) $(16x^4 + y^4)\ \text{m}^3$

**23.** If $\frac{a}{b} + \frac{b}{a} = 1$, then the value of $a^3 + b^3$ is

(a) 1 (b) $-1$ (c) 1/2 (d) 0

**24.** If $x^2 + 2x = 45$, then the value of $x^4 + 4x^3 + 4x^2 - 13$ is

(a) 2010 (b) 2015
(c) 2012 (d) 2025

**25.** If $a^2 + b^2 + c^2 + 3 = 2a - 2b + 2c$, then $(a+b-c)^3$ is equal to

(a) 0 (b) $-1$
(c) $-2$ (d) None of these

## 2 Marks Questions

**26.** Match the following:

| List I | List II |
|---|---|
| A. If $(ax+b)$ is a factor of $p(x)$, then | i. $n \in$ positive odd integer |
| B. $(x+a)$ is a factor of $(x^n+a^n)$, if | ii. $p\left(\frac{-b}{a}\right)=0$ |
| C. Factorize : $a^3b-b^3a$ is | iii. $\frac{4}{3}$ |
| D. Zeroes of polynomial $3x-4$ is | iv. $ab(a+b)(a-b)$ |

**Codes**

| | A | B | C | D |
|---|---|---|---|---|
| (a) | (i) | (ii) | (iii) | (iv) |
| (b) | (ii) | (i) | (iv) | (iii) |
| (c) | (i) | (iii) | (ii) | (iv) |
| (d) | (i) | (ii) | (iv) | (iii) |

**27.** Match the following:

| List I | List II |
|---|---|
| A. $98 \times 102$ is equal to | i. $a^3+b^3+c^3-3abc$ |
| B. $\frac{1}{2}(a+b+c)\{(a-b)^2+(b-c)^2+(c-a)^2\}$ is | ii. 18 |
| C. If $a^{1/3}+b^{1/3}+c^{1/3}=0$, then | iii. 9996 |
| D. $(-1)^3-(2)^3+(3)^3$ is equal to | iv. $(a+b+c)^3=27abc$ |

**Codes**

| | A | B | C | D |
|---|---|---|---|---|
| (a) | (i) | (ii) | (iii) | (iv) |
| (b) | (iii) | (i) | (iv) | (ii) |
| (c) | (ii) | (iv) | (i) | (iii) |
| (d) | (iv) | (ii) | (i) | (iii) |

**28.** If $x=\frac{1}{a}$, $y=\frac{1}{b}$ and $z=\frac{1}{c}$, then $\left(\frac{1}{x}+\frac{1}{y}+\frac{1}{z}\right)^2-\left(\frac{2}{xy}+\frac{2}{yz}+\frac{2}{zx}\right)$ is equal to

(a) $a^2+b^2+c^2$ (b) $\frac{1}{a^2}+\frac{1}{b^2}+\frac{1}{c^2}$

(c) 0 (d) 1

**29.** Study the given statements carefully.

**Statement I**

$$\frac{(a^2-b^2)^3+(b^2-c^2)^3+(c^2-a^2)^3}{(a+b)^3+(b+c)^3+(c+a)^3}=(a+b)(b+c)(c+a)$$

**Statement II**

$$a^2+b^2+c^2-ab-bc-ca=\frac{1}{2}[(a-b)^2+(b-c)^2+(c-a)^2]$$

Which of the following options holds?

(a) Both Statement-I and Statement-II are true

(b) Statement-I is true but Statement-II is false

(c) Statement-I is false but Statement-II is true

(d) Both Statement-I and Statement-II are false

**30.** Factorize : $x^4-81y^4$

(a) $(x-3y)(x+3y)(x^2+9y^2)$

(b) $(x+3y)^2(x^2+9y^2)$

(c) $(x-3y)(x+3y)^2$

(d) $(x^2+9y^2)(x-3y)$

**31.** If $x+y+z=1$, $xy+yz+zx=-1$ and $xyz=-1$, then the value of $x^3+y^3+z^3$ is

(a) 1 (b) $-1$

(c) 2 (d) 3

Chapter 03

# Linear Equations in Two Variables

## 1 Mark Questions

**1.** Which of the following are not linear equation?

(a) $3x^2 - 5x + 3 = x^2 + 7x - 1$

(b) $\frac{3 - x^2 + x}{2} = \frac{4x - 2x^2 + 5}{4}$

(c) $\frac{11x + 5}{13} - \frac{12x - 3}{4} = \frac{1}{5}$

(d) $\frac{4x^2 + 2x^3 + 5}{4} = \frac{x^3 + 2x^2 + x}{2}$

**2.** $ax + by + c = 0$ does not represent an equation in two variables, if

(a) $a = c = 0$ and $b \neq 0$

(b) $b = c = 0$ and $a \neq 0$

(c) $a = b = 0$

(d) $c = 0, a \neq 0$ and $b \neq 0$

**3.** The equation $x = 7$ in two variables can be written as

(a) $1 \cdot x + 1 \cdot y = 7$ (b) $1 \cdot x + 0 \cdot y = 7$

(c) $0 \cdot x + 1 \cdot y = 7$ (d) $0 \cdot x + 0 \cdot y = 7$

**4.** If (2, 0) is a solution of the linear equation $3x + 2y = k/2$, then the value of $k$ is

(a) 4 (b) 3

(c) 2 (d) 12

**5.** Which equation satisfies the values of the table?

| $x$ | $-1$ | 0 | 1 | 2 |
|---|---|---|---|---|
| $y$ | $-3$ | $-1$ | 1 | 3 |

(a) $y = x - 2$

(b) $y = 2x - 1$

(c) $y = 3x - 3$

(d) $y = x + 1$

**6.** If linear equation $2x + cy = 8$ has equal values of $x$ and $y$, then the value of $c$, when value of $x = 1$, will be

(a) 6 (b) 3

(c) 4 (d) 1

**7.** Any solution of the linear equation $2x + 0 \cdot y = 9$ in two variables is of the form

(a) $\left(\frac{9}{2}, 0\right)$

(b) $\left(\frac{9}{2}, n\right)$, where $n$ is a real number

(c) $\left(n, \frac{9}{2}\right)$, where $n$ is a real number

(d) $\left(0, \frac{9}{2}\right)$

**8.** If $x = -2$ and $y = 3$ is a solution of the equation $3x + 5y = a^2$, then the value of $a$ is

(a) 19 (b) $-21$ (c) $\pm 3$ (d) $-18$

**9.** If $[(a+b), (a-b)]$ is the solution of the equations $3x + 2y = 20$ and $4x - 5y = 42$, then the value of $b$ is

(a) 8 (b) $-2$ (c) $-4$ (d) 5

**10.** The value of $k$ in equation $2x + ky = 6$ if $(-2, 2)$ is a solution, is

(a) 5 (b) 4 (c) 8 (d) 6

**11.** The equation $y = 3x + 5n$ has .........

(a) Only two solutions

(b) Only one solutions

(c) Only three solutions

(d) Infinite many solutions

**12.** Point (4,1) lies on the line ...........

(a) $x + 2y = 5$ (b) $2x + y = -6$

(c) $x + 2y = 6$ (d) $x + y = 16$

**13.** The taxi fare in a city is as follows: For the first km, the fare is ₹ 8 and for the subsequent distance, it is ₹ 5 per km. Taking the distance covered as $x$ km and total fare as ₹ $y$. The linear equation for this information is

(a) $5x + y + 3 = 0$ (b) $5x - y + 3 = 0$

(c) $5x + y - 3 = 0$ (d) $5x - y - 3 = 0$

**14.** In an isosceles right angled triangle, if one of the angles is $x°$ and other angle is $y°$ (apart from right angle). Then, $x$ and $y$ are related with equation.

(a) $x - y = 180°$ (b) $x + y = 90°$

(c) $x + y = 180°$ (d) $x - y = 90°$

**15.** The equation of the line passing through the origin (0, 0) is

(a) $y = mx + c$ (b) $y = mx$

(c) $y = b$ (d) $x = a$

**16.** Megacity High School earned ₹ 5100 on tickets Sales for a play. The cost per ticket was ₹ 12. If $t$ represents the number of tickets sold to the play, which of the following equations could be used to determine the number of tickets sold for the play ?

(a) $12 = 5100t$ (b) $12t = 5100$

(c) $t = 5100 - 12$ (d) $t = 5100.12$

**17.** A fraction becomes $\frac{9}{11}$, if 2 is added to both the numerator and the denominator if 3 is added to both the numerator and the denominator it becomes $\frac{5}{6}$. The linear equation for this information is

(a) $6x - 5y = 3$ or $11x - 9y = -4$

(b) $6x - 5y = -3$ or $11x - 9y = -4$

(c) $6x - 5y = -3$ or $11x + 9y = 4$

(d) $-6x - 5y = 3$ or $11x - 9y = 4$

**18.** When numerator of a fraction is increased by 2, the fraction reduces to 1/3. Let numerator and denominator be $x$ and $y$, respectively. Write the given data in form of a linear equation in two variables.

(a) $3x - y + 6 = 0$ (b) $3x + y + 6 = 0$

(c) $3x - y + 8 = 0$ (d) $3x - 5y + 9 = 0$

**19.** If cost of a pen is 3 more than twice the cost of a pencil, then equation that describes the statement is (if cost of a pen is $x$ and cost of a pencil is $y$.)

(a) $2x = y + 3$ (b) $x = 2y + 3$

(c) $2x + y = 0$ (d) Both (a) and (b)

**20.** 5 yr ago, Raju told Rita that he was 10 yr older than your age. Taking Raju's and Rita's present age as $x$ yr and $y$ yr, respectively. Then, the linear equation which represents their age 5 yr ago, is

(a) $x + y = 10$ (b) $x - y = 20$

(c) $x - y = 10$ (d) $x + y = 20$

**21.** In a parking, the space occupied by 10 cars equals to the 4 motorbikes. There are total 140 vehicles in the parking. Then, how many cars are there?

(a) 100 (b) 50 (c) 40 (d) 90

**22.** The cost of 9 chairs and 3 tables is ₹ 306. If the cost of 1 chair is ₹ 25, the cost of 1 table is

(a) ₹ 25 (b) ₹ 27 (c) ₹ 30 (d) ₹ 24

**23.** During vegetable purchase, a shopkeeper tells that cost of 3 kg of potatoes is equal to 2 kg of tomatoes. If the total cost of 3 kg potatoes is 50 then cost of 1 tomato is

(a) ₹ 23 (b) ₹ 15 (c) ₹ 25 (d) ₹ 20

**24.** 2 yr later, a father will be 8 yr more than 3 times the age of his son. Taking the present ages of father and son as $x$ and $y$ respectively, write a linear equation for the above when the son's age is 10 yr. Then, father age will be

(a) 39 yr (b) 40 yr (c) 38 yr (d) 42 yr

**25.** Check whether $x=2$ and $y=1$ is a solution of which of equations ?

A. $2x+5y=9$ B. $\frac{5}{2}x+3y=14$

(a) (A) but not (B)
(b) Both (A) and (B)
(c) Neither (A) nor (B)
(d) None of the above

## 2 Marks Questions

**26.** Match the following:

| | List I | | List II |
|---|---|---|---|
| A. | The degree of a linear equation is | i. | $x+2y=500$ |
| B. | A player $A$ scored $x$ runs and other player $B$ scored $2y$ runs. If both together scored 500 runs, then the equation of this information is | ii. | 1 |
| C. | A linear equation of $ax+by+c=0$ have | iii. | $x-2y=0$ |
| D. | The cost of a book $x$ is twice the cost of a pen $y$, is represented by | iv. | infinite solutions |

**Codes**

| | A | B | C | D |
|---|---|---|---|---|
| (a) | (i) | (ii) | (iii) | (iv) |
| (b) | (ii) | (i) | (iv) | (iii) |
| (c) | (iii) | (iv) | (i) | (ii) |
| (d) | (iv) | (i) | (ii) | (iii) |

**27. Assertion** (A) For all values of $k$, $\left(-\frac{3}{2}, k\right)$ is a solution of the linear equation $2x+3=0$.

**Reason** (R) The linear equation $ax+b=0$ can be expressed as a linear equation in two variables as $ax+y+b=0$.

(a) If both (A) and (R) are correct and (R) in the correct explanation of (A).
(b) If both (A) and (R) are correct, but (R) is not the correct explanation of (A).
(c) If (A) is correct but (R) is incorrect.
(d) If (A) is incorrect but (R) is correct.

**28.** Match the linear equations in Column-I with their solutions in Column-II.

| | Column-I | | Column-II |
|---|---|---|---|
| (A) | $4x+3y=24$ | (i) | $(2,-3)$ |
| (B) | $\frac{x}{2}-\frac{y}{3}=2$ | (ii) | $(2,3)$ |
| (C) | $3x+5y=15$ | (iii) | $(3,4)$ |
| (D) | $\frac{x-2}{3}=y-3$ | (iv) | $\left(3,\frac{6}{5}\right)$ |

(a) (A) → (ii), (B) → (i), (C) → (iv), (D) → (iii)
(b) (A) → (iii), (B) → (i), (C) → (iv), (D) → (ii)
(c) (A) → (ii), (B) → (iv), (C) → (i), (D) → (iii)
(d) (A) → (iii), (B) → (iv), (C) → (i), (D) → (ii)

**29.** Match the following.

| | List I | | List II |
|---|---|---|---|
| A. | $8y=9$ in the form form of linear equation in two variable | (i) | $x-3y-7=0$ |
| B. | The line equation $3x=2y$ when expressed in form $ax+by+c=0$, then $a,b,c$ are | (ii) | 3 |
| C. | Age of father is 7 yr more than 3 times the present age of his son. The above statement can be expressed in a linear equation as | (iii) | $0\cdot x+8y=9$ |
| D. | The value of $\lambda$, if $x=-\lambda$ and $y=\frac{5}{2}$ is a solution of the equation $x+4y-7=0$ | (iv) | $3,-2,0$ |

**Codes**

| | A | B | C | D |
|---|---|---|---|---|
| (a) | (iii) | (iv) | (i) | (ii) |
| (b) | (iii) | (ii) | (i) | (iv) |
| (c) | (ii) | (iv) | (iii) | (i) |
| (d) | (ii) | (i) | (iii) | (iv) |

**30.** $X$ and $Y$ are friends. $X$ is elder to $Y$ by 5 yr. $Y$'s sister $Z$ is half the age of $Y$ while $X$'s father $M$ is 8 yr older than twice the age of $Y$. If the present age of $M$ is 48 yr. Find the present ages of $X, Y$ and $Z$ (in years)

(a) 10, 20, 35 (b) 25, 15, 10
(c) 25, 20, 10 (d) None of these

**31.** A library take charge of ₹ 5 for issuing a book for one day and ₹ 2 per day thereafter. If Ritu had taken a book for $x$ days and $y$ be the total amount needs to be paid, write the mathematical statement in two variables for the situation and find the amount (in ₹) to be paid for 5 days.

(a) $y=2x+3$; 13 (b) $y=x+3$; 9
(c) $y=x-3$; 10 (d) $y=2x-3$; 15

**32.** Match the following column.

| | Column I | | Column II |
|---|---|---|---|
| A. | $x+y=0$ | (i) | $\left(\frac{3}{2},3\right)$ |
| B. | $y-2x=0$ | (ii) | $(5,-2)$ |
| C. | $3x+5y=0$ | (iii) | $(1,-1)$ |
| D. | $2x-y=12$ | (iv) | $(-5,3)$ |

Choose the correct options :

(a) A-(iv), B-(i), C-(iii), D-(ii)
(b) A-(iii), B-(i), C-(iv), D-(ii)
(c) A-(i), B-(iii), C-(ii), D-(iv)
(d) A-(i), B-(iv), C-(iii), D-(ii)

**Direction** (Q. Nos. 33 and 34) *The linear equation that converts Fahrenheit (F) to Celsius (C) is given by the relation* $C=\dfrac{5F-160}{9}$

**33.** If the temperature is 35°C, then the temperature in Fahrenheit is

(a) 95° F (b) 96° F
(c) 98° F (d) 94° F

**34.** The numerical value of the temperature which same in both the scales is

(a) 40 (b) –40
(c) 50 (d)–50

Chapter 04

# Coordinate Geometry

## 1 Mark Questions

1. The coordinates of points $P$ and $Q$ are $(-5, 3)$ and $(-5, m)$ respectively. And if sum of abscissa and ordinate of both points are equal. Then, the possible value of $m$ is

(a) $-5$ (b) $-13$ (c) $-10$ (d) 3

2. If the perpendicular distance of a point $P$ from the $X$-axis is 5 units and the foot of the perpendicular lies on the negative direction of $X$-axis, then the point $P$ has

(a) $x$-coordinate $= -5$

(b) $y$-coordinate $= 5$ only

(c) $y$-coordinate $= -5$ only

(d) $y$-coordinate $= 5$ or $-5$

3. The value of '$x$' in the ordered pair $(x, -8)$, if the ordinate of the pair is 4 more than the abscissa is .........

(a) $-4$ (b) $-8$

(c) $-12$ (d) 4

4. The distance of the point (4, 3) from the origin is

(a) 3 units

(b) 4 units

(c) 5 units

(d) $-5$ units

5. The sign of abscissa and ordinate of a point in quadrant IIIrd are respectively

(a) $(+, -)$ (b) $(-, +)$ (c) $(-, -)$ (d) $(+, +)$

6. The point $(-4, 2)$ lies in

(a) Ist quadrant (b) IInd quadrant

(c) IIIrd Quadrant (d) IVth quadrant

7. If $(x + 11, 5) = (6, 7 + y)$, then the values of $x$ and $y$ respectively, are

(a) $-5, -2$ (b) $-5, 2$

(c) $5, -2$ (d) $5, 2$

8. Line $x + y = 2$ passes through the ......... quadrants.

(a) Ist and IIIrd both

(b) IInd and IIIrd both

(c) IIIrd and IVth both

(d) Ist, IInd and IVth

9. If $a > 0$ and $b < 0$, then the point $(a, b)$ lies in

(a) IV quadrant (b) II quadrant

(c) III quadrant (d) I quadrant

10. Which of the following point does not lie in IV quadrant ?

(a) $(4, -1)$ (b) $(2, -6)$

(c) $(1, -3)$ (d) $(-2, 4)$

**11.** The measures of the angle between the coordinate axes is

(a) 0° (b) 180°
(c)90° (d) 360°

**Directions** (Q. Nos. 12-15) *Study the graph and answer the following questions.*

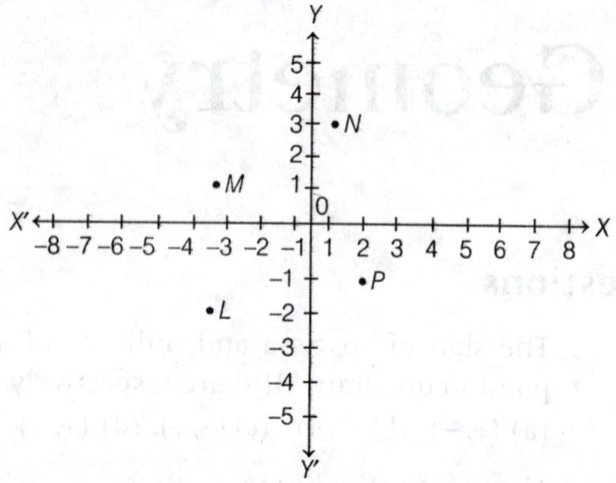


**12.** The coordinates of point $L$ are .........

(a) $(-3, 2)$
(b) $(3, -2)$
(c) $(3, 2)$
(d) $(-3, -2)$

**13.** Sum of ordinates of point $M$ and $N$ is .........

(a) 2 (b) 4 (c) $-5$ (d) $-6$

**14.** The point whose abscissa is 2 less than the ordinate is .........

(a) $M$ (b) $N$
(c) $L$ (d) $P$

**15.** The difference between abscissa of $P$ and $N$ is ...........

(a) 0 (b) 5
(c) 1 (d) 3

**16.** In the adjoining figure, the radius of a circle with centre $O$ is 8 units. If $O$ lies on the origin, then find the coordinates of $B$ and also find the area of circle.

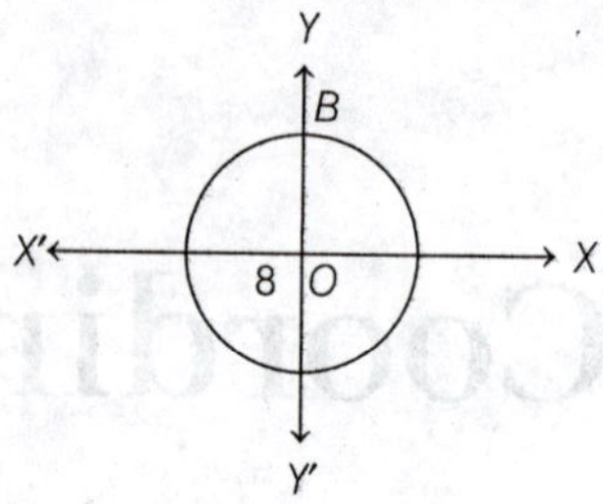


(a) (8, 0), 200.96 sq units
(b) (0, 8), 200.96 sq units
(c) (0, −8), 200 sq units
(d) None of the above

**17.** If the coordinate of two points $A$ and $B$ are $(10, 5)$ and $(-7, -4)$ respectively. Then, the value of ($x$-coordinates of $A$) − ($y$-coordinates of $B$) is

(a) $-14$ (b) 14 (c) $-10$ (d) $-12$

**18.** In the given figure, $PQR$ is an equilateral triangle in which coordinates of $Q$ and $R$ are $(0, 4)$ and $(0, -4)$ respectively. The coordinates of the vertex $P$ are

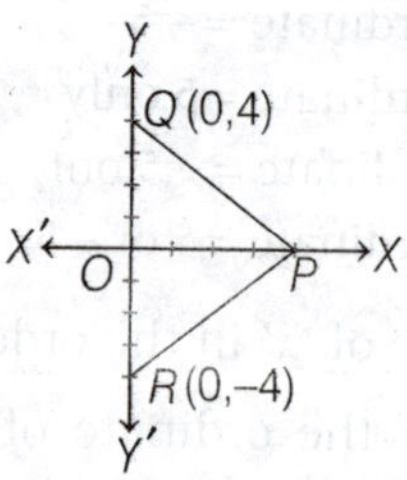


(a) $(-4\sqrt{3}, 0)$
(b) $(4\sqrt{3}, 0)$
(c) $(\sqrt{3}, 0)$
(d) $(4, 0)$

## 2 Marks Questions

**19.** Match the following columns.

| | Column I | | Column II |
|---|---|---|---|
| A. | Ordinate | (i) | (0, 0) |
| B. | Abscissa | (ii) | $x$ |
| C. | Ordered pair | (iii) | $y$ |
| D. | Coordinate of origin | (iv) | $(x, y)$ |

**Codes**

| | A | B | C | D | | A | B | C | D |
|---|---|---|---|---|---|---|---|---|---|
| (a) | (ii) | (iii) | (iv) | (i) | (b) | (iii) | (ii) | (iv) | (i) |
| (c) | (iii) | (ii) | (i) | (iv) | (d) | (ii) | (iii) | (iv) | (i) |

**20.** Match the following columns based on given graph.

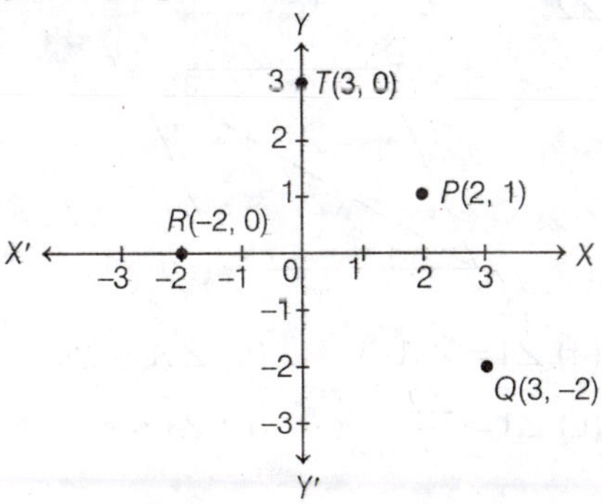


| | Column I | | Column II |
|---|---|---|---|
| (A) | Coordinate of point lies in the IV quadrant | (i) | (3, 0) |
| (B) | Distance of a point $R$ from origin. | (ii) | 2 |
| (C) | It we draw a perpendicular line from $Q$ to the axes, then the area of rectangle is equal to | (iii) | − 2 |
| (D) | Coordinate of a point on $Y$-axis | (iv) | (3,− 2) |
| | | (v) | 6 |

| | A | B | C | D |
|---|---|---|---|---|
| (a) | (iv) | (ii) | (i) | (v) |
| (b) | (ii) | (iv) | (i) | (v) |
| (c) | (iv) | (ii) | (v) | (i) |
| (d) | (iv) | (ii) | (i) | (v) |

**21.** In the given figure, $ABCD$ is a rhombus with diagonals $AC = 16$ cm and $BD = 8$ cm.

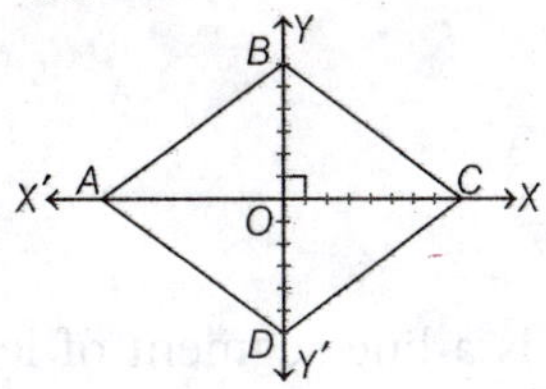


The coordinates of $A, B, C$ and $D$ are respectively.

(a) (−8,0), (0, 4), (8, 0), (0, −4)

(b) (−8,0), (0, 4), (0, 8), (0, − 4)

(c) (−8,0), (4,0), (8,0), (0, 4)

(d) None of the above

**22.** In the given figure, $PQRS$ is a rhombus whose diagonals $PR$ and $QS$ are along coordinate axes and $PR = 12$ units and $QS = 6$ units.

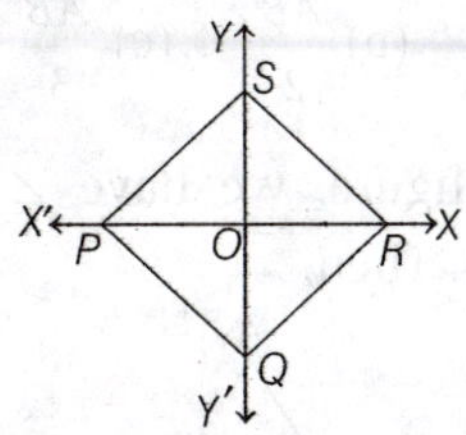


Now, if $T$ is a point which is 5 units right and 2 units above $S$, then find

(i) sum of abscissae of $P$ and $T$.

(ii) sum of ordinates of $Q, R$ and $T$.

| | (i) | (ii) |
|---|---|---|
| (a) | −1 | 2 |
| (b) | 1 | − 2 |
| (c) | 1 | 2 |
| (d) | − 1 | − 2 |

Chapter 05

# Lines and Angles

## 1 Mark Questions

**1.** If $PQ$ is a line segment of length 12 cm and $R$ is a point in its interior, then $PR^2 + QR^2 + 2PR \cdot QR$ equals

(a) 12 cm (b) 13 cm

(c) 144 cm (d) 169 cm

**2.** In the given figure, $C$ is the mid-point of the segment $AB$. $P$ and $Q$ are mid-points of the segments $AC$ and $BC$ respectively, then $AP$ is equal to

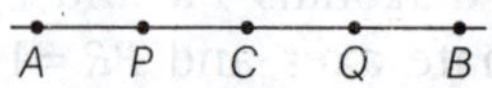


(a) $\frac{AB}{4}$ (b) $\frac{AB}{2}$ (c) $\frac{AB}{3}$ (d) $AB$

**3.** In the figure, we have $\angle ABC = \angle ACB$, $\angle 3 = \angle 4$. Then,

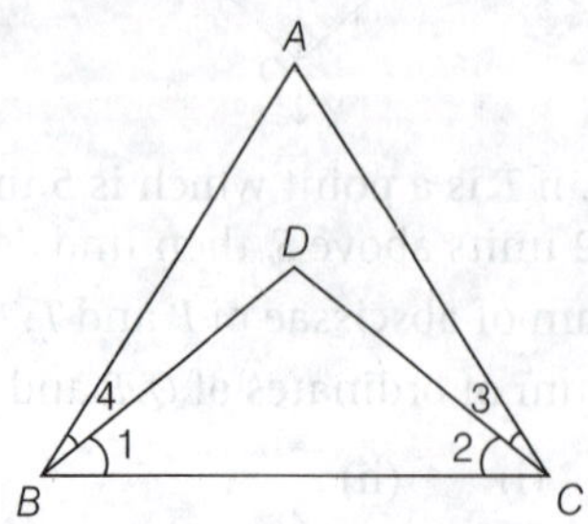


(a) $\angle 2 = \frac{3}{2} \angle 1$ (b) $\angle 1 = \frac{1}{2} \angle 2$

(c) $\angle 1 = \angle 2$ (d) $\angle 1 = 2\angle 2$

**4.** In the figure, if $\angle 1 = \angle 3$, $\angle 2 = \angle 4$ and $\angle 3 = \angle 4$, the relation between $\angle 1$ and $\angle 2$.

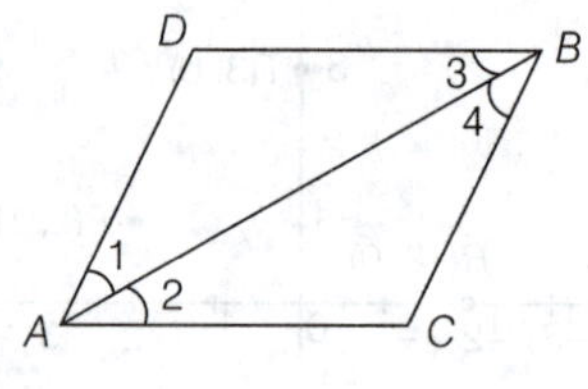


(a) $\angle 1 = \angle A$ (b) $\angle A = \angle B$

(c) $\angle 1 = \frac{\angle 2}{2}$ (d) $\angle 1 = \angle 2$

**5.** In the given figure, we have $\angle 1 = \angle 2$, $\angle 2 = \angle 3$.

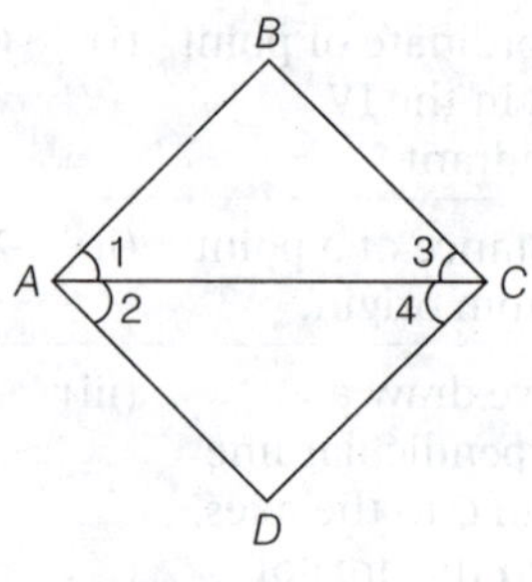


(a) $\angle 1 = \angle 2 + \angle 3$

(b) $\angle 2 = \angle 1 + \angle 3$

(c) $\angle 3 = \angle 1 + \angle 2$

(d) $\angle 1 = \angle 3$

6. In the given figure, find the value of $\angle EOD$.

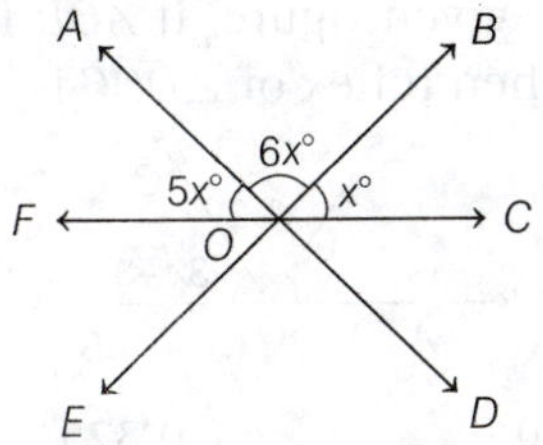


(a) 15° (b) 70°
(c) 45° (d) 90°

7. If two complementary angles are such that one angle is $1\frac{1}{2}$ times the other, then the smallest angle among them is
(a) 36° (b) 54°
(c) 72° (d) 18°

8. In the given figure, $\angle COD$ is a right angle. If $\angle AOC : \angle BOD = 3:2$, then $\angle BOD$ is equal to

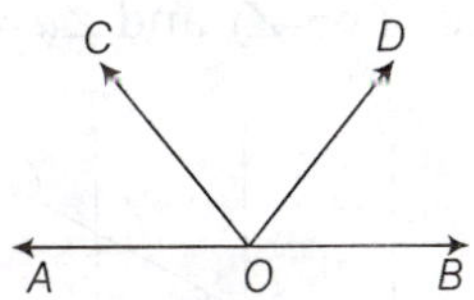


(a) 40° (b) 50°
(c) 54° (d) 36°

9. If two supplementary angles $A$ and $B$ are such that the difference between them is 30°, then the angles are respectively
(a) 110° and 80° (b) 75° and 105°
(c) 80° and 100° (d) 30° and 60°

10. In the given figure (not drawn to scale), find the value of $\angle DOC$.

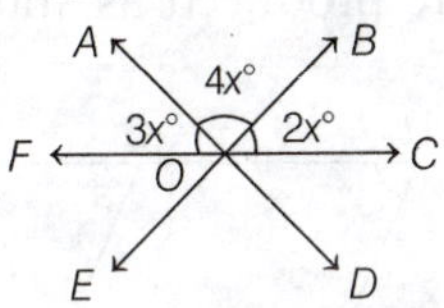


(a) 50° (b) 60°
(c) 30° (d) 75°

11. If two complementary angles are in the ratio 7 : 11, then the angles are .........
(a) 30°, 50° (b) 40°, 50°
(c) 20°, 60° (d) 35°, 55°

12. $\angle a$ and $\angle b$ form a linear pair of angles and $\angle a - 2\angle b = 30°$, then the value of $\angle a$ is
(a) 60° (b) 50°
(c) 120° (d) 130°

13. Angles with measures $x$ and $y$ form a complementary pair, then angles with which of the following measures will form a supplementary angles?
(a) $(\angle y + 35°), (\angle x + 65°)$
(b) $(\angle x - 30°), (\angle y - 30°)$
(c) $(\angle x - 43°), (\angle y - 47°)$
(d) $(\angle x - 20°), (\angle y - 50°)$

14. Which of the following angles cannot be constructed by using ruler and a pair of compasses only?
(a) $22\frac{1}{2}°$ (b) 45°
(c) 70° (d) 90°

15. If two angles $A$ and $B$ such that $A$ is complementary of itself and $B$ is supplementary of itself. Then, the values of $\angle A$ and $\angle B$ are, respectively
(a) 45° and 180° (b) 45° and 90°
(c) 90° and 45° (d) 180° and 0°

16. Choose the correct statement.
(a) The angle between the bisectors of a linear pair of angles is a right angle.
(b) The angle between the bisectors of a linear pair of angles is a complementary angle to itself.
(c) If two lines intersect, then the vertically opposite angles are supplementary.
(d) All of the above

**17.** In the given figure, $PQ$ and $RS$ are two intersecting lines. If $\angle POS = 75°$, then $x$ will be

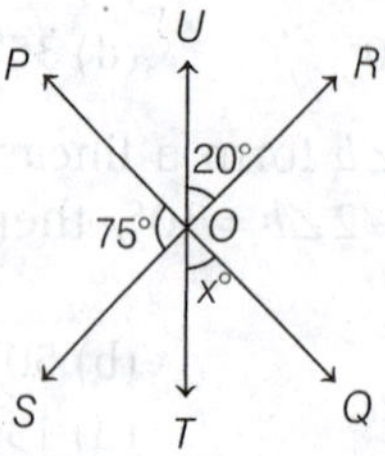


(a) 120° (b) 130°
(c) 140° (d) 85°

**18.** If $AOB$ is a line, then the relation between $\angle x, \angle y, \angle z$ and $\angle w$ will be

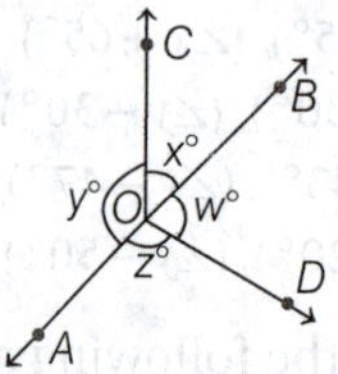


(a) $\angle x + \angle y = \angle w + \angle z$
(b) $\angle y + \angle z = \angle x + \angle w$
(c) $\angle x + \angle y + \angle w + \angle z = 180°$
(d) None of the above

**19.**

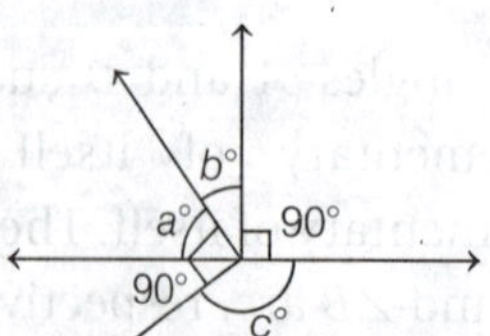


In the above figure, if $\angle a : \angle b = 2:3$, then $\angle c$ is equal to
(a) 54° (b) 126° (c) 36° (d) 144°

**20.** In the given figure, $\angle COE = 90°$. Find the value of $x$.

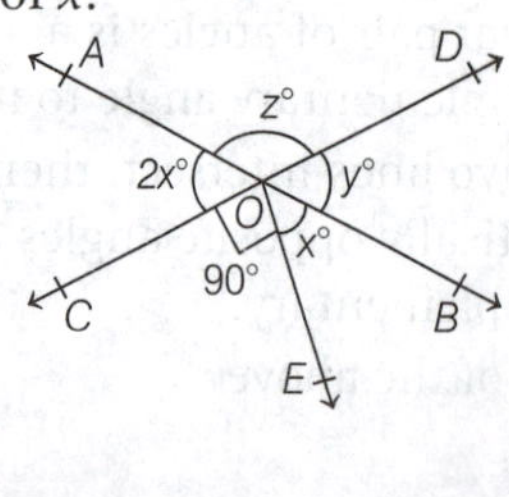


(a) 60° (b) 30°
(c) 45° (d) 10°

**21.** In the given figure, if $AOB$ is a straight line, then reflex of $\angle DOC$ is

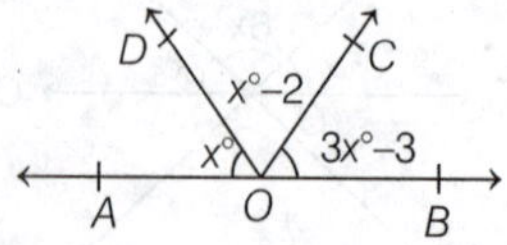


(a) 320° (b) 325°
(c) 328° (d) 330°

**22.** In the given figure, the value of $\angle d$ is

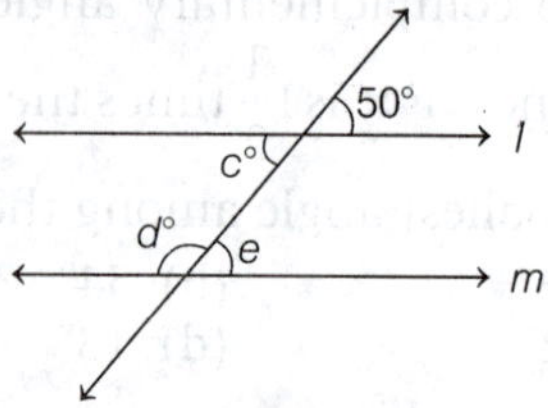


(a) 50° (b) 130°
(c) 90° (d) 100°

**23.** In figure, $\angle x = \angle y$ and $\angle a = \angle b$. Then,

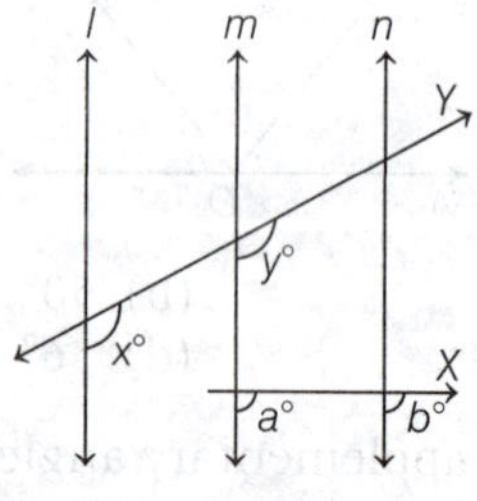


(a) $l \parallel y$
(b) $l$ is transversal of $m$ and $n$.
(c) $l \parallel n$
(d) $x \parallel y$

**24.** The sides $BA$ and $DC$ of the parallelogram $ABCD$ are produced as shown in figure. Then,

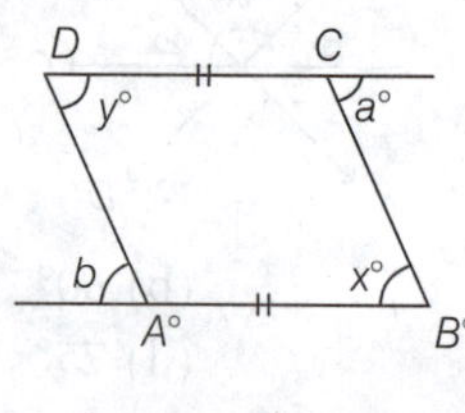

(a) $\angle a = \angle x + \angle y$

(b) $\angle a = \angle b = \frac{1}{2}(\angle x + \angle y)$

(c) $\angle y = \angle a - \angle b$

(d) $\angle a + \angle b = \angle x + \angle y$

**25.** In the given figure (not drawn to scale), $AB \parallel CD$ and $PQ, QR$ intersects $AB$ and $CD$ both at $E, F$ and $G, H$ respectively. Find the value of $x$.

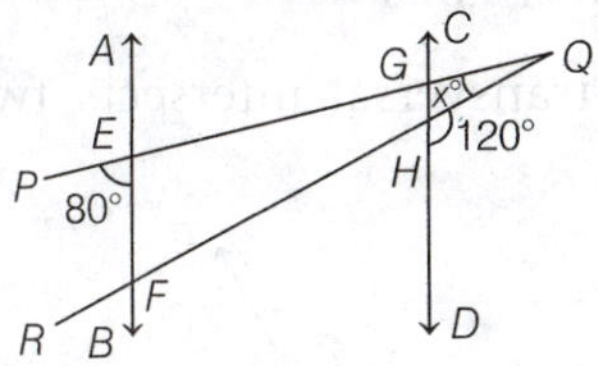


(a) 40° (b) 20°
(c) 100° (d) 30°

**26.** In the given figure (not drawn to scale), $PQ \parallel RS$ and $EF \parallel QS$. If $\angle PQS = 55°$, then the measure of $\angle RFE$ is

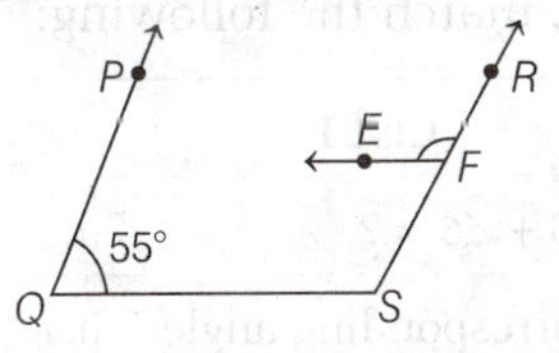


(a) 115° (b) 125°
(c) 60° (d) 180°

**27.** In the given figure, if $AB \parallel CD$, $\angle APQ = 50°$ and $\angle PRD = 127°$, then the value of $(\angle x + \angle y)$ is

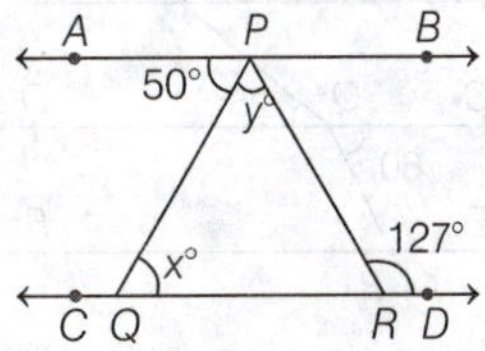


(a) 137° (b) 127° (c) 53° (d) 27°

**28.** In the given figure, $AB \parallel CD$. Find the value of $x$.

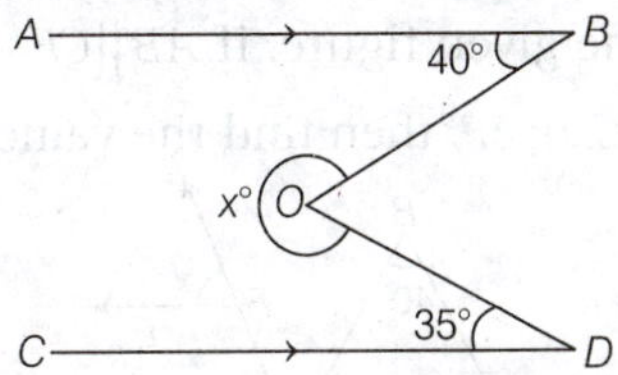


(a) 189° (b) 215° (c) 285° (d) 280°

**29.** In the figure, if $OP \parallel RS$, $\angle OPQ = 110°$ and $\angle QRS = 130°$, then $\angle PQR$ is equal to

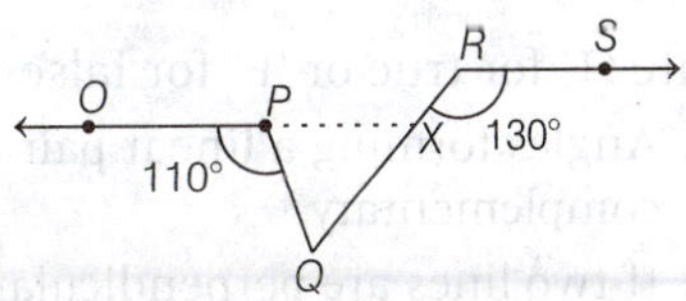


(a) 40° (b) 50° (c) 60° (d) 70°

## 2 Marks Questions

**30.** In the given figure, if $AB \parallel CD$, $CD \parallel EF$ and $y : z = 3 : 7$, then the values of $(\angle x + \angle y)$ and $(\angle x + \angle z)$ are, respectively

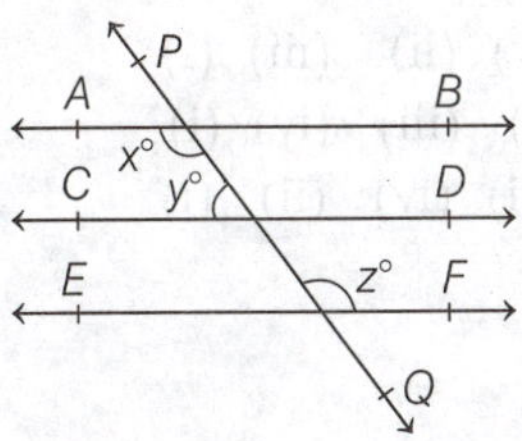


(a) 250° and 90° (b) 180° and 252°
(c) 180° and 126° (d) 270° and 252°

**31.** In figure, a transversal $PQ$ intersect two parallel lines $AB$ and $CD$ at $L$ and $M$ respectively. If $\angle 1 = 95°$ and $\angle 2 =$

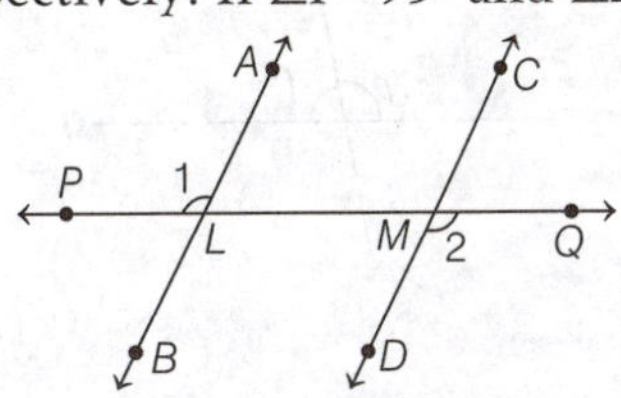


(a) 95° (b) 70°
(c) 85° (d) 75°

**32.** In the given figure,

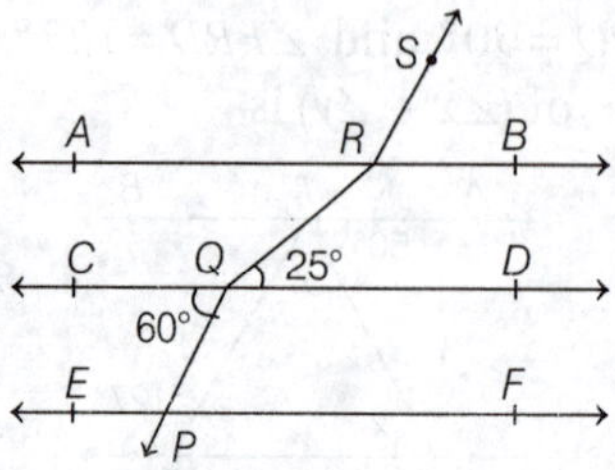


if $AB \| CD \| EF$, $PQ \| RS$, $\angle RQD = 25°$ and $\angle CQP = 60°$, then $\angle QRS$ is equal to

(a) 160° (b) 145°
(c) 170° (d) 150°

**33.** In the given figure, if $AB \| CF$ and $CD \| EF$, then find the value of $x$.

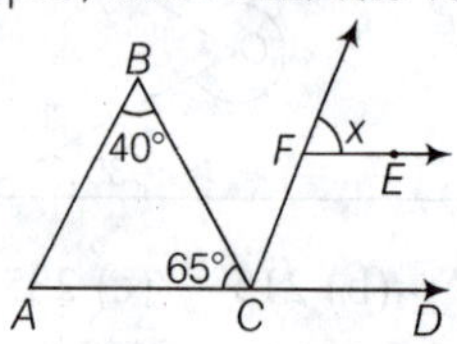


(a) 105° (b) 60°
(c) 40° (d) 75°

**34.** State 'T' for true or 'F' for false.

I. Angles forming a linear pair are complementary.

II. If two lines are perpendicular to the third line, then those two lines are perpendicular to each other.

III. In the given figure, if $\angle a = 50°$, then $\angle f$ is equal to 130°.

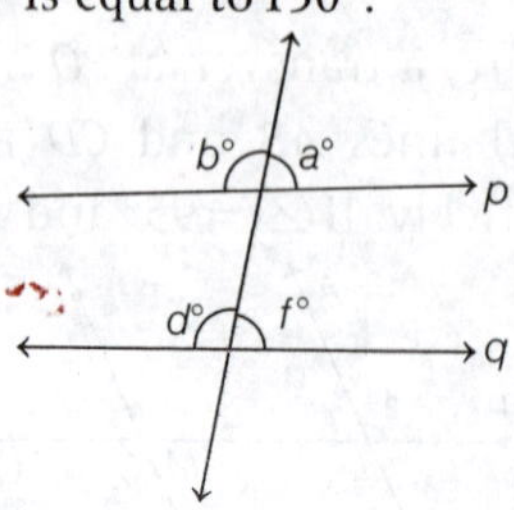


IV. A rotating ray after making a complete rotation coincides with its initial position. The angle formed is reflex angle.

**Codes**

| | I | II | III | IV |
|---|---|---|---|---|
| (a) | F | F | F | F |
| (b) | T | T | T | T |
| (c) | F | F | T | F |
| (d) | T | T | F | F |

**35.** If a transversal intersects two parallel lines.

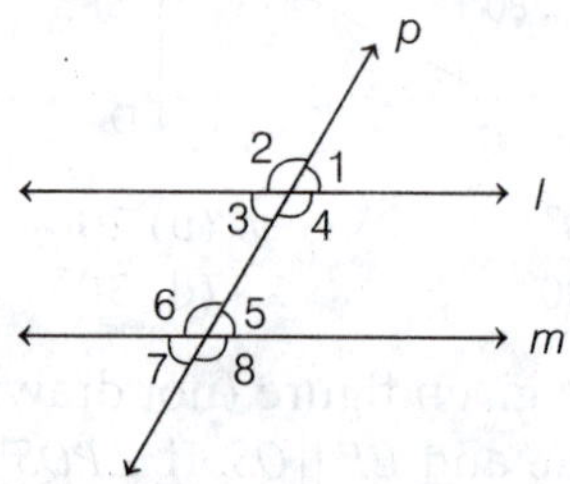


Then, match the following:

| | List I | | List II |
|---|---|---|---|
| A. | $\angle 3 + \angle 6 = ?$ | i. | $\angle 2$ and $\angle 8$ |
| B. | Corresponding angle pair | ii. | $\angle 3$ and $\angle 7$ |
| C. | Vertically opposite angles | iii. | $\angle 5$ and $\angle 7$ |
| D. | Alternate angles | iv. | $\angle 4 + \angle 5$ |

**Codes**

| | A | B | C | D |
|---|---|---|---|---|
| (a) | (i) | (ii) | (iii) | (iv) |
| (b) | (iv) | (ii) | (iii) | (i) |
| (c) | (ii) | (iii) | (iv) | (i) |
| (d) | (iii) | (iv) | (ii) | (i) |

Chapter 06

# Triangles

## 1 Mark Questions

**1.** Which of the following figures represent isosceles triangles?

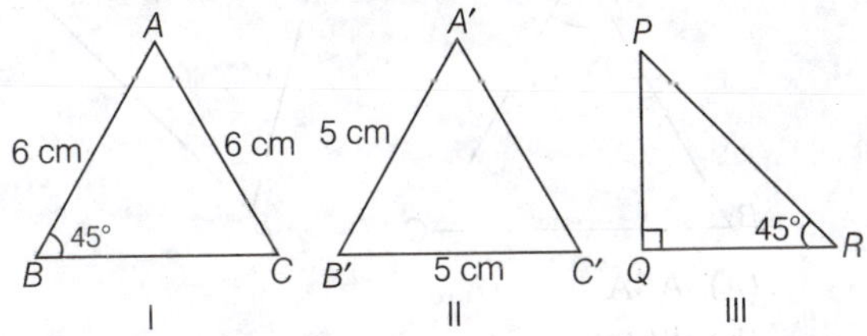


(a) Only I
(b) Both I and II
(c) Both II and III
(d) All I, II and III

**2.** If a triangle has lengths $AB = 4$ cm, $BC = 5$ cm and $\angle ABC = 90°$. Then, the side which is greatest among all the sides, is

(a) $AB$ (b) $AC$
(c) $BC$ (d) Can't say

**3.** In the given figure, if bisector of $\angle A$ divides $BC$ in the ratio $1:1$ and $\angle D = 90°$. Then, $\Delta ABC$ is of the type

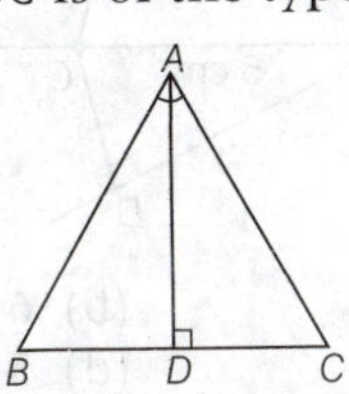


(a) a right angled triangle
(b) an isosceles triangle
(c) an equilateral triangle
(d) None of the above

**4.** In the given figure, the length of side $AC$ is equal to

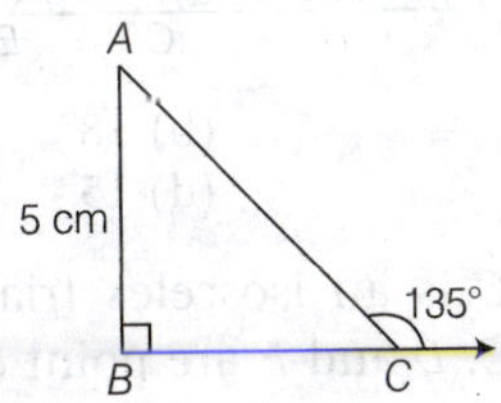


(a) $5\sqrt{2}$ cm (b) 4 cm
(c) 3 cm (d) 5 cm

**5.** Which of the following figures are right angled triangles?

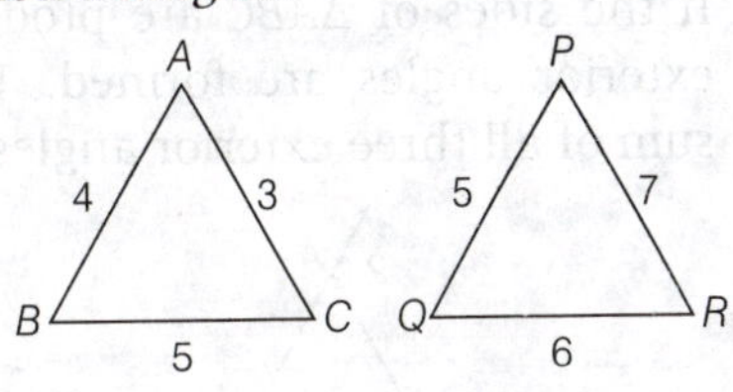


(a) Only I
(b) Only II
(c) Both I and II
(d) Neither I nor II

6. In the given figure, $\angle ABC = 90°$ and $AB = BC$. If $BD$ is bisector of $\angle ABC$, then in $\Delta BDC$, the longest side is

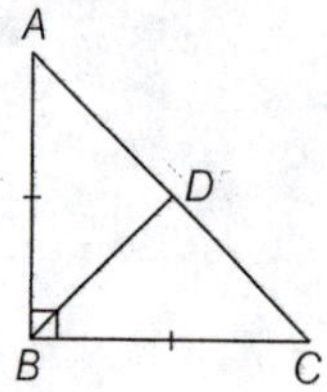


(a) $BC$
(b) $BD$
(c) $CD$
(d) None of the above

7. In the figure given, what are the values of $\angle a$.

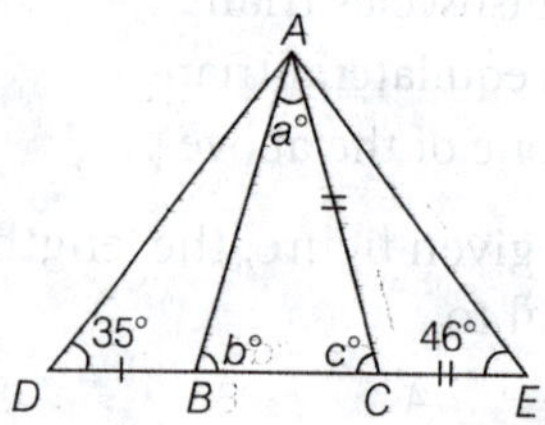


(a) 92°  (b) 18°
(c) 20°  (d) 15°

8. If $\Delta ABC$ is an isosceles triangle where $AB = AC$, $D$ and $E$ are point on $BC$, such that $BE = CD$. Then, which of the following relation is true?

(a) $AD = AB$  (b) $AE = DE$
(c) $AD = DE$  (d) $AD = AE$

9. If the sides of $\Delta ABC$ are produced and exterior angles are formed. Then, the sum of all three exterior angles, is

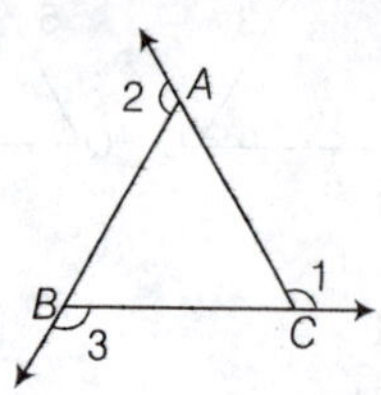


(a) 180°  (b) 360°
(c) 90°  (d) 0°

10. In the given figures, both triangles, $AB$ and $BC$ are equal to the $PQ$ and $QR$ respectively. If $\Delta ABC \cong \Delta PQR$, then which angles must not be equal?

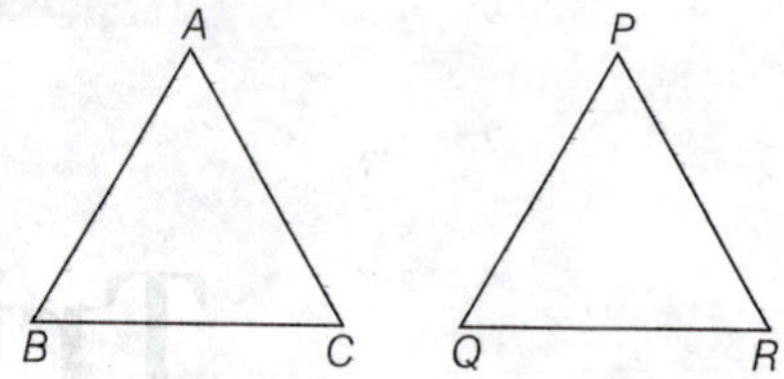


(a) $\angle A$ and $\angle Q$  (b) $\angle B$ and $\angle Q$
(c) $\angle A$ and $\angle P$  (d) $\angle C$ and $\angle R$

11. Which of the following criteria of congruency is shown?

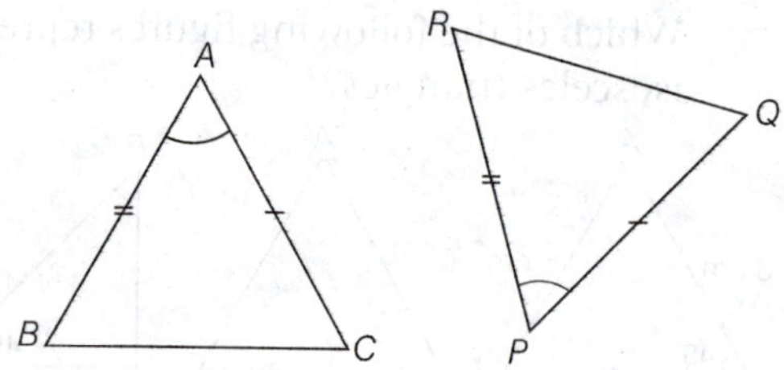


(a) ASA
(b) SSS
(c) SAS
(d) None of the above

12. In $\Delta ABC$ and $\Delta DEF$, $AB = DE$ and $\angle A = \angle D$. Two triangles are congruent by SAS, if

(a) $BC = EF$  (b) $AC = DF$
(c) $AC = EF$  (d) $BC = DE$

13. In the given figure, if $AC$ is bisector of $\angle BAD$ such that $AD = 3$ cm and $AC = 5$ cm, then the value of $CD + BC$ is

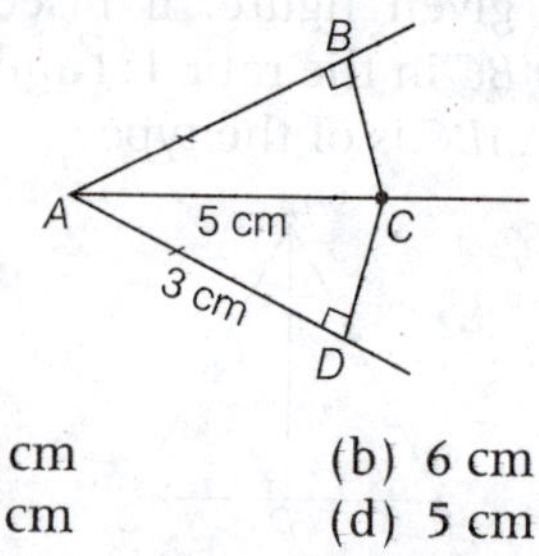


(a) 4 cm  (b) 6 cm
(c) 8 cm  (d) 5 cm

**14.** If $AD$ is bisector of $\angle A$ and $\angle D$ is perpendicular to $BC$. Then, $\Delta ABC$ is ......... triangle.

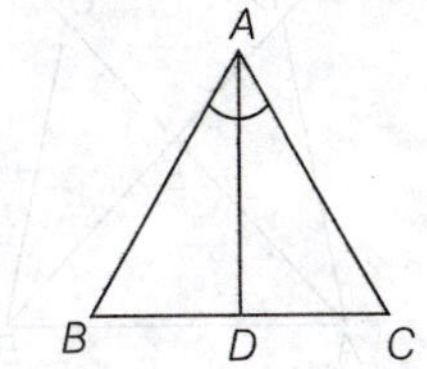

(a) Scalene
(b) Equilateral
(c) Isosceles
(d) None of the above

**15.** In the given figure, if $PA = PD$ and $PB = PC$.
Then, $\Delta PAB$ is congruent to $\Delta PDC$ by

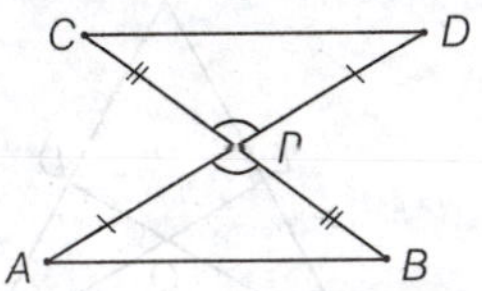

(a) $\Delta$AAS (b) $\Delta$SAS
(c) $\Delta$SSA (d) $\Delta$SSS

**16.** In $\Delta DEF$ and $\Delta PQR$, $DE = DF$, $\angle F = \angle P$ and $\angle E = \angle Q$. The two triangles are
(a) Isosceles but not necessarily congruent
(b) Isosceles and congruent
(c) Congruent but not isosceles
(d) Neither congruent nor isosceles

**17.** If $AB = DE$, $AC = DF$, $\angle A = \angle D = 90°$ and $BC = 5$ cm, then $DF$ is equal to

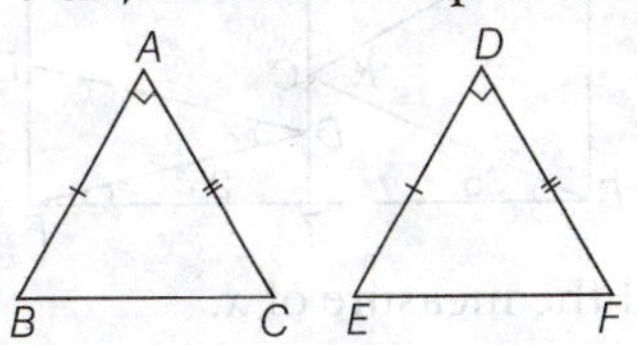

(a) 5 cm
(b) 4.5 cm
(c) 5.5 cm
(d) Can't say

**18.** In the given figure, if $\angle 1 = \angle 2$ and $\angle 3 = \angle 4$. Then, by which congruence property, two $\Delta ABC$ and $\Delta ABD$ shown in figure are congruent?

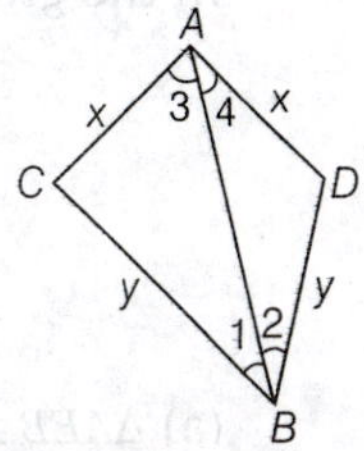

(a) SAS (b) SSS (c) RHS (d) SSA

**19.** In the given figure, if $AB = CF$, $EF = BD$ and $\angle AFE = \angle DBC$. Then, $\Delta AFE$ and $\Delta CBD$ are congruent by which of the following criterion?

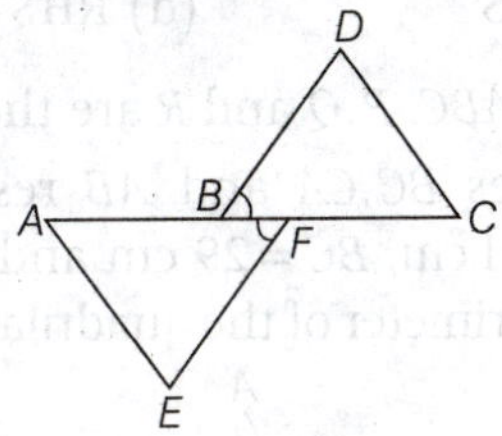

(a) SAS (b) SSS
(c) ASA (d) None of these

**20.** In the given figure, $AB \perp BE$ and $FE \perp BE$.
If $AB = FE$ and $BC = DE$, then

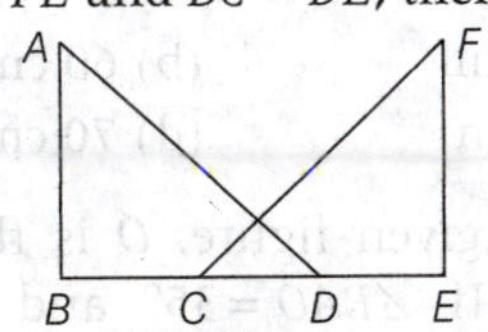

(a) $\Delta ABD \cong \Delta FCE$ (b) $\Delta ABD \cong \Delta FEC$
(c) $\Delta ABD \cong \Delta EFC$ (d) $\Delta ABD \cong \Delta CEF$

**21.** In the given figure, if $AE = AD$ and $BD = CE$, then .........

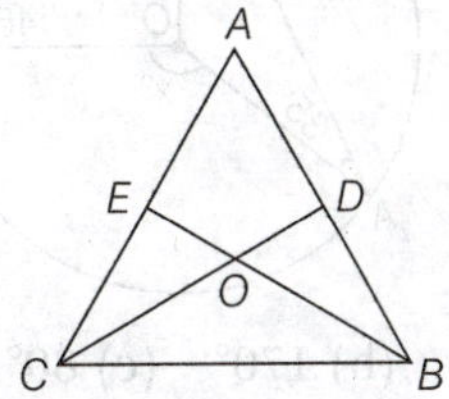

(a) $\Delta BEC \cong \Delta BCD$ (b) $\Delta AEB \cong \Delta ADC$
(c) $BC = CD$ (d) None of these

**22.** In the given figure, if $BE = CF$, then

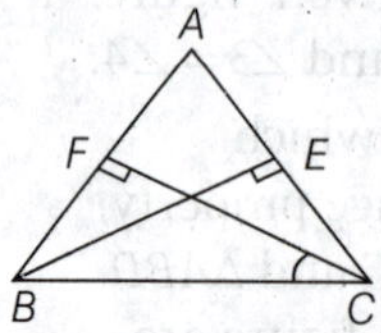


(a) $\Delta AEB \cong \Delta AFC$  (b) $\Delta ABE \cong \Delta AFC$
(c) $\Delta ABE \cong \Delta CAF$  (d) $\Delta ABE \cong \Delta ACF$

**23.** In quadrilateral $ABCD$, $AB$ is a diagonal. If $AC = AD$ and $AB$ bisects $\angle A$, by which congruence property is $\Delta ACB \cong \Delta ADB$?
(a) SAS  (b) ASA
(b) SSS  (d) RHS

**24.** In a $\Delta ABC$, $P, Q$ and $R$ are the mid-points of sides $BC, CA$ and $AB$ respectively. If $AC = 21$ cm, $BC = 29$ cm and $AB = 30$ cm. The perimeter of the quadrilateral $ARPQ$ is

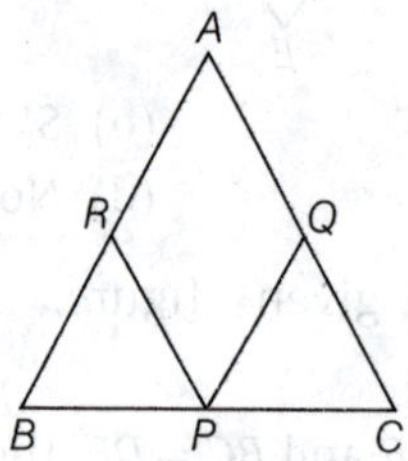


(a) 91 cm  (b) 60 cm
(c) 51cm  (d) 70 cm

**25.** In the given figure, $O$ is the centre of circle. If $\angle BAO = 35°$ and $\angle BCO = 45°$ then the value of $x$ will be

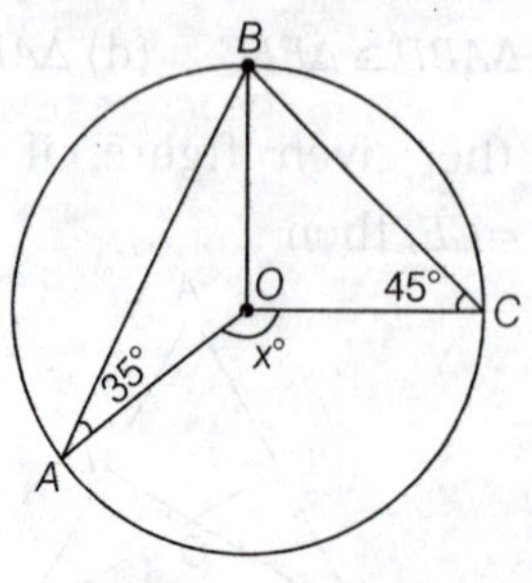


(a) 160°  (b) 170°  (c) 80°  (d) 140°

**26.** In the given figure, if $ED = EC$ and $\angle ADF = \angle BCG$, then $\Delta ABE$ is a/an

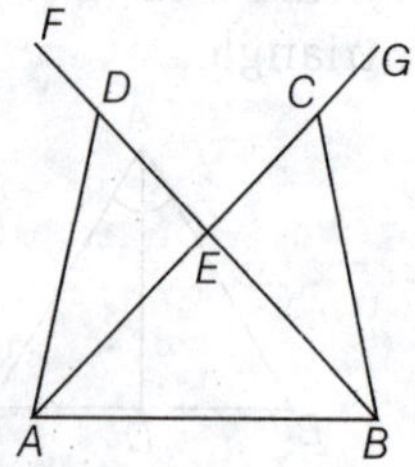


(a) Equilateral triangle
(b) Isosceles triangle
(c) Scalene triangle
(d) Non-isosceles right angled triangle

**27.** In the given figure, $\angle A = \angle C$ and $AB = BC$, then which of following is correct ?

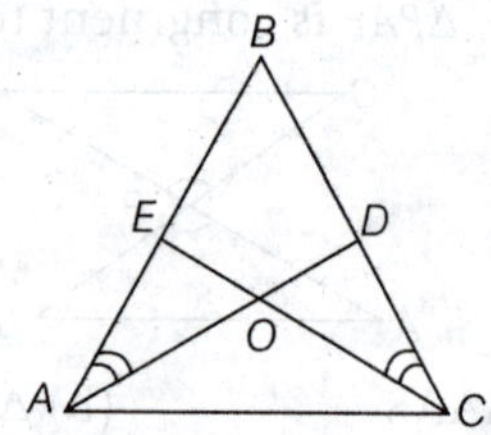


(a) $\angle OEB = \angle ODB$
(b) $\Delta ABD \cong \Delta CBE$
(c) $\angle AEO = \angle CDO$
(d) All of the above

**28.** In the given figure, it is given that
(i) $AB \perp BF$ and $EF \perp BF$
(ii) $AC = BC$
(iii) $KD$ is perpendicular to $BC$ and $DE$.

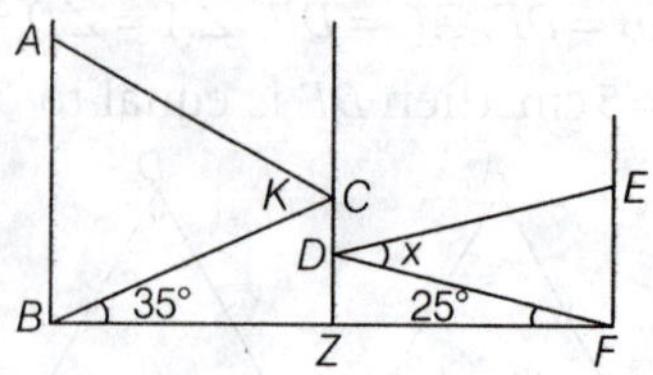


Find the measure of $x$.
(a) 75°  (b) 30°
(c) 60°  (d) 45°

## 2 Marks Questions

**29.** State 'T' for true or 'F' for false.

I. If two triangles have their corresponding sides equal, then they are always congruent.

II. If the sides of any triangle are 3 : 4 : 5, then the greatest angle is opposite to the side 5.

III. $O$ is a point inside the $\Delta ABC$, then $\angle BOC = \angle BAC + \angle ABO + \angle ACO$.

IV. Two right angled triangles are congruent, if hypotenuse and a side of one triangle are respectively equal to the hypotenuse and a side of the other triangle.

**Codes**

| | I | II | III | IV |
|---|---|---|---|---|
| (a) | T | F | F | T |
| (b) | T | T | F | T |
| (c) | T | T | T | T |
| (d) | F | F | T | T |

**30.** Match the following:

| List I | List II |
|---|---|
| A. Equilateral triangle is | i. Right isosceles triangle |
| B. 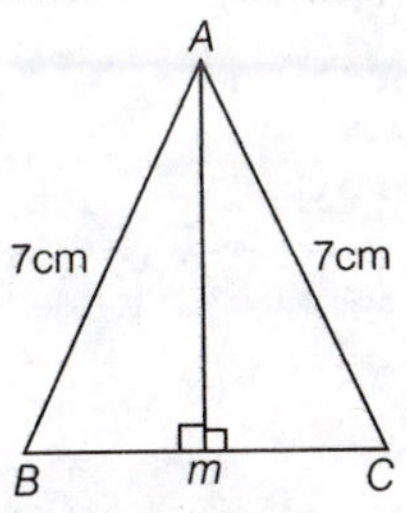 $\Delta AMB \cong \Delta AMC$ by | ii. SSS Rule |
| C. 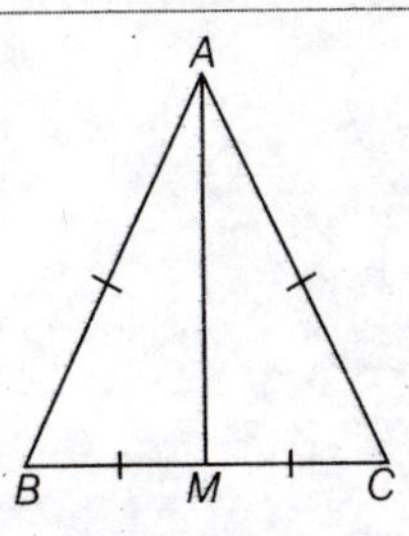 $\Delta AMB \cong \Delta AMC$ by | iii. RHS Rule |
| D. The triangle in which one angle is 90° and other two sides are equal, is | iv. Acute angled triangle |



**Codes**

| | A | B | C | D |
|---|---|---|---|---|
| (a) | (iv) | (iii) | (ii) | (i) |
| (b) | (i) | (ii) | (iii) | (iv) |
| (c) | (ii) | (i) | (iii) | (iv) |
| (d) | (iv) | (i) | (ii) | (iii) |

**31.** Match the following :

| List I | List II |
|---|---|
| A. 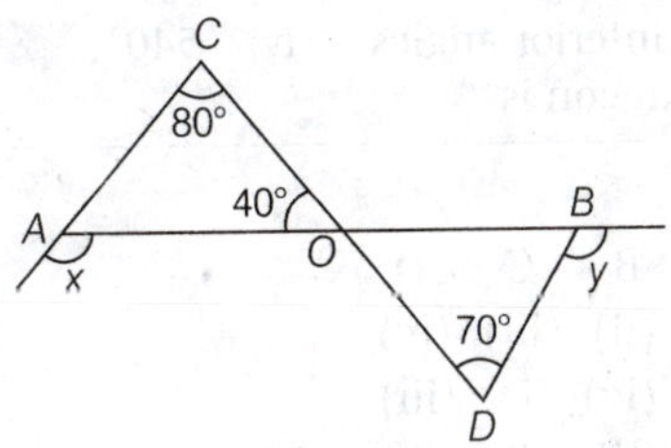 | i. $\angle x = 37°$ $\angle y = 53°$ |
| B. $\Delta\ ABC = \Delta\ EFG$ 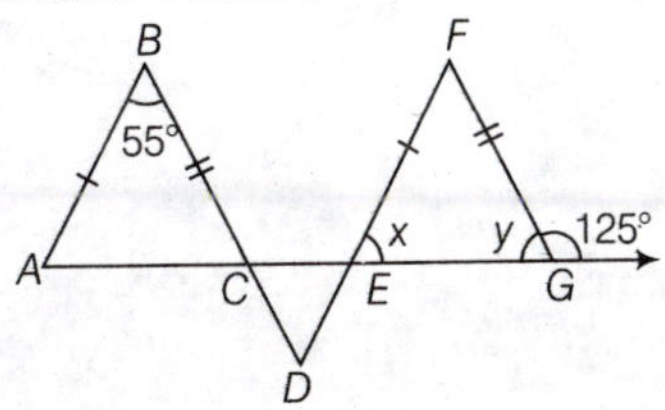 | ii. $\angle x = 120°$ $\angle y = 110°$ |
| C. 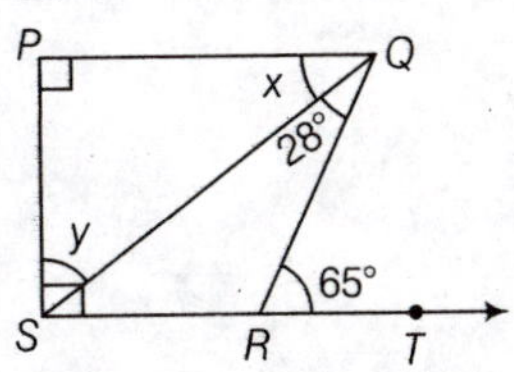 | iii. $\angle x = 70°$ $\angle y = 55°$ |



**Codes**

| | A | B | C |
|---|---|---|---|
| (a) | (i) | (ii) | (iii) |
| (b) | (ii) | (iii) | (i) |
| (c) | (i) | (iii) | (ii) |
| (d) | (ii) | (i) | (iii) |

**32.** Match the following:

| | List I | | List II |
|---|---|---|---|
| A. | In an equilateral triangle | i. | 55° |
| B. | If 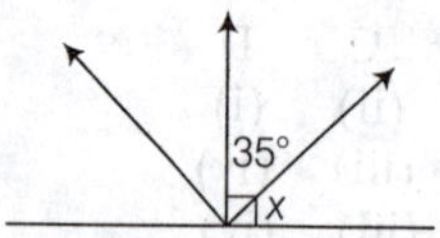 then, $\angle x$ is equal to | ii. | 45° |
| C. | A right angled isosceles triangle has other angles equal to | iii. | All angles are equal |
| D. | Sum of interior angles of a pentagon is | iv. | 540° |



**Codes**

| | A | B | C | D |
|---|---|---|---|---|
| (a) | (i) | (ii) | (iii) | (iv) |
| (b) | (ii) | (iv) | (i) | (iii) |
| (c) | (iii) | (i) | (ii) | (iv) |
| (d) | (iv) | (iii) | (i) | (ii) |

**33.** Match the two columns.

In right $\Delta ABC$, right angled at $C$, $M$ is the mid-point of hypotenuse $AB$. $C$ is joined to $M$ and produced to a point $D$ such that $DM = CM$. Point $D$ is joined to point $B$.

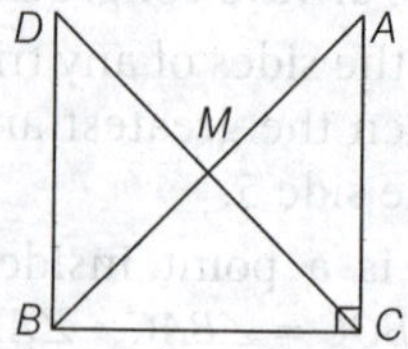


| Column-I | Column-II |
|---|---|
| (A) $\Delta AMC$ | (i) congruent $\Delta BMD$ |
| (B) $\angle DBC$ | (ii) a right angle |
| (C) $\Delta DBC$ | (iii) congruent $\Delta ACB$ |
| (D) $CM$ | (iv) (1/2) $AB$ |

Choose the correct option :

(a) (A) → (iv); (B) → (i); (C) → (ii); (D) → (iii)

(b) (A) → (ii); (B) → (iii); (C) → (i); (D) → (iv)

(c) (A) → (i); (B) → (iii); (C) → (iv); (D) → (ii)

(d) (A) → (i); (B) → (ii); (C) → (iii); (D) → (iv)

Chapter 07

# Quadrilaterals

## 1 Mark Questions

**1.** The length of the parallel sides of a trapezium are 14 cm and 7 cm. If the length of third side is 8 cm and of fourth side is $x$ cm, then the number of possible integral value of $x$ is

(a) 12 (b) 13

(c) 14 (d) 17

**2.** In a concave quadrilateral, out of all angles, the number of angles whose measure is more than 180°, is

(a) 2 (b) 1 (c) 3 (d) 0

**3.** If two segments $AC$ and $BD$ bisect each other at $O$, then $ABCD$ is a

(a) trapezium (b) parallelogram

(c) Both (a) and (b) (d) None of these

**4.** The diagonal of rectangle $ABCD$ intersect each other at $O$. If $\angle BOC = 44°$, then the value of $\angle OAD$ will be

(a) 120° (b) 68°

(c) 90° (d) 44°

**5.** In the following figure, the values of $\angle x$ and $\angle y$ are

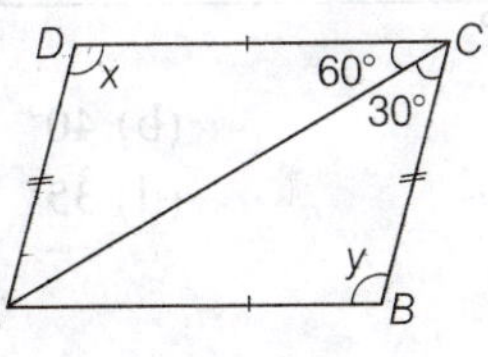


(a) $\angle x = \angle y = 90°$

(b) $\angle x = 30°, \angle y = 150°$

(c) $\angle x = 60°, \angle y = 120°$

(d) $\angle x = 40°, \angle y = 140°$

**6.** If the diagonals of a rhombus are 30 cm and 40 cm, then the length of side of rhombus is

(a) 20 cm (b) 22 cm

(c) 25 cm (d) 45 cm

**7.** Two parallel line $l$ and $m$ intersected by a transversal $p$. The quadrilateral formed by the bisectors of interior angles is a

(a) Trapezium (b) Kite

(c) Parallelogram (d) Square

**8.** If the difference between the interior and exterior angles of a regular polygon is zero, then the number of sides in the polygon is

(a) 4 (b) 6

(c) 8 (d) 12

**9.** $ABCD$ is a parallelogram. If $AB$ is produced to $E$ such that $ED$ bisects $BC$ at $O$. Then, which of the following is correct?

(a) $AB = OE$ (b) $OE = OC$

(c) $AB = BE$ (d) None of these

**10.** In a parallelogram $ABCD$ diagonals $AC$ and $BD$ intersects at $O$ and $AC = 14$ cm and $BD = 17$ cm, then the measure of $OC$ and $OD$ respectively equal to

(a) 7 cm and 6.4 cm (b) 6.5 cm and 7.5 cm
(c) 3.8 cm, 3.8 cm (d) 7 cm and 8.5 cm

**11.** If the sides $BA$ and $DC$ of quadrilateral $ABCD$ are produced as shown in the following figure, then the value of $\angle x + \angle y$ is

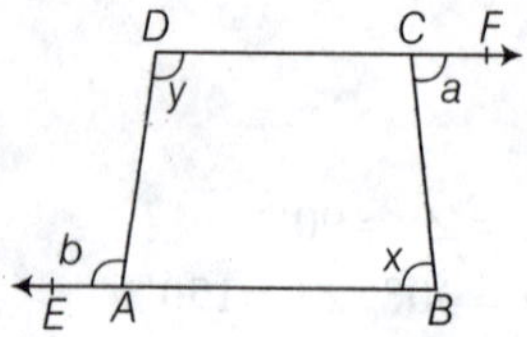


(a) $2\angle a$ (b) $2\angle b$
(c) $\angle a - \angle b$ (d) $\angle a + \angle b$

**12.** In a trapezium $ABCD$, if $AB \parallel CD$, then $(AC^2 + BD^2)$ is equal to

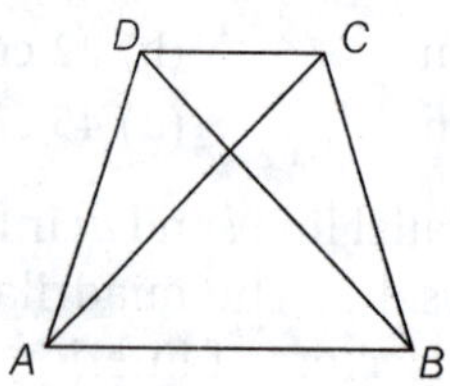


(a) $BC^2 + AD^2 + 2BC \cdot AD$
(b) $AB^2 + CD^2 + 2AB \cdot CD$
(c) $AB^2 + CD^2 + 2AD \cdot BC$
(d) $BC^2 + AD^2 + 2AB \cdot CD$

**13.** In figure, $ABCD$ is a rectangle in which diagonal $AC$ is produced to $E$. If $\angle ECD = 146°$, then find $\angle AOB$.

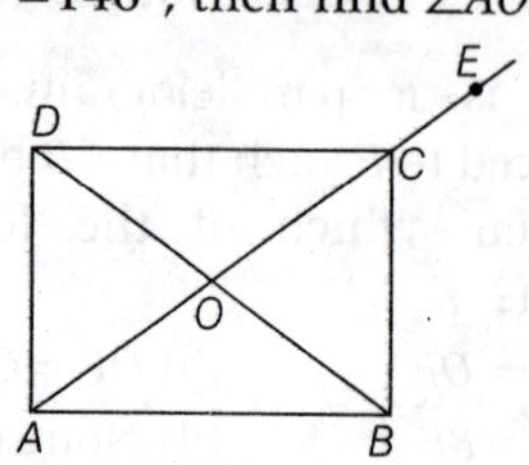


(a) 110°
(b) 115°
(c) 112°
(d) None of the above

**14.** The quadrilateral formed by the bisectors of the angles of a parallelogram is a

(a) parallelogram (b) kite
(c) rhombus (d) rectangle

**15.** Points $P$ and $Q$ have been taken on opposite sides $AB$ and $CD$ respectively of a parallelogram $ABCD$ such that $AP = CQ$.

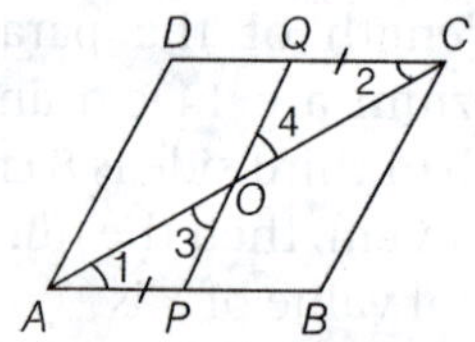


Then,

(a) $AC$ and $PQ$ bisect each other
(b) $AC$ and $PQ$ are equal to each other
(c) $AC = CD$
(d) None of the above

**16.** In a $\Delta ABC$, if $D$ and $E$ are the mid-points of sides $AB$ and $AC$ respectively, the quadrilateral formed is a

(a) rectangle (b) rhombus
(c) trapezium (d) square

**17.** In the given figure, $PQRS$ is an isosceles trapezium. Find $x$ :

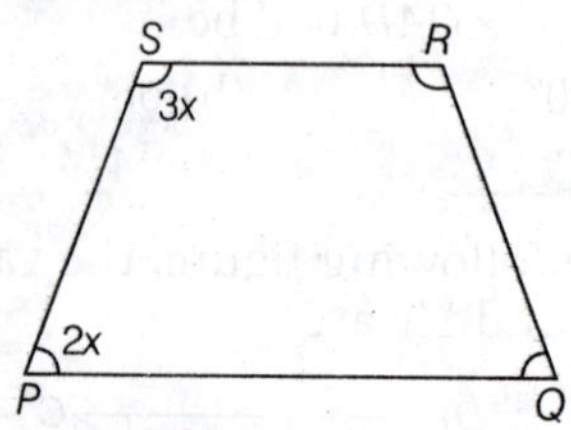


(a) 30° (b) 40°
(c) 36° (d) 35°

**18.** In the following figure, if $ABCD$ is a rectangle and $P$, $Q$ are the mid-points of $AD$, $DC$ respectively. Then, the ratio of lengths $PQ$ and $AC$ is equal to

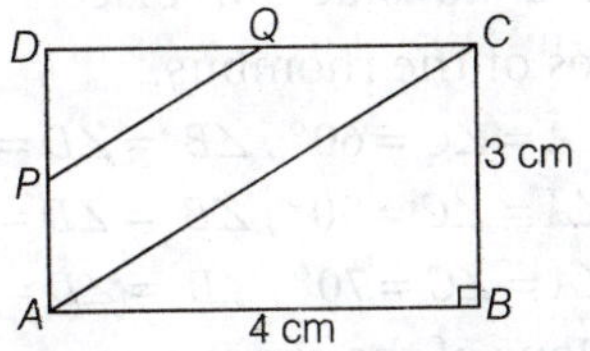


(a) 1 : 1 (b) 1 : 2
(c) 2 : 1 (d) 3 : 2

**19.** In figure, $PQRS$ is a rhombus in which the diagonal $PR$ is produced to $T$. If $\angle SRT = 152°$, then find $x, y$ and $z$.

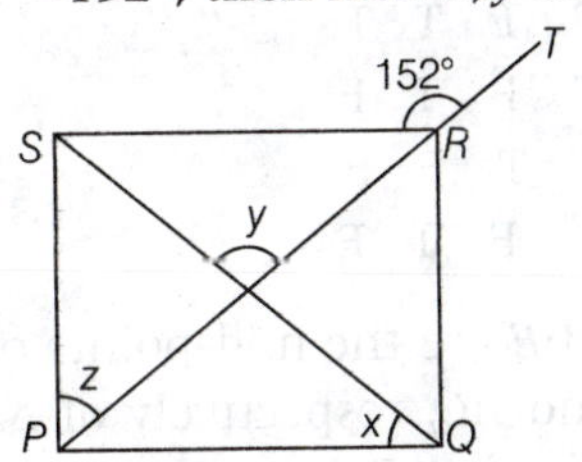


(a) $x = 60°, y = 90°, z = 28°$
(b) $x = 62°, y = 80°, z = 28°$
(c) $x = 62°, y = 90°, z = 28°$
(d) None of the above

**20.** In the following figure, $PQRS$ is a square. $M$ is the mid-point of $PQ$ and $RM \perp AB$. $RA$ is equal to

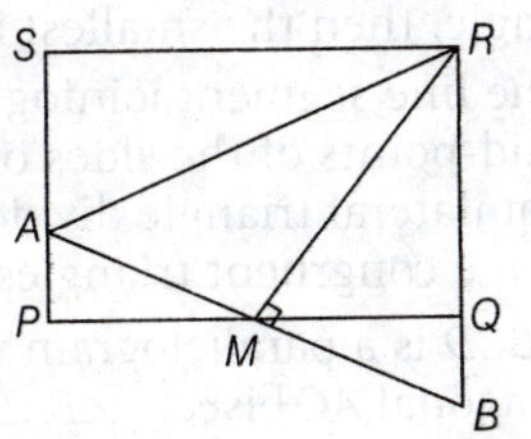


(a) $RM$ (b) $RB$
(c) $MB$ (d) None of these

**21.** In the adjoining figure, $PQRS$ is a parallelogram. $L$ is the mid-point of $RS$ and through $S$ is a line segment drawn parallel to $LQ$ to meet $RQ$ produced at $M$ and intersect $PQ$ at $N$. Then, which of the following is true.

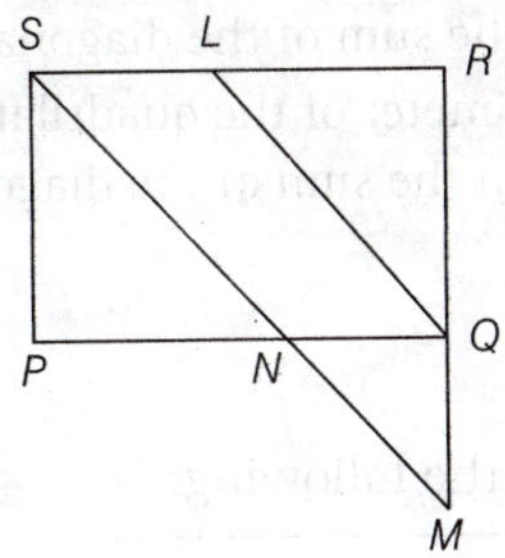


(a) $PS = SL$
(b) $PS = RM - RQ$
(c) $SR = PN$
(d) $SR = NQ$

**22.** In a parallelogram $ABCD$, $E$ and $F$ are the mid-points of sides $AB$ and $CD$ respectively. $AF$ and $CE$ meet the diagonal $BD$ of length 12 cm at $P$ and $Q$. Then, length of $PQ$ is

(a) 6 cm (b) 4 cm
(c) 3 cm (d) 5 cm

**23.** In figure, $X$ is a point in the interior of square $ABCD$. $AXYZ$ is also a square. If $DY = 3$ cm and $AZ = 2$ cm, then $BY$ is equal to

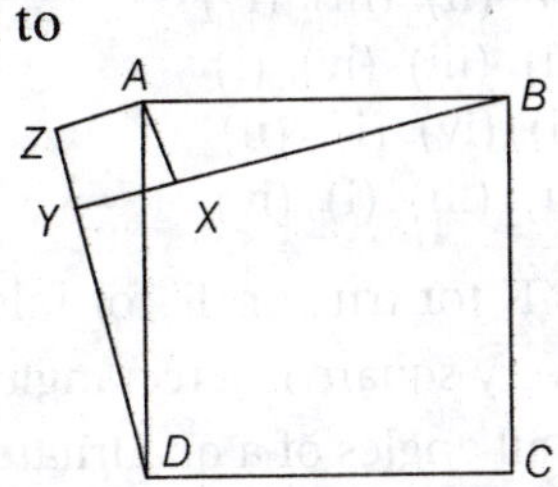


(a) 5 cm (b) 6 cm
(c) 7 cm (d) 8 cm

**24.** *ABCD* is quadrilateral. If *AC* and *BD* are its diagonals, then the
(a) sum of the squares of the sides of the quadrilateral is equal to the sum of the squares of its diagonals.
(b) perimeter of the quadrilateral is equal to the sum of the diagonals
(c) perimeter of the quadrilateral is less than the sum of the diagonals
(d) perimeter of the quadrilateral is greater than the sum of the diagonals

**25.** *ABCD* is a rhombus in which altitude from *D* to side *BC* bisects *BC*. Then, angles of the rhombus.
(a) $\angle A = \angle C = 60°$, $\angle B = \angle D = 120°$
(b) $\angle A = \angle C = 50°$, $\angle B = \angle D = 130°$
(c) $\angle A = \angle C = 70°$, $\angle B = \angle D = 110°$
(d) None of the above

## 2 Marks Questions

**26.** Match the following:

| | List I | | List II |
|---|---|---|---|
| A. | A quadrilateral having all angles and sides equal. | i. | Rectangle |
| B. | A quadrilateral having one pair of parallel sides. | ii. | Square |
| C. | A quadrilateral having all sides equal. | iii. | Trapezium |
| D. | A quadrilateral whose opposite sides and opposite angles are equal. | iv. | Rhombus |

**Codes**

| | A | B | C | D |
|---|---|---|---|---|
| (a) | (i) | (ii) | (iii) | (iv) |
| (b) | (ii) | (iii) | (iv) | (i) |
| (c) | (ii) | (iv) | (i) | (ii) |
| (d) | (ii) | (iii) | (i) | (iv) |

**27.** State 'T' for true or 'F' for false.
I. Every square is a rectangle.
II. If all angles of a quadrilateral are equal, then it is a parallelogram.
III. The sum of all interior angles of a quadrilateral is 180°.
IV. A rhombus is a quadrilateral, whose all sides are equal and each angle is 90°.

**Codes**

| | I | II | III | IV |
|---|---|---|---|---|
| (a) | T | T | T | T |
| (b) | T | F | T | F |
| (c) | T | T | F | F |
| (d) | F | F | T | F |

**28.** *D* and *E* are the mid-points of the sides *AB* and *AC*, respectively of $\Delta ABC$. *DE* is produced to *F*. To prove that *CF* is equal and parallel to *DA*, we need an additional information which is
(a) $\angle DAE = \angle EFC$ (b) $AE = EF$
(c) $DE = EF$ (d) $\angle ADE = \angle ECF$

**29.** State 'T' for true or 'F' for false.
I. If one of the angles of a parallelogram is 60° less than twice the smallest angle, then the smallest angle is 80°.
II. The line segment joining the mid-points of the sides of an equilateral triangle divides it into three congruent triangles.
III. *ABCD* is a parallelogram in which diagonal *AC* bisects $\angle BAD$. If $\angle BAC = 35°$, then $\angle ABC$ is equal to 110°.

**Codes**

| | I | II | III |
|---|---|---|---|
| (a) | F | F | F |
| (b) | T | F | T |
| (c) | T | F | T |
| (d) | F | F | T |

**30.** Fill in the blanks with the help of options, given in the box.

(i) 1.5 cm, (ii) square, (iii) 40°, (iv) 3 cm, (v) 6 cm, (vi) trapezium, (vii) 60°, (viii) 4 cm

I. In the following figure, $S$, $T$ and $U$ are mid-points of the given sides. If the line joining $QT$ and $RS$ intersect $SU$ and $TU$ at $L$ and $M$ respectively, then $LM =$ ___ .

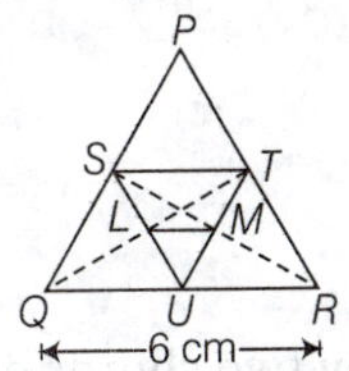


II. In the following figure, $ABCD$ is parallelogram in which $P$ is mid-point of $CD$ and $PA$ is bisector of $\angle DAB$, then $PC =$ ___, if $BC = 4\text{cm}$.

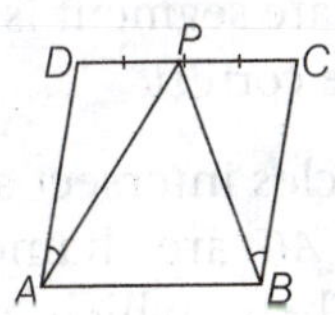


III. In the following figure, $ABCD$ is a parallelogram. If $\angle DAB = 60°$ and $\angle DBC = 80°$, then $\angle CDB =$ ___ .

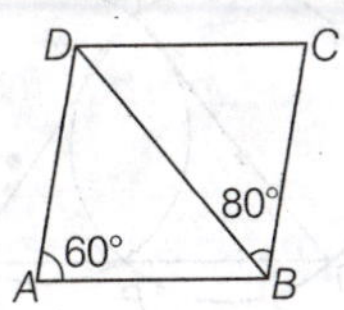


**Codes**

| | I | II | III |
|---|---|---|---|
| (a) | (i) | (viii) | (iii) |
| (b) | (ii) | (iii) | (iv) |
| (c) | (v) | (iv) | (iii) |
| (d) | (i) | (ii) | (iv) |

**31.** $LMNO$ is a trapezium with $LM \parallel NO$. If $P$ and $Q$ are the mid-points of $LO$ and $MN$ respectively and $LM = 10$ cm and $ON = 12$ cm, then $PQ$ is equal to

(a) 2.5 cm
(b) 5 cm
(c) 11 cm
(d) 15 cm

**32.** The parallelogram $PQRS$ is formed by joining together four equilateral triangles of side 1 unit, as shown in the figure.

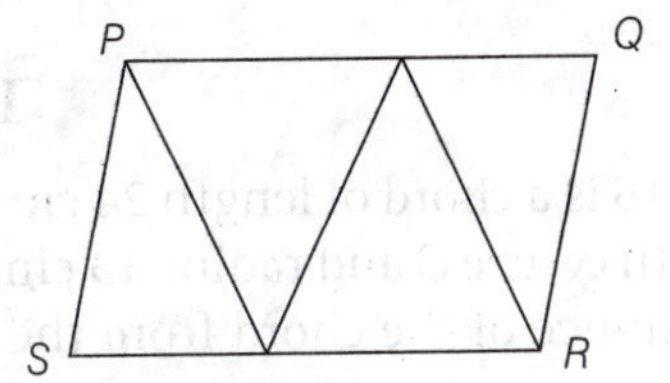


What is the length of the diagonal $SQ$?

(a) $\sqrt{7}$ units
(b) $\sqrt{8}$ units
(c) $\sqrt{6}$ units
(d) $\sqrt{5}$ units

**33.** $ABCD$ is a trapezium in which $AB \parallel DC$ and $AD = BC$. If $P, Q, R, S$ are respectively, the mid-points of $BA, BD, CD$ and $CA$,

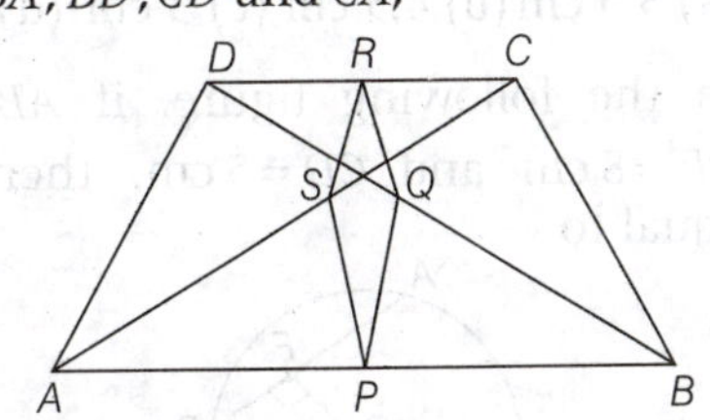


(a) rectangle
(b) square
(c) rhombus
(d) None of the above

Chapter
08

# Circle

## 1 Mark Questions

**1.** If $AB$ is a chord of length 24 cm of a circle with centre $O$ and radius 13 cm, then the distance of the chord from the centre is

(a) 5 cm (b) 6 cm
(c) $\sqrt{407}$ cm (d) 7 cm

**2.** In the given figure, $AB = 10$ cm, $OM = ON = 4$ cm. Then $CD$ is .........

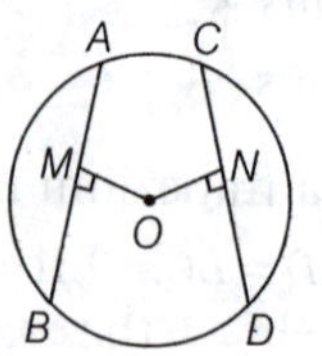


(a) 3.5 cm (b) 4.5 cm (c) 3 cm (d) 10 cm

**3.** In the following figure, if $AB = 8$ cm, $DE = 8$ cm and $CD = 5$ cm, then $CF$ is equal to

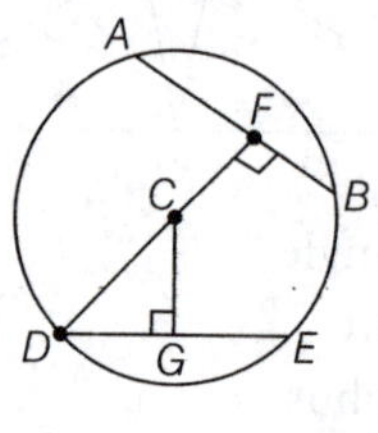


(a) 3 cm (b) 2 cm (c) 5 cm (d) 4 cm

**4.** Choose the incorrect statement.

(a) If two circles intersect at two points, then the line through the centres is the perpendicular bisector of the common chord.

(b) Of any two chords of a circle, the one which is nearer to the centre, is larger.

(c) The arc of a circle subtending a right angle at any point of the circle in its alternate segment is a semi-circle.

(d) All are correct

**5.** If two circles intersect at two points $A$, $B$ and $AD$, $AC$ are diameters to the two circles. Then, which of the following steps is wrong in order to prove that $B$ lies on the line segment $DC$?

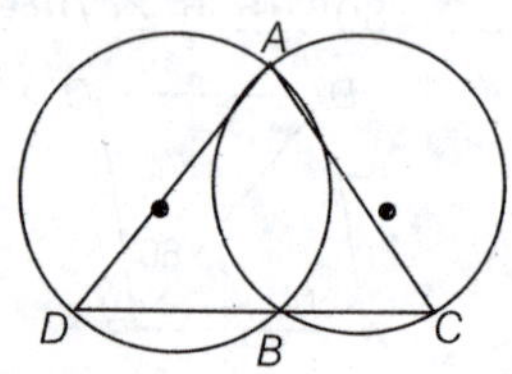


I. Join $AB$.

II. $\angle ABD = 90°$, $\angle ABC = 90°$ (angles in a semi-circle)

III. $\angle ABD + \angle ABC = 180° + 180°$

IV. If $DBC$ is a straight line segment, then $B$ lies on the line segment $DC$.

(a) I
(b) II
(c) III
(d) IV

**6.** In the following figure, $\angle AOB$, the angle subtended by chord $AB$ of the circle, is $60°$. If $OA = 5$ cm, then the length of chord $AB$ is

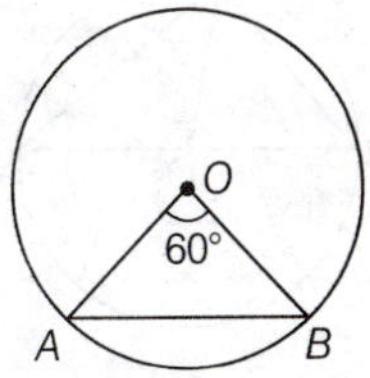


(a) $\frac{5}{2}$ cm (b) $\frac{5\sqrt{3}}{2}$ cm

(c) 5 cm (d) $\frac{5\sqrt{3}}{4}$ cm

**7.** $PQ$ and $RS$ are two parallel chords of circle whose centre is at $O$ and radius is 10 cm. If $PQ = 16$ cm and $RS = 12$ cm, then find out the distances between $PQ$ and $RS$, when they lie on the same side of $O$.

(a) 14 cm

(b) 2 cm

(c) 4 cm

(d) None of the above

**8.** In the given circle with centre '$O$', the mid-points of two equal chords $AB$ and $CD$ are $M$ and $L$ respectively.

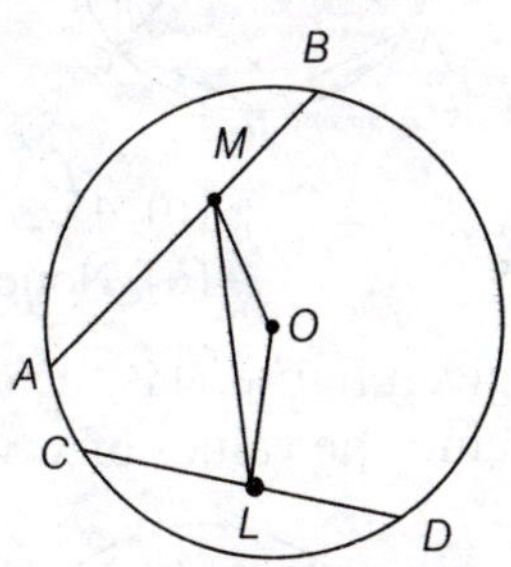


If $\angle OLM = 35°$, Then $\angle LMB$ is equal to

(a) 125° (b) 115°

(c) 105° (d) 90°

**9.** In the following figure, two intersecting circles with centres $O$ and $O'$, intersect each other at points $A$ and $B$. The length of their common chords is 12 cm and the radii are respectively 10 cm and 8 cm. Find the distance between their centres.

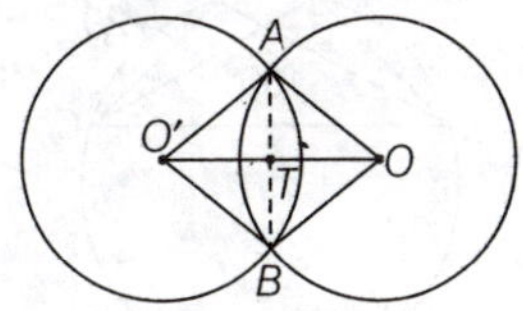


(a) $(\sqrt{8} + \sqrt{28})$ cm (b) $(8 + \sqrt{28})$ cm

(c) $(8 + 2\sqrt{7})$ cm (d) None of these

**10.** In the given figure, if $PQRS$ is a cyclic quadrilateral with respective angles. Then, the ratio of $x$ and $y$ is .........

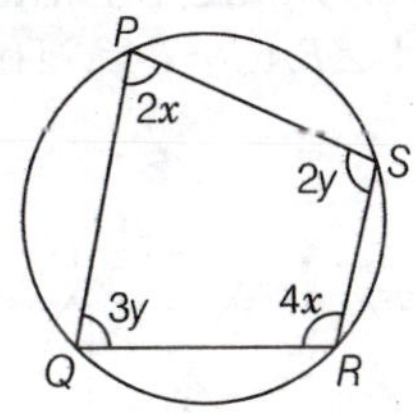


(a) 1 : 3 (b) 5 : 6

(c) 2 : 3 (d) None of these

**11.** In the following figure, $AB$ and $BC$ are two chords of the circle with centre $O$, where $\angle BAO = 40°$; $\angle BCO = 30°$, then $\angle AOC$ is equal to

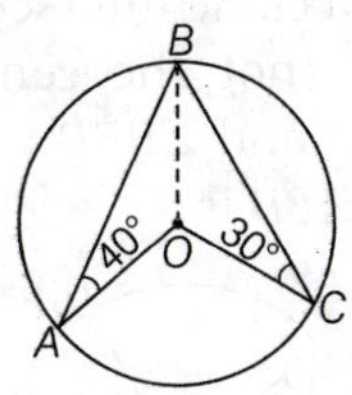


(a) 120°

(b) 70°

(c) 140°

(d) None of the above

**12.** In the following figure, $A, B, C$ and $D$ are four points on the circle. If $AC$ and $BD$ intersect at a point $E$ such that $\angle BEC = 130°$ and $\angle ECD = 20°$. Then, $\angle BAC$ is equal to

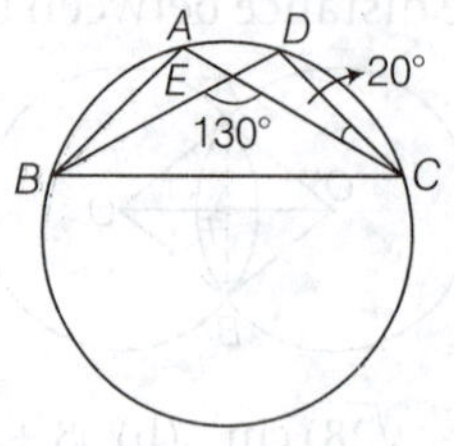


(a) 50°
(b) 160°
(c) 110°
(d) None of the above

**13.** In the given figure, $O$ is the centre of the circle and $\angle BAC = 64°$. The measure of $\angle BDC$ is .........

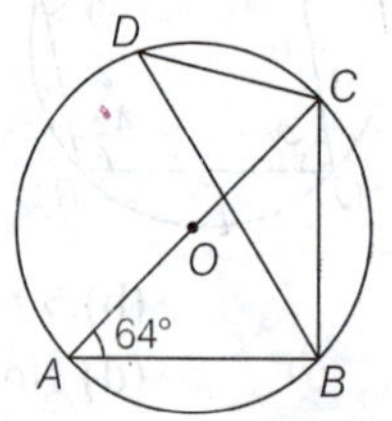


(a) 46° (b) 40°
(c) 64° (d) 50°

**14.** In the following figure, if two chords $AB$ and $CD$ of a circle intersect each other at a point $E$ (not the centre) such that $\angle BAC = 45°$ and $\angle BED = 120°$. Then, the value of $\angle ABD$ is

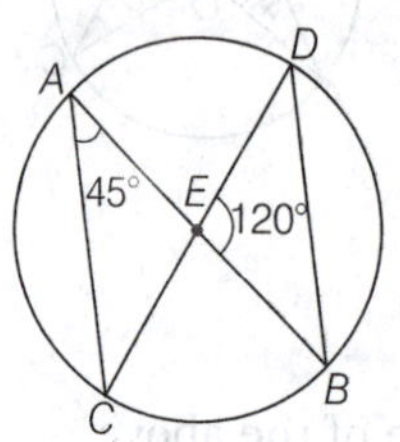


(a) 15° (b) 30°
(c) 45° (d) 60°

**15.** In the following figure, if $AC$ is a diameter of the circle and $\overset{\frown}{AXB}$ is equal to one-third of $BYC$. Then, $\angle BOC$ is equal to

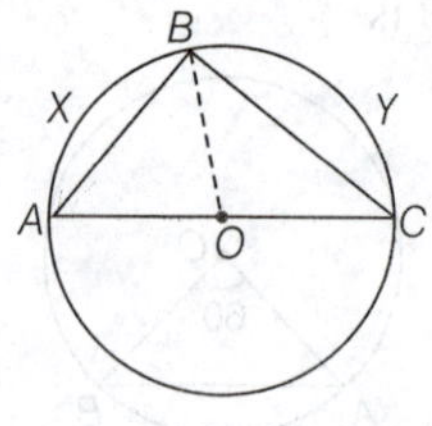


(a) 90° (b) 45° (c) 135° (d) 75°

**16.** In the following figure, the values of $\angle 4, \angle 5$ and $\angle 6$ are, respectively

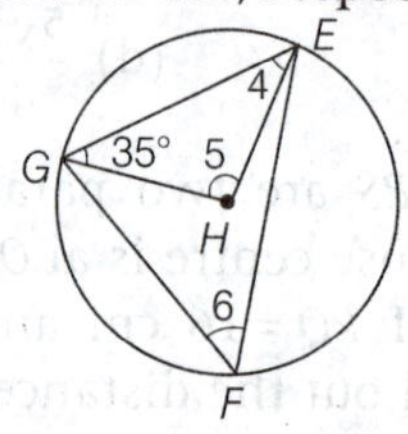


(a) 35°, 120° and 55° (b) 35°, 110 and 60°
(c) 30°, 120° and 55° (d) 35°, 110° and 55°

**17.** In the following figure, $O$ is the centre of the circle. If $\angle CEA = 45°$, then the value of $x + y - z$ is

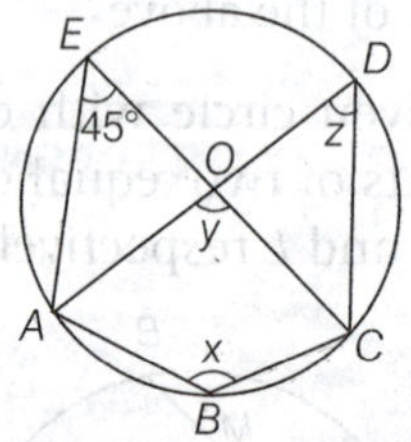


(a) 90° (b) 45°
(c) 135° (d) None of these

**18.** In the given figure, $O$ is the centre of the circle. Find the values of $x, y$ and $z$.

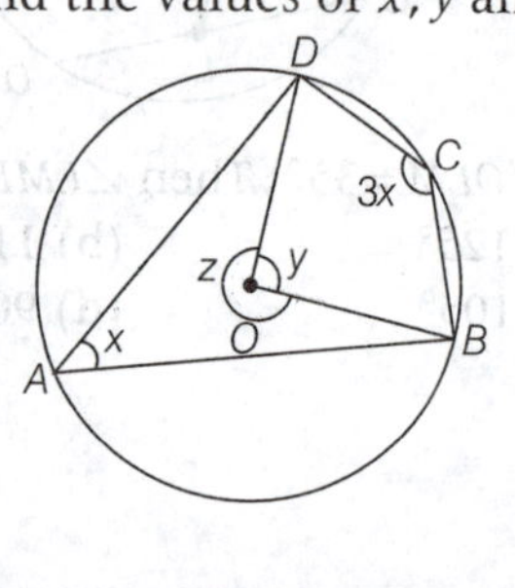

(a) 40°, 90°, 250°
(b) 45°, 90°, 270°
(c) 45°, 80°, 270°
(d) None of the above

**19.** In the following figure, the values of $x$ and $y$ are, respectively

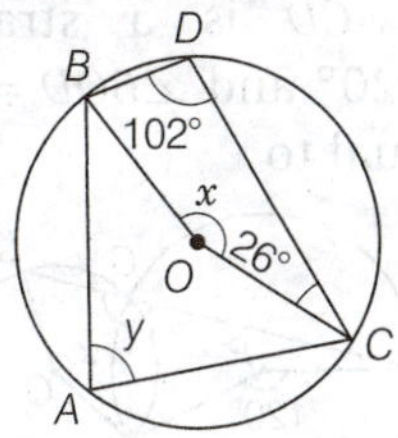


(a) 160° and 78° (b) 156° and 78°
(c) 160° and 80° (d) 144° and 72°

**20.** In the figure given below, if $\angle AOP = 70°$ and $\angle AOB = 120°$, then what is $\angle AQP$?

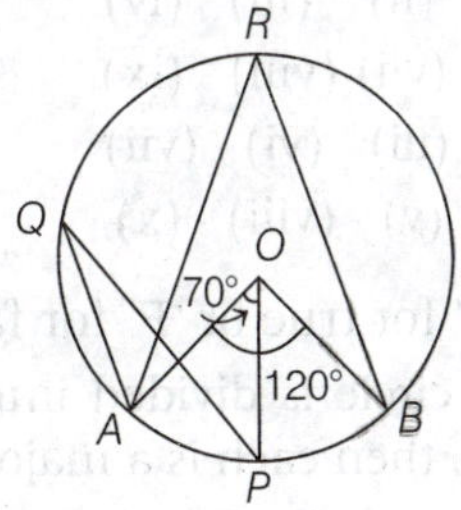


(a) 45° (b) 37.5° (c) 35° (d) 22.5°

## 2 Marks Questions

**21.** Match the following:

| | List I | List II |
|---|---|---|
| A. | 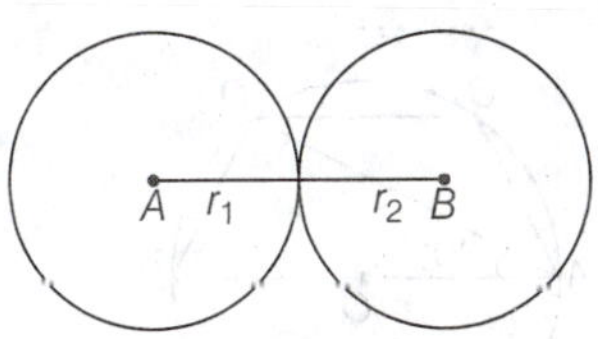 | i. $r_1 + r_2 > AB$ |
| B. | 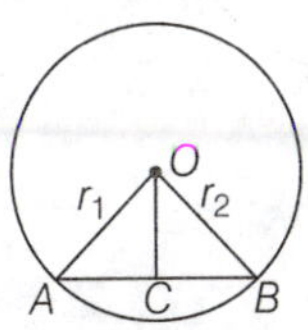 | ii. $r_1 + r_2 = AB$ |
| C. | 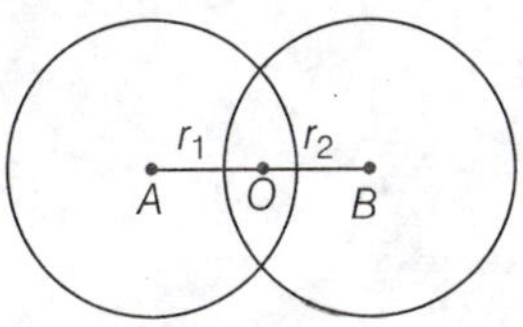 | iii. $r_1 = r_2$ |
| D. | 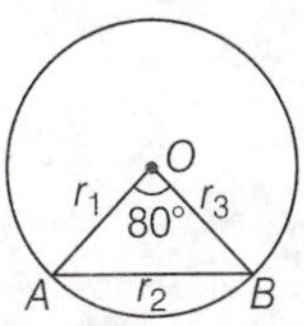 | iv. $r_1 < r_2$ |

**Codes**

| | A | B | C | D |
|---|---|---|---|---|
| (a) | (i) | (ii) | (iii) | (iv) |
| (b) | (ii) | (iii) | (i) | (iv) |
| (c) | (ii) | (iii) | (iv) | (i) |
| (d) | (ii) | (iv) | (i) | (iii) |

**22.** Fill in the blanks with the help of options, given in the box.

(i) 45°, (ii) 90°, (iii) supplementary, (iv) complementary, (v) chord, (vi) centre, (vii) quadrant of circle, (viii) chord, (ix) opposite angle, (x) opposite angles of its interior angle

I. In the following figure, the value of $x$ is ___ .

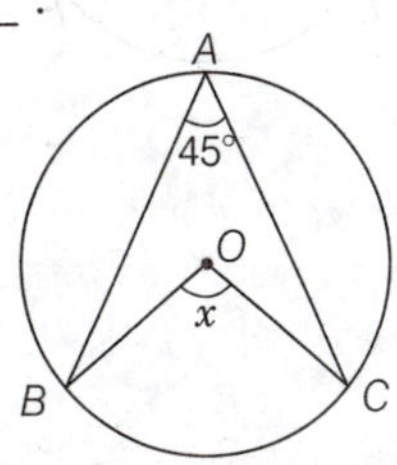


II. Opposite angles of a cyclic quadrilateral are ___ .

III. Congruent arcs of a circle subtend equal angles at the ___ .

IV. The arc of a circle subtending a right angle at the centre is called the ___ .

**Codes**

| | I | II | III | IV |
|---|---|---|---|---|
| (a) | (i) | (ii) | (iii) | (iv) |
| (b) | (vi) | (vii) | (viii) | (ix) |
| (c) | (ii) | (iii) | (vi) | (vii) |
| (d) | (ii) | (v) | (viii) | (x) |

**23.** State 'T' for true or 'F' for false.

I. If a circle is divided into three equal arcs, then each is a major arc.

II. The sum of a pair of opposite angles of a cyclic quadrilateral is 360°.

III. Segment is a region between the chord and its corresponding arc.

IV. Angles inscribed in the same arc of a circle are equal.

| | I | II | III | IV | | I | II | III | IV |
|---|---|---|---|---|---|---|---|---|---|
| (a) | T | F | T | T | (b) | F | F | T | T |
| (c) | T | T | F | T | (d) | F | T | F | T |

**24.** In figure, $O$ is the centre of the circle. Then

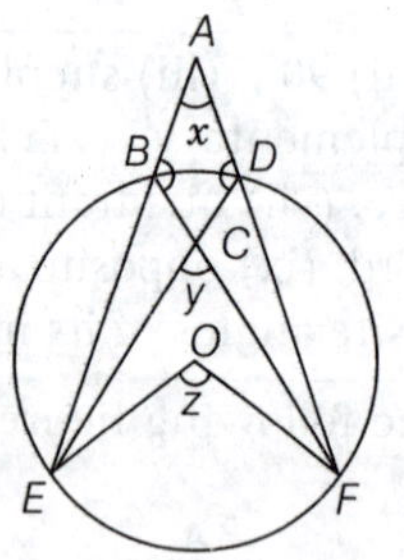


(a) $x + y = z$

(b) $y = z$

(c) $x + 2y = z$

(d) $2x = z$

**25.** In the following figure, $P$ and $Q$ are centres of two circles, intersecting at $B$ and $C$. $ACD$ is a straight line. If $\angle APB = 120°$ and $\angle BQD = x$, then value of $x$ is equal to

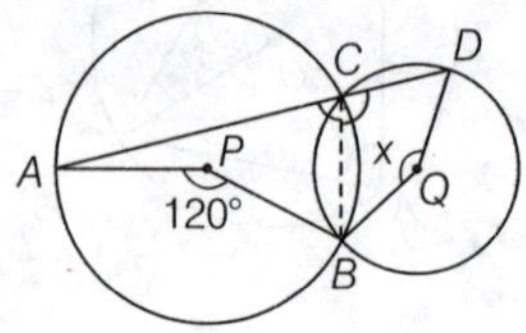


(a) 60° (b) 120°

(c) 30° (d) 90°

**26.** In the given figure, $AOB$ is the diameter of a circle and $CD \parallel AB$. If $\angle BAD = 40°$ then $\angle CAD =$ ………

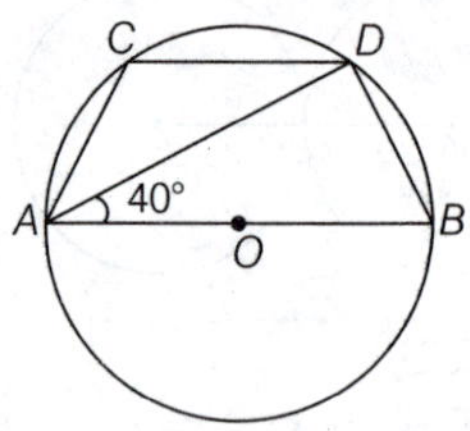


(a) 10°

(b) 60°

(c) 45°

(d) 50°

Chapter 9

# Surface Area of Solid Figures

## 1 Mark Questions

1. The height of a cone is 60 cm. A small cone is cut-off at the top by a plane parallel to its base. If its volume be $\frac{1}{8}$ of the volume of the give n cone, at which height above the base is the section cut ?

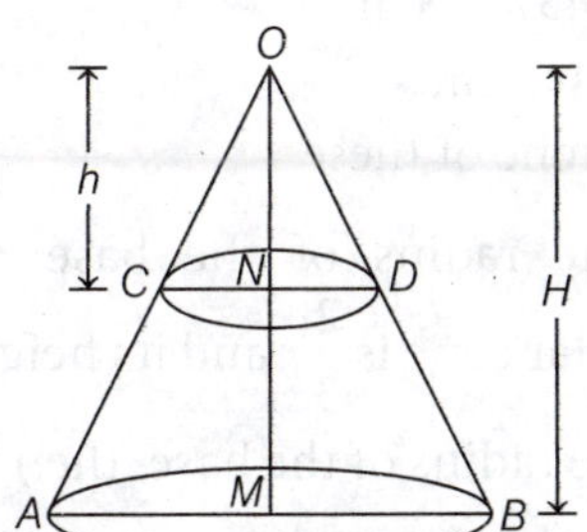


(a) 50 cm (b) 40 cm
(c) 30 cm (d) 35 cm

2. The surface area of a solid metallic sphere is $314 \text{ cm}^2$. It is melted and recast into solid right circular cone of radius 2.5 cm and height 8 cm. Then, the number of cones recast. (take $\pi = 3.14$)
(a) 70 (b) 10
(c) 20 (d) 5

3. A sphere and right circular cone of same radius have equal volumes. How much percentage does the height of the cone exceeds its diameter ?
(a) 50% (b) 70%
(c) 60% (d) 100%

4. The radius of a sphere is increased by 10%, then its surface area increases by
(a) 10% (b) 15%
(c) 20% (d) 21%

5. The volume of the two spheres are in the ratio 64 : 27. The difference of their surface areas, if the sum of their radii is 7, is
(a) $28 \text{ cm}^2$ (b) $88 \text{ cm}^2$
(c) $64\pi \text{ cm}^2$ (d) $36\pi \text{ cm}^2$

6. How many metres of cloth 12 m wide, will be required to make a conical tent, the radius of whose base is 6 m and height is 8 m?
(a) 12 m (b) 12.57 m
(c) 11.5 m (d) 12.9 m

**7.** If the volumes of two cones are in the ratio 1:5 and their diameter are in the ratio 4:5, then the ratio of their heights is

(a) 16:5 (b) 5:16
(c) 2:3 (d) 4:3

**8.** A cone and cylinder are having the same base. Then, the ratio of their heights if their volumes are equal.

(a) 3:1 (b) 1:2
(c) 2:5 (d) 3:4

**9.** A toy is in the form of a cone of radius 3.5 cm surmounted on a hemisphere of same radius. The total height of the toy is 15.5 cm. Find the total surface area of the toy.

(a) 214.5 $cm^2$ (b) 214 $cm^2$
(c) 215 $cm^2$ (d) 216 $cm^2$

**10.** A solid metallic sphere of base radius 3 cm is melted to make a solid cone of height 3 cm and base radius 2 mm. What is the number of cones?

(a) 1350 (b) 4500
(c) 13500 (d) 900

**11.** The slant height of a cone increased by 20%. If the radius remains the same, then curved surface area is increased by

(a) 10% (b) 20%
(c) 21% (d) 12%

**12.** A conical tent is to accommodate 14 persons. Each person must have 6 sq m of the space on the ground and 22 cu m of air to breadth. Find the height of the cone.

(a) 14 m (b) 16 m (c) 13 m (d) 11 m

**13.** A sector of a circle of radius 12cm and central angle of 120°. It is rolled up so that the two bounding radii are joined together to form a cone. Find the volume of the cone.

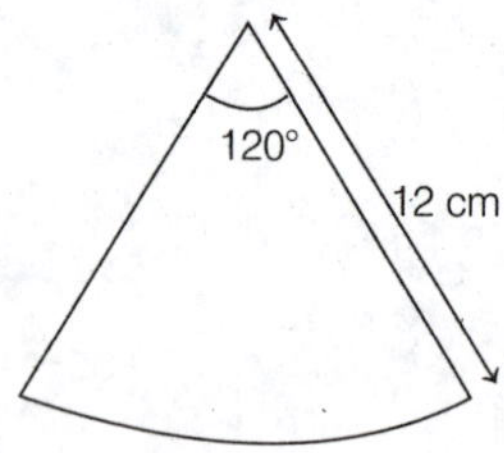


(a) $\frac{128}{3}\sqrt{2}\,\pi\text{ cm}^3$ (b) $\frac{256}{3}\sqrt{2}\,\pi\text{ cm}^3$
(c) $256\sqrt{2}\,\pi\text{ cm}^3$ (d) $\frac{256}{3}\text{ cm}^3$

**14.** A hemispherical tank of radius 3 cm is full of milk. It is connected to a pipe, through which liquid is emptied at the $\frac{1}{14}$ litre per second. The time taken to empty the tank completely is

(a) 0.302 sec (b) 0.396 sec
(c) 0.453 sec (d) 0.792 sec

**15.** The largest sphere is carved out of a cube of 14 cm. The volume of the sphere is

(a) 1450 $cm^3$
(b) 1437.33 $cm^3$
(c) 1440 $cm^3$
(d) None of these

**16.** If the radius of the base of a right circular cone is $\frac{2}{3}r$ and its height is equal to the radius of the base, then its volume is

(a) $\frac{4}{21}\pi r^3$ (b) $16\pi r^3$
(c) $\frac{8\pi}{81}r^3$ (d) $\frac{27}{4}r^3$

**17.** The diameter of two cones are equal. If their slant heights are in the ratio 2:3, then the ratio of their curved surface area is

(a) 4:9 (b) 6:5
(c) 25:16 (d) 2:3

**18.** A corn cob (see below figure), shaped somewhat like a cone, has the radius of its broadest end as 2.1 cm and length as 20 cm. If each 1 $cm^2$ of the surface of the cob carries an average of four grains, then find how many grains you would find on the entire cob?

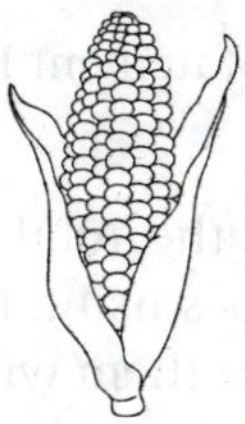

(a) 520
(b) 535
(c) 531
(d) 540

**19. Assertion** A semi-circular sheet of metal of diameter 28 cm is bent into an open conical cap. Then, the depth and capacity of cap is 12.12 cm and 622.26 $cm^3$, respectively.

**Reason** When the semi-circular sheet is bent into an open conical cap, the radius of the sheet becomes the slant height of the cap and the circumference of the sheet becomes the circumference of the base of the cone.

(a) Both Assertion and Reason are correct and Reason is the correct explanation of Assertion
(b) Both Assertion and Reason are correct, but Reason is not the correct explanation of Assertion
(c) Assetion is correct but Reason is incorrect
(d) Assertion is incorrect but Reason is correct

**20.** The radius and height of a right solid circular cone *PQR* are respectively 6 cm and $2\sqrt{7}$ cm. A coaxial cone (*UVW*) of radius and height are respectively 3 cm and $\sqrt{7}$ cm.

Find the whole surface area of solid thus formed.

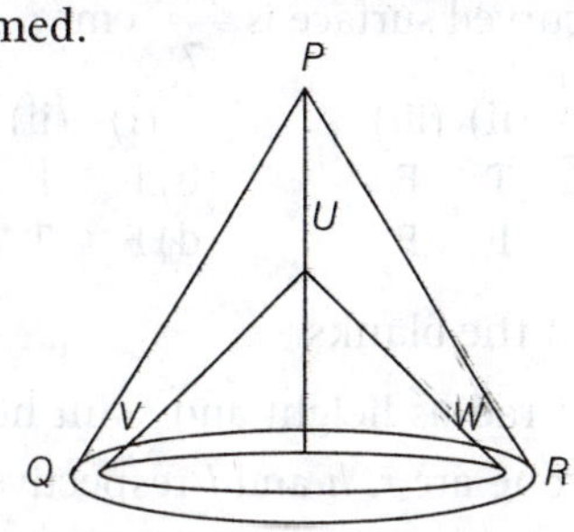


(a) $86\pi$ (b) $88\pi$
(c) $87\pi$ (d) $90\pi$

**21.** The internal and external diameter of a hollow hemispherical vessel are 24 cm and 25 cm respectively. The cost to paint 10 $cm^2$ surface is ₹ 0.2. Then, the total cost to paint the vessel all over

(a) ₹ 38.51 (b) ₹ 51.25
(c) ₹ 48.51 (d) ₹ 41.50

**22.** If the diameter of a sphere is decreased 20%. Then, its curved surface area decreased is

(a) 40% (b) 32%
(c) 56% (d) 36%

## 2 Marks Questions

**23.** True (T) and false (F) statements

(i) A right circular cone is generated by revolving a right angled triangle about one of the sides containing the obtuse angle.

(ii) In a sphere the number of faces is 2.

(iii) The radius of cone is 4 cm and vertical height is 3 cm. Then, the area of the curved surface is $\frac{440}{7}$ cm$^2$.

| | (i) | (ii) | (iii) | | (i) | (ii) | (iii) |
|---|---|---|---|---|---|---|---|
| (a) | F | T | F | (b) | F | F | T |
| (c) | T | F | F | (d) | F | T | T |

**24.** Fill in the blanks.

I. If radius height and slant height of a cone are $r$, $h$ and $l$ respectively, then. Total surface area of a cone is P.

II. If total surface area of sphere is 88 cm$^2$, then radius of sphere is Q.

III. The total surface area of a cone whose radius is 4 cm and slant height 7 cm is R.

Choose the values from the box

(i) $\pi rl$, (ii) $\pi r(l + r)$, (iii) 6 cm, (iv) $\sqrt{7}$ cm, (v) 138.28 cm$^2$, (vi) 7 cm

| | P | Q | R |
|---|---|---|---|
| (a) | (i) | (iii) | (iv) |
| (b) | (ii) | (iii) | (v) |
| (c) | (ii) | (iv) | (v) |
| (d) | (i) | (iv) | (v) |

**25.** **Statement I** If diameter of a sphere is decreased by 20%, then its curved surface area is decreased by 36%.

**Statement II** Curved surface area of sphere is increased when diameter increase.

(a) Both Statement I and Statement II are true

(b) Statement I is true but Statement II is false

(c) Statement I is false but Statement II is true

(d) Both Statement I and Statement II are false

**26.** Calculate the total surface area of the solid shapes using the data in column I and match them with column II

| Column I | Column II |
|---|---|
| A. A hemisphere of radius 10.5 cm | p. 6600 cm$^2$ |
| B. A cone of base radius 30 cm and slant height 40 cm | q. 1039.5 cm$^2$ |
| C. A hemisphere of radius 21 cm. | r. 282.85 cm$^2$ |
| D. A cone of base radius 5 cm and height is 12 cm. | s. 4158 cm$^2$ |

Choose the correct option :

| | A | B | C | D | | A | B | C | D |
|---|---|---|---|---|---|---|---|---|---|
| (a) | q | p | s | r | (b) | r | s | p | q |
| (c) | q | s | p | r | (d) | s | p | r | q |

**27.** Fill in the blanks.

(I) The volume of hemisphere of radius 7 cm is P.

(II) A hollow sphere of internal and external radii 2 cm and 4 cm respectively is melted into a cone of base radius 4 cm. Then, the height of the cone is Q.

(III) A metallic sphere of radius 10.5 cm is melted and thus recast into small, sphere of radius 3.5 cm. Then, the number of small sphere is R.

(IV) If the diameter and height of a right circular cone are 6 cm and 7 cm respectively, then the volume of the right circular cone is S.

Choose the values of the box

| (i) $21\pi$ cm$^3$, (ii) 27, (iii) $23\pi$ cm$^3$, (iv) 340 cm$^3$, (v) $(x+2z)(y+2z)z$, (vi) $486\pi$ cm$^3$, (vii) 14 cm, (viii) $480\pi$ cm$^3$ |
|---|

| | P | Q | R | S |
|---|---|---|---|---|
| (a) | (iv) | (v) | (ii) | (i) |
| (b) | (vi) | (vii) | (ii) | (i) |
| (c) | (vi) | (vii) | (iv) | (i) |
| (d) | (iv) | (v) | (i) | (ii) |

**28.** Match the two columns.

| | Column I | Column II |
|---|---|---|
| P. | If a cone and a hemisphere have equal base and equal volume. Then, the ratio of their heights is | (i) 9 : 25 |
| Q. | The base radii of two right circular cones of the same height are in the ratio 3:5. Then, the ratio of their volume is | (ii) 4 : 1 |
| R. | A cone and a hemisphere have equal base and the ratio of volume of cone to volume of hemisphere is 2, then the ratio of height to radius is | (iii) 2 : 1 |
| S. | Eight solid iron spheres each of radius $r$ and surface area $S$ are melted to form a sphere with surface area $S'$, then ratio of $S$ and $S'$ is | (iv) 1 : 2 |

Choose the correct option :

| | P | Q | R | S |
|---|---|---|---|---|
| (a) | (iv) | (iii) | (ii) | (i) |
| (b) | (iii) | (ii) | (i) | (iv) |
| (c) | (iii) | (i) | (ii) | (iv) |
| (d) | (ii) | (iii) | (iv) | (i) |

**29.** If a solid sphere of radius 10 cm is moulded into 8 spherical solid balls of equal radius, then the surface area of each ball is

(a) $75\pi$ cm$^2$
(b) $100\pi$ cm$^2$
(c) 150 cm$^2$
(d) 50 cm$^2$

**30.** A solid wooden toy is in the shape of a right circular cone mounted on a hemisphere. If the radius of the hemisphere is 5.2 cm and the total height of the toy is 11.2 cm, then the volume of the wooden toy is

(a) 464.57 cm$^3$
(b) 646.75 cm$^3$
(c) 465 cm$^2$
(d) 614 cm$^3$

Chapter

10

# Statistics

## 1 Mark Questions

**1.** A frequency polygon is constructed by plotting frequency of the class interval and the
(a) upper limit of the class
(b) lower limit of the class
(c) mid-value of the class
(d) any values of the class

**2.** In a histogram the area of each rectangle is proportional to
(a) the class mark of the corresponding class interval
(b) the class size of the corresponding class interval
(c) frequency of the corresponding class interval
(d) cumulative frequency of the corresponding class interval

**3.** In the 'less than' type of ogive the cumulative frequency is plotted against
(a) the lower limit of the concerned class interval
(b) the upper limit of the concerned class interval
(c) the mid-value of the concerned class interval
(d) any value of the concerned class interval

**4.** In a histogram the class intervals or the groups are taken along
(a) $Y$-axis
(b) $X$-axis
(c) both of $X$-axis and $Y$-axis
(d) in between $X$ and $Y$-axes

**5.** A histogram is a pictorial representation of the grouped data in which class intervals and frequency are respectively taken along
(a) vertical axis and horizontal axis
(b) vertical axis only
(c) horizontal axis only
(d) horizontal axis and vertical axis

**6.** In a histogram, each class rectangle is constructed with base as
(a) frequency
(b) class-intervals
(c) range
(d) size of the class

**Directions** (Q. Nos. 7-9) *The bar graph shown in figure represents the circulation of newspaper in 10 languages.*

Study the bar graph and answer the following questions :

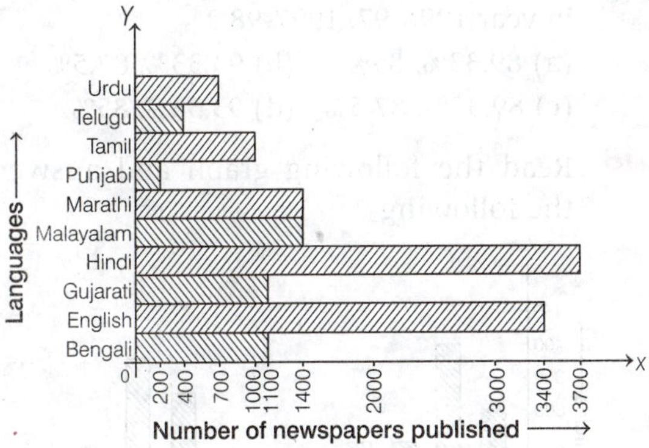


**7.** What is the total number of newspaper published in Hindi, Punjabi, Urdu, Bengali, English and Tamil ?

(a) 9500 (b) 10,000

(c) 10,200 (d) 10,100

**8.** Pair of languages which publish same number of newspaper ?

(a) Bengali and Tamil

(b) Hindi and English

(c) Gujarati and Marathi

(d) Bengali and Gujarati

**9.** How much the total number of newspapers published in Marathi and English both is more than the total number of newspapers published in Tamil and Hindi both ?

(a) 700 (b) 0

(c) 100 (d) 200

**10.** In the following frequency distribution, the adjusted frequency for the class 25-45 is

| Class Interval | 5-10 | 10-15 | 15-25 | 25-45 | 45-75 |
|---|---|---|---|---|---|
| Frequency | 6 | 12 | 10 | 8 | 15 |

(a) 6 (b) 5 (c) 3 (d) 2

**11.** The bar graph shows the export/import for 5 consecutive years for any goods.

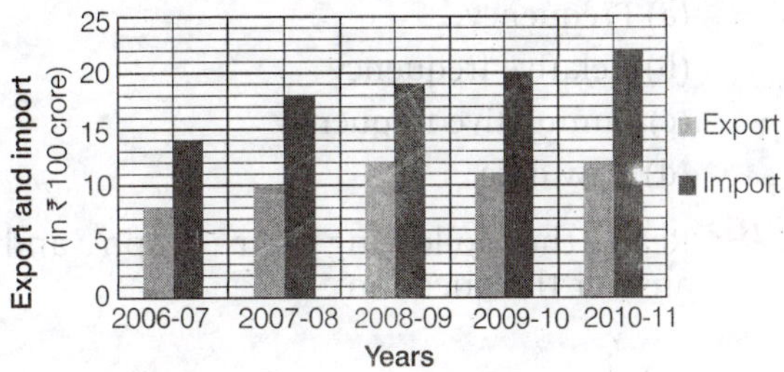


What is the mean of export and import of the years 2007-08 and 2009-10?

(a) 16.75 (b) 29.5

(c) 15.75 (d) 27.5

**12.** The mean of prime numbers between 1 and 20 is

(a) 9.5 (b) 10.5

(c) 9.6 (d) 10.6

**13.** Read the following bar graph and answer the following questions :

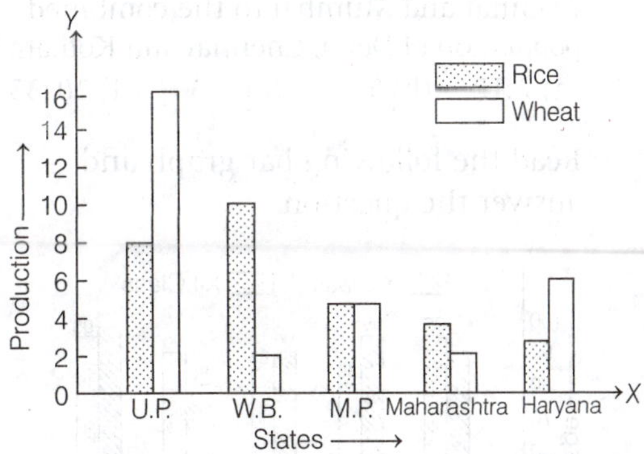


What is the percentage of total production of wheat to the total production of wheat and rice ?

(a) 50% (b) 51.67%

(c) 51.75% (d) 50.82%

**14.** Which one of the following is not the graphical representation of statistical data?

(a) Bar graph (b) Histogram

(c) Frequency polygon

(d) Cumulative frequency distribution

**15.** In a frequency distribution, ogives are graphical representation of

(a) Frequency

(b) Relative frequency

(c) Cumulative frequency

(d) Raw data

**16.** Read the following bar graph and answer the question

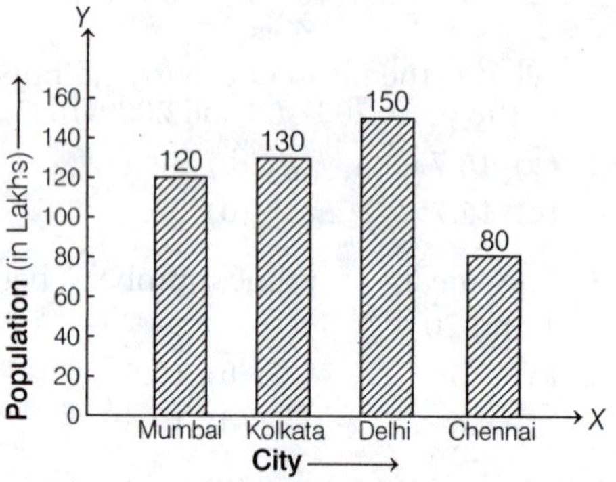


The ratio of combined population of Chennai and Mumbai to the combined population of Delhi, Chennai and Kolkata?

(a) 7:12 (b) 5:9 (c) 2:3 (d) 20:33

**17.** Read the following bar graph and answer the question

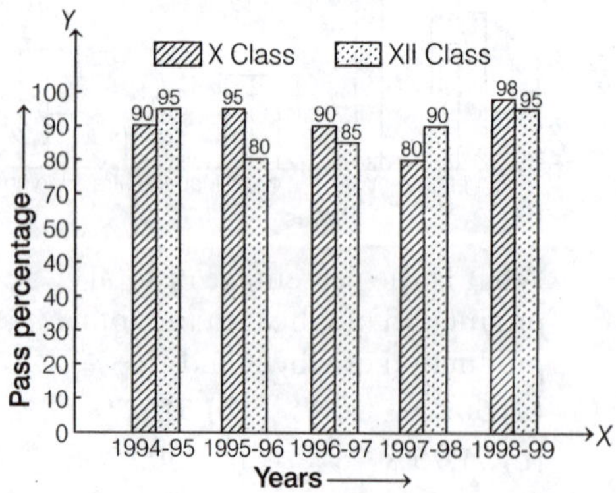


What is the average pass percentage of X class in year 1994-95, 1997-98, 1998-99 and average pass percentage of XII class in year 1996-97, 1997-98 ?

(a) 89.33%, 85% (b) 93.33%, 87.5%

(c) 89.33%, 87.5% (d) 93.33%, 85%

**18.** Read the following graph and answer the following-

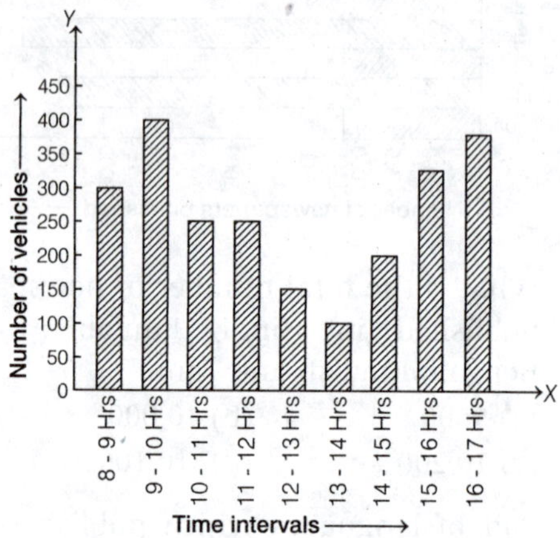


What is the total number of vehicles passing through a crossing during a particular day ?

(a) 2300 (b) 2350 (c) 2250 (d) 2400

**19.** Read the graph and check which statement is true ?

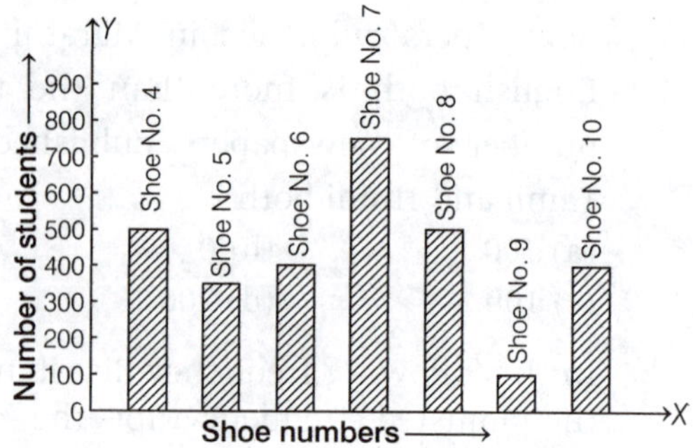

**Statement I** The number of students wearing shoe number 10 is less than three times the number of students wearing shoe number 9 ?

**Statement II** The number of students wearing shoe number 4 is equal to the number of students wearing shoe number 8 ?

(a) Statement I is true but statement II is false.

(b) Statement II is true but statement I is false

(c) Both statement are true.

(d) Both statement are false

## 2 Marks Questions

**20.** If $\bar{x}$ is the mean of $x_1, x_2, \ldots, x_n$ then for $a \neq 0$, the mean of $ax_1, ax_2, \ldots\ldots, ax_n$ $\frac{x_1}{a}, \frac{x_2}{a}, \ldots, \frac{x_n}{a}$ is

(a) $\left(a+\frac{1}{a}\right)\bar{x}$

(b) $\left(a+\frac{1}{a}\right)\frac{\bar{x}}{2}$

(c) $\frac{\bar{x}}{n}$

(d) $\frac{\left(a+\frac{1}{a}\right)\bar{x}}{2n}$

# PRACTICE SET 01

## 1 Mark Questions

**1.** If $x = 1$ and $y = 0$ is the solution of equation $2x + \sqrt{3}y - 4a = 0$, then the value of $a$ is

(a) 7 (b) $-\frac{1}{2}$

(c) $\frac{1}{2}$ (d) $\frac{1}{3}$

**2.** In the following figure, the value of $\angle x$ is

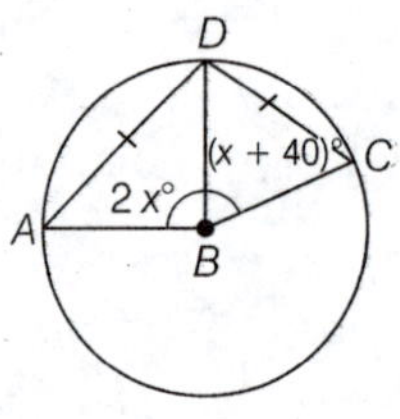


(a) 60° (b) 40°

(c) 20° (d) None of these

**3.** A race car driver kept track of the number of laps he drove in the past 5 days. Which day had the highest laps driven?

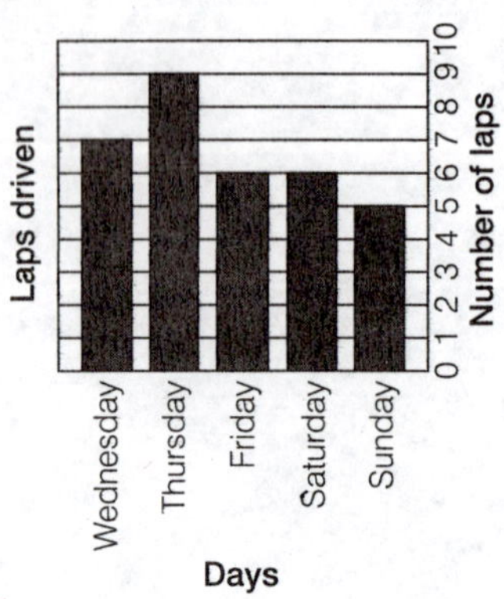


(a) Sunday (b) Friday

(c) Saturday (d) Thursday

**4.** The value of $l$, so that $y - 2p$ is a factor of $\frac{y^3}{4p^2} - 2y + lp$.

(a) 0 (b) 1

(c) 2 (d) 3

**5.** Number of zeroes of the zero polynomial is

(a) 0 (b) 1

(c) 2 (d) Infinite

**6.** $\frac{7\sqrt{2}}{(3+\sqrt{2})} - \frac{2\sqrt{5}}{(\sqrt{6}+\sqrt{5})} - \frac{3\sqrt{2}}{(\sqrt{15}+3\sqrt{2})}$ is equal to

(a) 0 (b) 1

(c) 2 (d) None of these

**7.** The minute hand of a clock is $\frac{x}{2}$ cm long. Then, the area of the face of the clock described by the minute hand in 35 min, is

(a) $\frac{11x^2}{24}$ (b) $\frac{7x^2}{24}$ (c) $\frac{5x^2}{24}$ (d) $\frac{13x^2}{24}$

**8.**

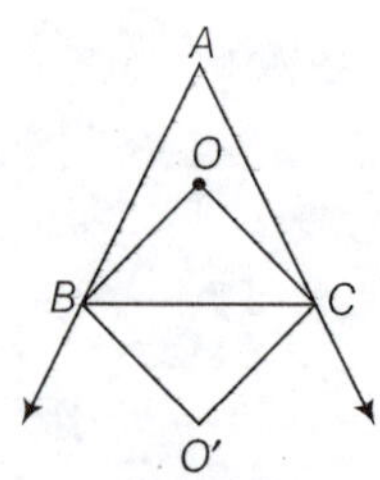


In the above figure, $OB$ and $O'B$ are internal and external bisectors respectively, then which of the following is true?

(a) $\angle BOC = \angle BO'C + \angle A$
(b) $\angle BOC = \angle BO'C$
(c) $\angle BO'C = \angle BOC + \angle A$
(d) Can't say

**9.** If $AB$ is a line segment, $C$ is a point such that $\angle ACB = 90°$ and $D$ is a point such that $\angle ADB = 90°$. Then, which of the following can be true?
(a) $ABCD$ is a rhombus.
(b) $ABCD$ is a parallelogram.
(c) $ABCD$ is a cyclic quadrilateral.
(d) Can't say

**10.**

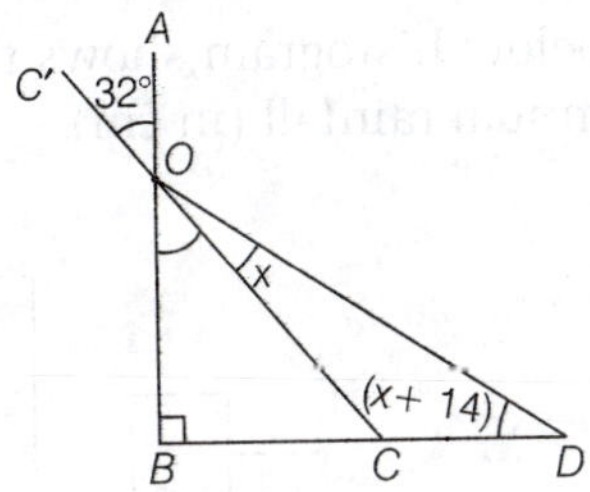


In the above figure, if $AB \perp BC$, then $\angle x$ is equal to
(a) 18° (b) 22° (c) 25° (d) 32°

**11.** The given values of $x$ and $y$ are thought to satisfy a linear equation $y = 4x - 2$. When we draw the graph using the values of $x$ and $y$ as given in the table.

| $x$ | 1 | 2 |
|---|---|---|
| $y$ | 2 | 6 |

At what point the graph of the linear equation intersects the $X$-axis?
(a) (1, 0) (b) (2, 0)
(c) $\left(\frac{1}{2}, 0\right)$ (d) $\left(\frac{1}{4}, 0\right)$

**12.** How many spherical bullets can be made out of a solid cone of lead whose radius and height 12 cm and 44 cm respectively, each bullet being 4 cm in diameter?
(a) 1541 (b) 2541 (c) 2041 (d) 2341

**13.** $\sqrt[5]{\sqrt[4]{(2^4)^3}} - 5\sqrt[5]{8} + 2\sqrt[5]{\sqrt[4]{(2^3)^4}}$ is equal to
(a) $2(\sqrt[5]{8})$
(b) $-2(\sqrt[5]{8})$
(c) $3(\sqrt[5]{8})$
(d) $-3(\sqrt[5]{8})$

**14.** In a $\Delta ABC$, if $AB = AC$ and the bisectors of angles $B$ and $C$ intersect at point $O$. Then, which of the following is true?
(a) $BO = OC$
(b) $AO$ is bisector of $\angle BAC$
(c) $OA = OB = OC$
(d) Both (a) and (b)

**15.** The aggregate monthly expenditure of a family was ₹ 6240 during the first 3 months, ₹ 6780 during the next 4 months and ₹ 7236 during the last 5 months of a year. If the total savings during the year is ₹ 7080, then the average monthly income of the family is
(a) ₹ 7425
(b) ₹ 7500
(c) ₹ 8425
(d) ₹ 8500

**16.** In the following figure, if $MK$ bisects $\angle JKL$, then which of the following is incorrect?

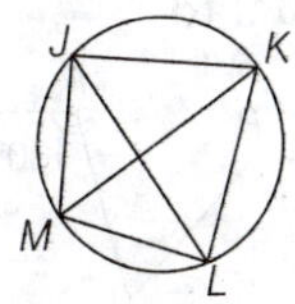


(a) $JM = ML$
(b) $\angle JKM = \angle LKM$
(c) $\Delta JML$ is an isosceles
(d) None of the above

**17.** Edward walked around two sides of a square field from $A$ to $B$. Misha walked diagonally from $A$ to $B$.

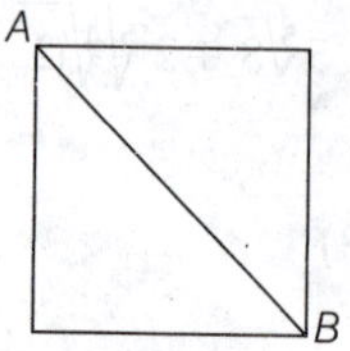


Approximately, what percentage of the distance Edward walked was the distance Misha walked?

(a) 50% (b) 71%
(c) 100% (d) 141%

**18.** The price $p$ that a make up company can charge for a certain kit is $p = 40 - 4x^2$, where $x$ is the number of kits produced. It costs the make up company ₹ 15 to make each kit. Then, the polynomial (function) expressing the company's profit $p$ by subtracting the total cost to make $x$ kits from the total revenue is

(a) $-4x^3 + 4x$ (b) $-4x^3 + 25x$
(c) $-4x^2 + 5x$ (d) $-4x^2 + 25x$

**19.** $(\sqrt{2} + \sqrt{3})(\sqrt{3} - \sqrt{2})$ is

(a) a rational number
(b) an irrational number
(c) zero
(d) None of the above

**20.** In the adjoining figure, if $OP \parallel RS$, then $\angle PQR$ is equal to

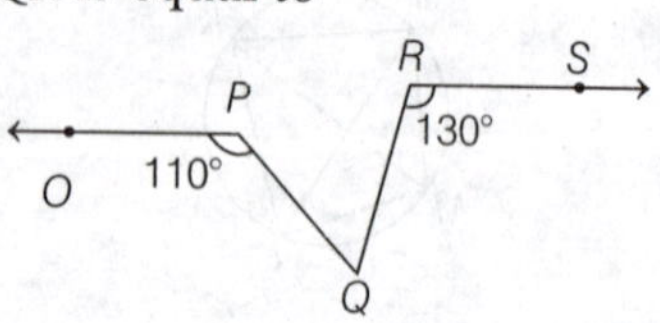


(a) 50° (b) 30° (c) 40° (d) 60°

**21.** If $x = \left(\frac{\sqrt{3}+1}{2}\right)$, then the value of $4x^3 + 2x^2 - 8x + 7$ is

(a) 8 (b) 10
(c) 15 (d) 14

**22.** If $p + q = 10$ and $pq = 5$, then the value of $\frac{p}{q} + \frac{q}{p}$ will be

(a) 22 (b) 18
(c) 20 (d) 21

**23.** The percentage increase in the area of an equilateral triangle, if its each side is tripled, is

(a) 200% increase
(b) 400% increase
(c) 600% increase
(d) 800% increase

**24.** The below histogram shows the data of the annual rainfall (in cm).

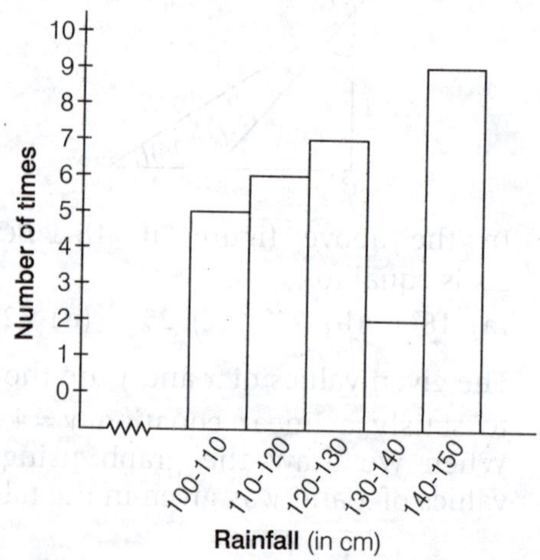


The number of times annual rainfall below 120 cm is what percent of the number of times the annual rainfall above 130 cm.

(a) 100% (b) 200%
(c) 50% (d) 40%

**25.** Choose the incorrect statement.
In a parallelogram,

(a) diagonals divide it into congruent triangles
(b) opposite sides are equal
(c) opposite angles are equal
(d) the diagonals bisect each other at 90°

**26.** The following graphs gives the amount of manure (in thousand tonnes) manufactured by a company during some years.

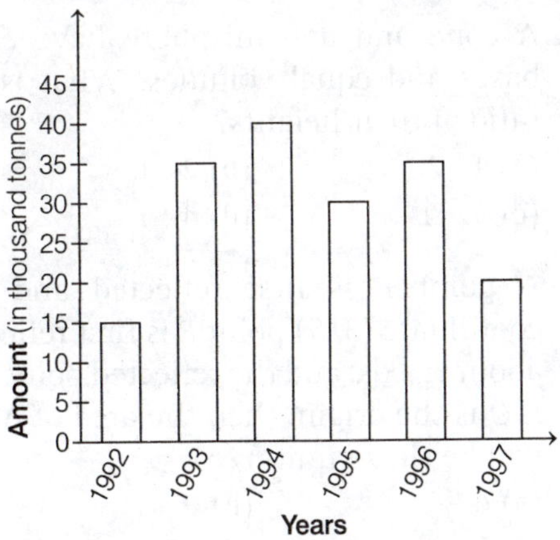


In which year the amount of manure manufactured by the company was maximum ?

(a) 1993 (b) 1994
(c) 1996 (d) 1997

**27.** If $\dfrac{(7+4\sqrt{5})+(4-2\sqrt{5})-(10+5\sqrt{5})}{6}$ $= p+q\sqrt{5}$, then $\sqrt{p-q}$ is equal to

(a) $\sqrt{6}$
(b) $\dfrac{\sqrt{6}}{2}$
(c) $\dfrac{\sqrt{6}}{3}$
(d) $\dfrac{1}{\sqrt{6}}$

**28.** $ABCD$ is a cyclic quadrilateral whose diagonals $AC$ and $BD$ intersect at $P$. If $AB = DC$, then which of the following is/are correct?

(a) $AD \parallel BC$
(b) $\Delta PAB \cong \Delta PDC$
(c) $PA = PB$ and $PC = PD$
(d) All of the above

**29.** In the given figure, $ABCD$ is a rectangle. $BD = BE$, $\angle BED = 40°$ and $\angle EDA = 260°$. Find $\angle CDB$.

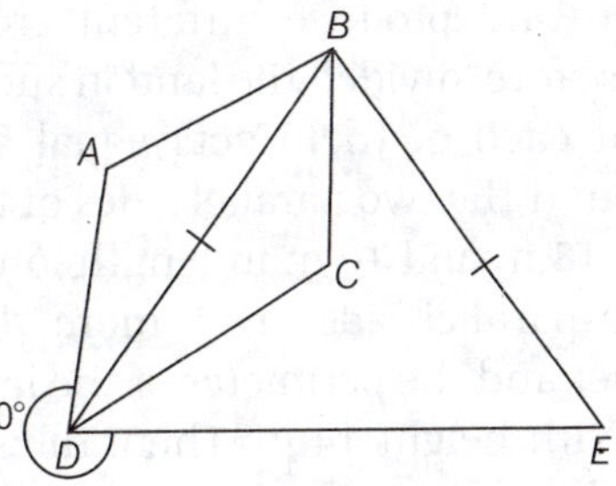


(a) 25° (b) 30°
(c) 40° (d) 45°

**30.** In isosceles $\Delta ABC$, $BA$ and $BC$ are congruent. If $M$ and $N$ are points on $AC$ such that $MA$ is congruent to $MB$ and $NB$ is congruent to $NC$. Then, which of the following is true?

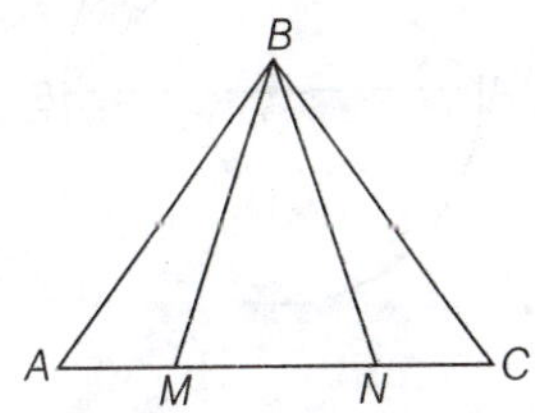


(a) $\Delta ABN \cong \Delta CNB$ (b) $\Delta AMB \cong \Delta CNB$
(c) $\Delta AMB \cong \Delta MNB$ (d) $\Delta CNB \cong \Delta MBN$

**31.** $ABC$ is a triangle and $M$ is the mid-point of $AC$. If $I$ and $J$ are points on $BM$ such that $AI$ and $CJ$ are perpendicular to $BM$. Then, which of the following is incorrect?

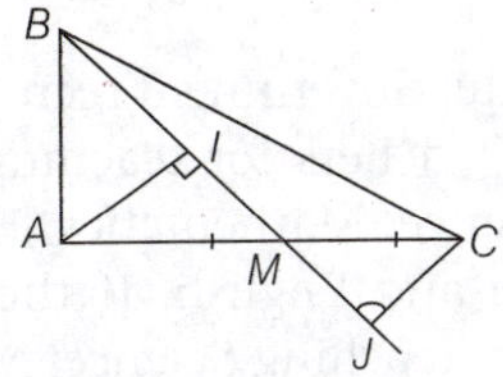


(a) $\angle AMI = \angle CMJ$ (b) $\angle IAM = \angle JCM$
(c) $\Delta AIM \cong \Delta CJM$ (d) $\angle ABM = \angle CBM$

**32.** Megha has a piece of land which is in the shape of a trapezium. She wants her one daughter and one son to work on the land and produce different crops and therefore, divided the land in such a way that each of them gets equal share of land. If the two parallel sides of the land are 18 m and 10 m in length, one of the non-parallel sides is 1 more than the other and the perimeter of the land is 62 m with height 14 m. Then, the share of land each one gets, is

(a) 196 $m^2$ (b) 98 $m^2$
(c) 150 $m^2$ (d) 100 $m^2$

**33.** In the given figure '$O$' is the centre of the circle, then the value of $x$ is

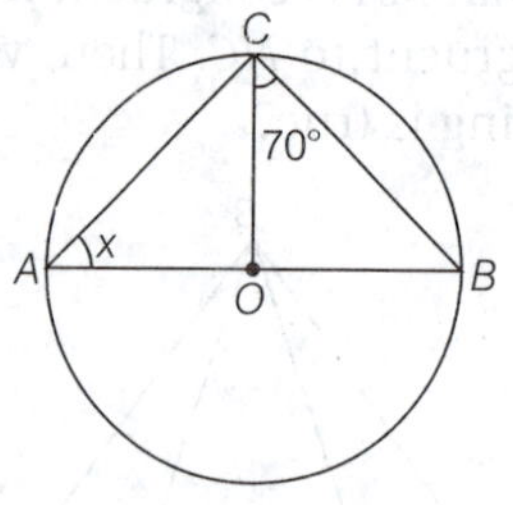


(a) 90° (b) 50°
(c) 20° (d) 40°

**34.** The value of question mark (?) in the expression $x^4 - 7x^2 + 1 = ?$, if $x = \frac{\sqrt{3}+2}{\sqrt{2}}$, is

(a) $\frac{1}{4}$ (b) $\frac{3}{4}$
(c) 1 (d) 3

**35.** In a state, Government recruited average of 800 teachers for teaching 5 subjects *viz*. Science, Mathematics, Hindi, Social Science and English. If the average of teachers teaching Science, Mathematics and Social Science is 656 and the number of teachers teaching Hindi is 20% of the total number of teachers. Then, the number of teachers teaching English is

(a) 1200 (b) 600
(c) 168 (d) 1232

**36.** A cone and a hemisphere have equal bases and equal volumes. What is the ratio of their heights?

(a) 1 : 2 (b) 2 : 1
(c) $\sqrt{2}$ :1 (d) 4 : 1

**37.** A point $P$ is first reflected and has coordinate (3, 5) point $P$ is first reflected about $Y$-axis, and the reflected point is $Q$. If $O$ is the origin, then the area of $\Delta POQ$ will be (in sq units)

(a) 6 (b) 9
(c) 12 (d) 15

**38.** The value of $\angle y$, if $AB \| PQ$ is

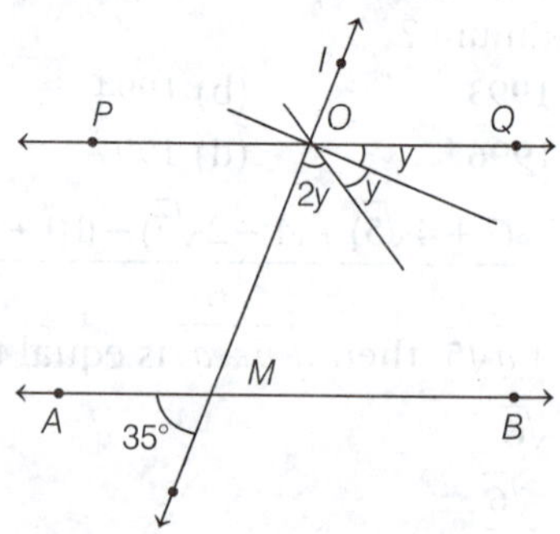


(a) 9° (b) 29°
(c) 27° (d) 7°

**39.** A circle has it centre (3, 5) has its point of tangency (3, 0). The area of circle will be (in sq units)

(a) $25\pi$ (b) $9\pi$
(c) $16\pi$ (d) $4\pi$

**40.** If the point $A(3, 5)$ and $B(1, 4)$ lie on the graph of line $ax + by - 7 = 0$, then $(a, b)$ will be

(a) (1, 2) (b) (1, − 2)
(c) (− 1, 2) (d) (− 1, − 2)

## 2 Marks Questions

**41.** In the following figure, parallel sides of a trapezium are $a$ and $b$, respectively.

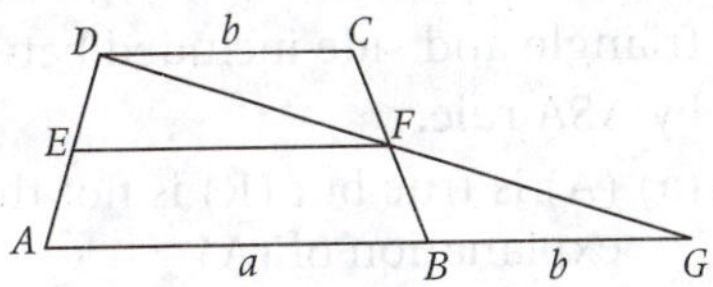


(a) $DF = FG$ (b) $DC = 2BG$
(c) $DF = 2FG$ (d) $DC = 3BG$

**42.** The value of

$$\left(\frac{x^{1/a}}{x^{1/b}}\right)^{\frac{a^2b^2}{b-a}} \cdot \left(\frac{x^{1/b}}{x^{1/c}}\right)^{\frac{b^2c^2}{c-b}} \cdot \left(\frac{x^{1/c}}{x^{1/a}}\right)^{\frac{a^2c^2}{a-c}}$$ is

(a) 0 (b) 1
(c) $x^{1/a+1/b+1/c}$ (d) $x^{ab+bc+ca}$

**43. Assertion** (A) If $ABCD$ is a rhombus in which $\angle C = 60°$, then $AC : BD = \sqrt{3} : 1$.

**Reason** (R) All sides of rhombus are equal and diagonals of rhombus are perpendicular to each other.

Which of the following is true?

(a) (A) is true and (R) is the correct explanation of (A)
(b) (A) is true and (R) is not the correct explanation of (A)
(c) (A) is true and (R) is false
(d) Both (A) and (R) are false

**44.** Match the following :

| | List I | List II |
|---|---|---|
| A. | 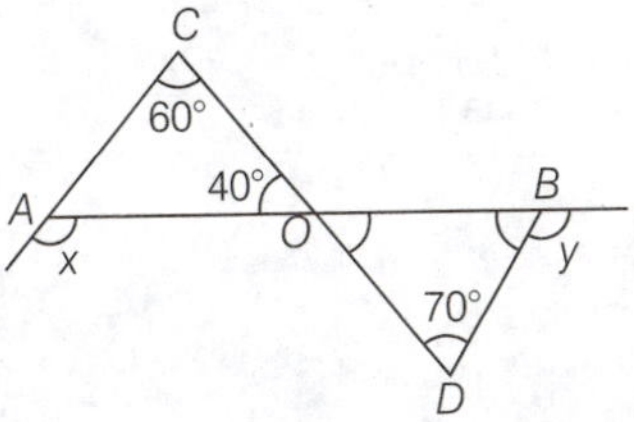 | i. $x = 18°$ $y = 72°$ |
| B. | 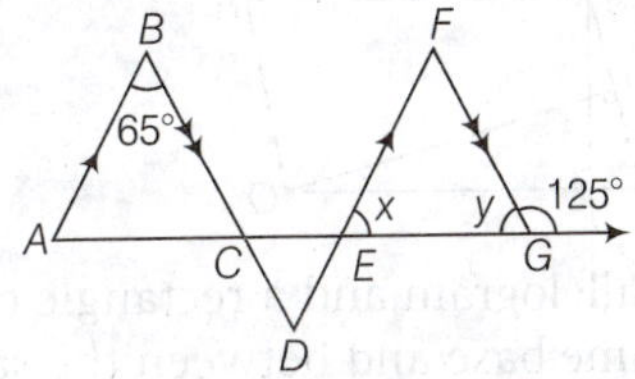 | ii. $x = 100°$ $y = 110°$ |
| C. | 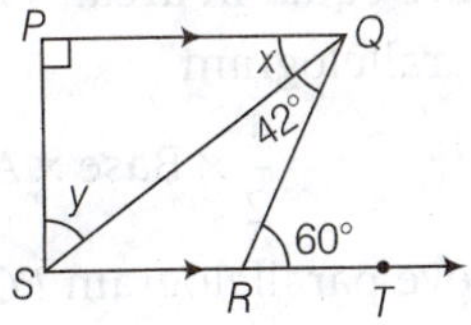 | iii. $x = 70°$ $y = 55°$ |

| | A | B | C |
|---|---|---|---|
| (a) | (i) | (ii) | (iii) |
| (b) | (ii) | (iii) | (i) |
| (c) | (i) | (iii) | (ii) |
| (d) | (ii) | (i) | (iii) |

**45.** $ABCD$ is a parallelogram. If $AB$ is produced to $E$ such that $ED$ bisects $BC$ at $O$. Then, which of the following is correct?

(a) $AB = OE$
(b) $AB = BE$
(c) $OE = OC$
(d) None of these

**46.** Match the following :

| | List I | | List II |
|---|---|---|---|
| A. | If $\sqrt{x} - \sqrt{12} = \sqrt{4} - \sqrt{x}$, then find $x$. | i. | $\frac{16}{25}$ |
| B. | If $\sqrt{x} + \sqrt{x - \sqrt{1-x}} = 1$, then $x = ?$ | ii. | 0 |
| C. | If $x = 3 + 3^{1/3} + 3^{2/3}$, then $x^3 - 9x^2 + 18x - 12 =$ | iii. | $4 + 2\sqrt{3}$ |

| | A | B | C |
|---|---|---|---|
| (a) | (i) | (ii) | (iii) |
| (b) | (iii) | (i) | (ii) |
| (c) | (iii) | (ii) | (i) |
| (d) | (ii) | (iii) | (i) |

**47.** Consider the following statements below:

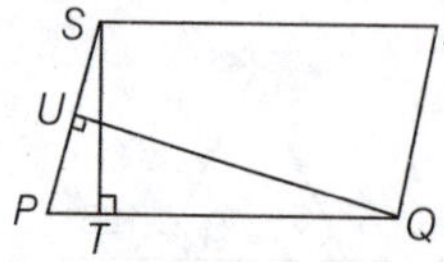


I. A parallelogram and a rectangle on the same base and between the same parallels are equal in area.

II. Area of parallelogram

$$= \frac{1}{2} \times \text{Base} \times \text{Altitude}.$$

III. In the above parallelogram *PQRS*, it is given that $PQ = 20$ cm. If the altitudes *ST* and *QU* being 12 cm and 16 cm respectively, then $PS = 15$ cm.

Which of the following is/are true?

(a) Only I (b) I and III

(c) Only II (d) II and III

**48. Assertion** (A) *ABCD* is a square. If $C'$ is a point on *BA* and $B'$ is a point on *AD* such that $BB'$ and $CC'$ are equal. Then, $\Delta AB'B$ and $\Delta BC'C$ are congruent.

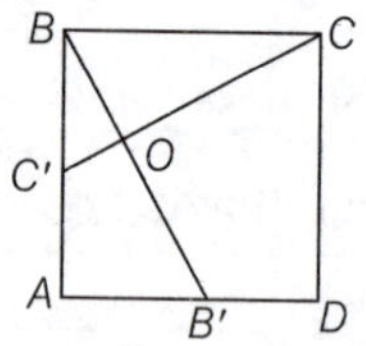


**Reason** (R) Two triangles are congruent, if two angles of a triangle and side included between them are equal to the corresponding two angles of other triangle and side included between them by ASA rule.

(a) (A) is true but (R) is not the correct explanation of (A)

(b) (A) is false and (R) is the correct explanation of (A)

(c) (A) is true and (R) is false

(d) Both (A) and (R) are false

**49.** A rectangular reservoir is 120 m long and 75 m wide. At what speed per hour must water flow into it through a square pipe of 20 cm wide so that the water rises by 2.4 m in 18 h?

(a) 40 km/h

(b) 30 km/h

(c) 45 km/h

(d) 60 km/h

**50.** If the equation, $x - y + (\sqrt{x} + \sqrt{y}) = 10$ and the value of $x$ is 9, then value of $y$ will be

(a) 4 (b) – 4

(c) 9 (d) 16

# PRACTICE SET 02

## 1 Mark Questions

**1.** The ratio of the numbers of sides of two regular polygons is 1 : 2. If each interior angle of the first polygon is 120, then the measure of each interior angle of the second polygon is

(a) 140° (b) 135°
(c) 150° (d) 160°

**2.** The value of $k$, if $x = 2$, $y = -1$ is a solution of the equation $2x + 3y = k$ is

(a) 6 (b) 7
(c) 5 (d) 1

**3.** In the following figure, $ABCD$ and $AEFG$ are two parallelograms. If $\angle C = 55°$ and $\angle F$.

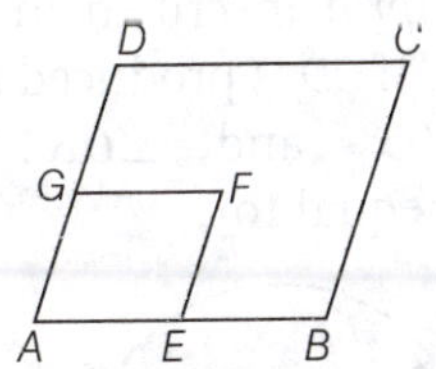


(a) 65° (b) 75°
(c) 85° (d) 55°

**4.** Find the area of the shaded region

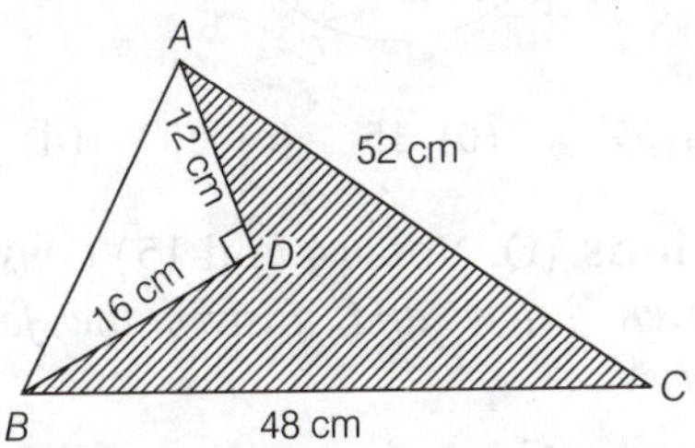


(a) 278 $cm^2$ (b) 384 $cm^2$
(c) 364 $cm^2$ (d) 284 $cm^2$

**5.** $ABCD$ is a cyclic quadrilateral with centre $O$ in the given figure. Chord $AB$ is produced to $E$ where $\angle CBE = 130°$, the value of $x$ is equal to

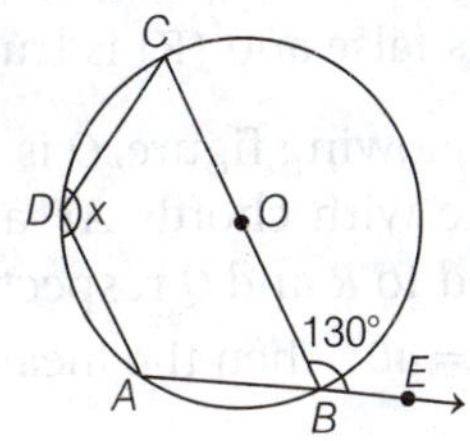


(a) 130° (b) 260°
(c) 140° (d) 280°

**6.** In the following statements which is/are required to find the cost of 4 oranges and 5 apples?

I. Cost of 5 oranges and 3 apples is ₹ 43.
II. Suppose cost of one orange is ₹ 5.

(a) Both the Statements I and II are required to answer the question
(b) Any one of the statement is sufficient to answer the question
(c) Both the statements together are not sufficient to answer the question
(d) None of the above

**7.** The length of a rectangle is decreased by 50% and its width is increased by 50%. What impact does this have on the area of the rectangle?

(a) The area does not change
(b) The area increases by $\frac{3}{4}$
(c) The area decreases by 25%
(d) None of the above

**8.** **Assertion** (A) If $a+b+c=0$, then $x^{a^2 b^{-1} c^{-1}} \cdot x^{a^{-1} b^2 c^{-1}} \cdot x^{a^{-1} b^{-1} c^2}$ is equal to 1.

**Reason** (R) If $a+b+c=0$, then $a^3+b^3+c^3=3abc$.

Which of the following is true?

(a) (A) is true and (R) is correct explanation of (A)
(b) (A) is false and (R) is correct explanation of (A)
(c) (A) is true and (R) is false
(d) (A) is false and (R) is true

**9.** In the following figure, $O$ is the centre of the circle with chords $AP$ and $BP$ being produced to $R$ and $Q$ respectively. If $\angle QPR = 40°$, then the measure of $\angle AOB$ is

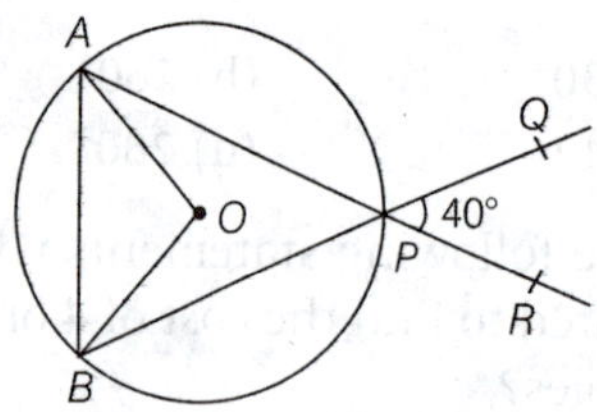


(a) 130° (b) 60° (c) 120° (d) 80°

**10.** In the given figure, $ABCD$ is a parallelogram, then $\angle DBA$ and $\angle BDA$ are respectively equal to

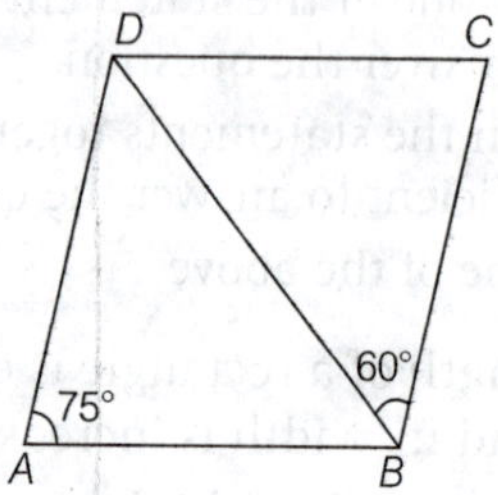


(a) 45°, 60° (b) 60°, 45°
(c) 70°, 35° (d) 35°, 70°

**11.** In the given figure, $ABCD$ and $BPQ$ are straight lines. If $BP = BC$ and $DQ$ is parallel to $CP$.
Find $\angle BDQ$?

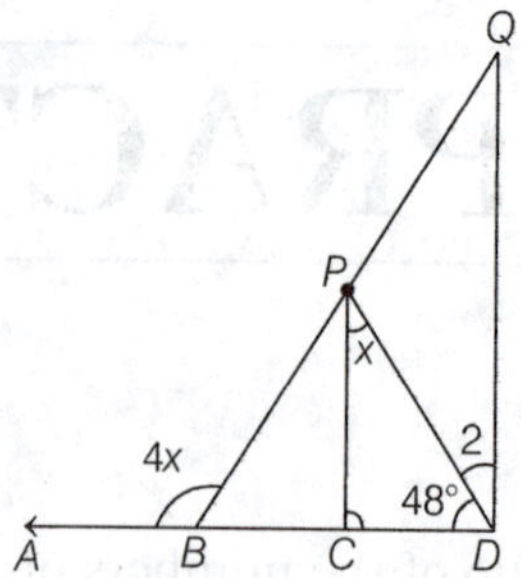


(a) 48° (b) 45° (c) 90° (d) 96°

**12.** Match the following:

| List I | List II |
|---|---|
| A. $16^{3/4}$ | i. 3 |
| B. $81^{0.25}$ | ii. $(8^{1/3})^3$ |
| C. $\sqrt[3]{625^{0.75}}$ | iii. 5 |

| | A | B | C | | A | B | C |
|---|---|---|---|---|---|---|---|
| (a) | (i) | (ii) | (iii) | (b) | (ii) | (i) | (iii) |
| (c) | (iii) | (ii) | (i) | (d) | (i) | (iii) | (ii) |

**13.** In the following figure, $ABCD$ is a quadrilateral inscribed in a circle with centre $O$. If $CD$ is produced to $E$ such that $\angle ADE = 95°$ and $\angle OBA = 30°$. Then, $\angle OAC$ is equal to

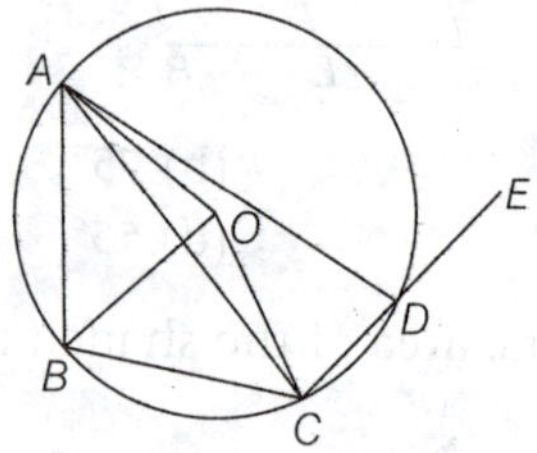


(a) 5° (b) 15° (c) 20° (d) 25°

**Directions** (Q. Nos. 14 and 15) *Consider the data given below and answer the following questions.*

If a transversal intersects two parallel lines, then

(i) each pair of corresponding angles are equal

(ii) each pair of alternate interior angles are equal

(iii) each pair of cointerior angles are supplementary.

**14.** In the given figure, $AB || PQ$. The value of $x$ and $y$ respectively, are

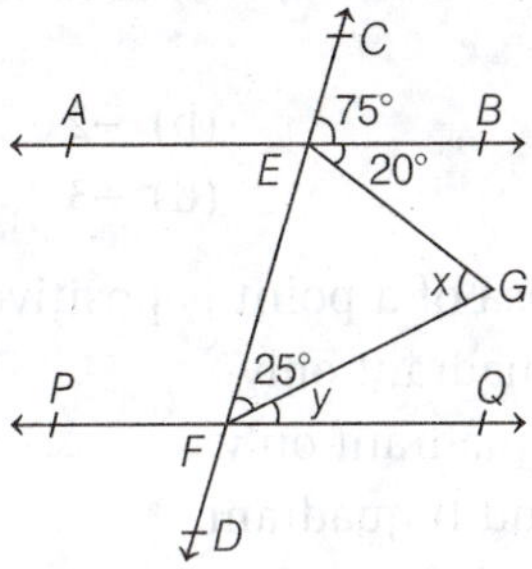


(a) 50°, 70° (b) 70°, 50°
(c) 75°, 45° (d) 20°, 75°

**15.** In the given figure, $AB || CD$. Then, the value of $p+q-r=$

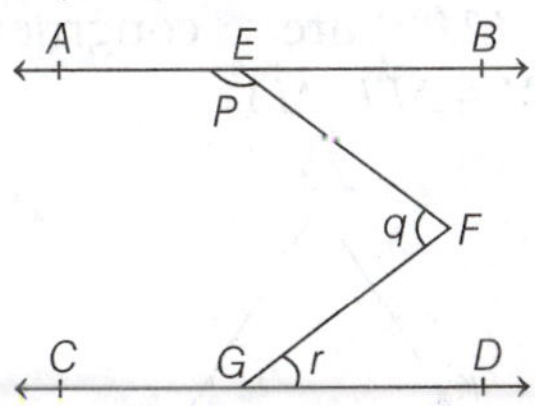


(a) 80° (b) 180°
(c) 100° (d) 360°

**16.** The area of triangle formed by points $A(3,0), B(0,-4), C(0,4)$ will be (in sq. units)

(a) 6 (b) 12
(c) 24 (d) 10

**17.** The value of the expression $\sqrt{(x+y+z)(x+y-z)+(z^2-x^2-y^2)-2xy}$ is

(a) 0
(b) $2x$
(c) $2y$
(d) $x+y+z$

**18.** Consider the following figure :

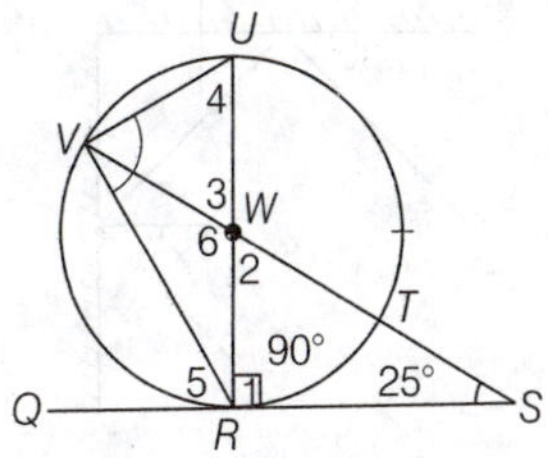


I. $\angle 2 = 65°$
II. $\angle 3 = 75°$
III. $\angle 4 = 57.5°$
IV. $\angle 5 = 60°$

Mark the incorrect matched option.

(a) II and III
(b) I and III
(c) III and IV (d) II and IV

**19.** The point is at a distance of 5 units from $X$-axis and 7 units from $Y$-axis, then the coordinates of point could be

(a) (5, 7) (b) (7, 5)
(c) (0, 7) (d) (7, 0)

**20.** A hemispherical dome of a building needs to be painted. If the circumference of the base of the dome is 17.6 cm, then find the cost of painting it, given that cost of painting is ₹5 per 100 cm$^2$.

(a) ₹24640
(b) ₹25640
(c) ₹22540
(d) None of the above

**21.** If $x = \dfrac{\sqrt{6}+\sqrt{5}}{\sqrt{6}-\sqrt{5}}$ and $y = 1$, then the value of $\dfrac{x+y}{x-y}$ is

(a) $\dfrac{6}{5}$ (b) $\dfrac{6-\sqrt{30}}{5-\sqrt{30}}$

(c) $\dfrac{6+\sqrt{30}}{5}$ (d) None of these

**22.** Find the value of $\angle x$ in the given figure.

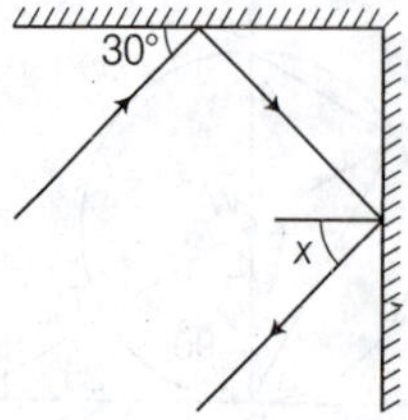


(a) 30° (b) 35° (c) 40° (d) 45°

**23.** Which of the following is a homogenous expression?

(a) $5x^2 - 4xy + 6x^2y + 9y^2$

(b) $4x + 5y + 100$

(c) $15x^3 + 14x^2y + 17y^2x + 12y^3$

(d) $y^2 + x^2 + x + y + 1$

**24.** The sum of $0.\bar{6}$ and $\overline{0.7}$ is

(a) $1.\bar{3}$

(b) 1.3

(c) $1.\bar{4}$

(d) an irrational number

**25.** A point $A$ in Ist quadrant has its coordinate (3, 2) is reflected about $X$-axis, The image of point $A$ about $X$-axis is point $Q$, and then the point $Q$ is reflected about $Y$-axis. The coordinates of final point will be

(a) $(-3, -2)$ (b) $(-3, 2)$

(c) $(3, -2)$ (d) $(-2, -3)$

**26.** $x^3 + 6x^2 + 11x + 6$ is divisible by

(a) $x + 1$

(b) $x + 2$

(c) Both (a) and (b)

(d) None of the above

**27.** $ABC$ is an equilateral triangle inscribed in a circle. $D$ is any point on the arc $BC$. What is $\angle ADB$ equal to?

(a) 90° (b) 60°

(c) 45° (d) None of these

**28.** Simplify $\dfrac{\sqrt{5}+\sqrt{3}}{\sqrt{80}+\sqrt{48}-\sqrt{45}-\sqrt{27}}$.

(a) 0 (b) 1

(c) $\sqrt{5}$ (d) $\sqrt{3}$

**29.** If (3, 4) is a solution of the linear equation $3kx + 5y = 2$, then the values of $k$ is

(a) 2 (b) $-2$

(c) 3 (d) $-3$

**30.** Abscissa of a point is positive in

(a) I quadrant only

(b) II quadrant only

(c) I and II quadrant

(d) I and IV quadrant

**31.** $ABC$ is an isosceles triangle with $BA$ and $BC$ congruent. Point $K$ is on $AB$ and point $L$ is on $BC$. Both $KK'$ and $LL'$ are perpendicular to $AC$. If the segments $KK'$ and $LL'$ are congruent. Then, $\Delta KK'M \cong \Delta LL'M$ is

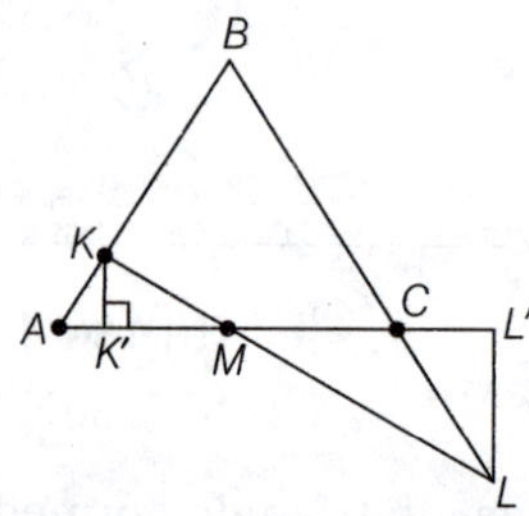


(a) true (b) false

(c) Can't say (d) None of these

**32.** If $2a - 3 = 5$ and $3b + 1 = 2$, then $3b - 2a$ is

(a) 7 (b) $-9$

(c) $-3$ (d) $-7$

**33.** A number is 27 more than the number obtained by revising its digits. If one of the digits is 3, then the other digit is

(a) 5 (b) 6

(c) 3 (d) 9

**34.** If $h, C, V$ are respectively the height, curved surface area and the volume of a cone, then $3\pi Vh^3 - C^2h^2 + 9V^2 =$

(a) 3 (b) 0 (c) 4 (d) 6

**35.** In the figure given above, $PQ$ is a diameter of the circle whose centre is at $O$. If $\angle ROS = 44°$, then what is the value of $\angle RTS$?

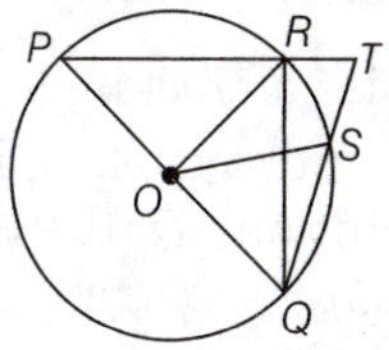


(a) 46° (b) 64°
(c) 69° (d) None of these

**36.** The value of $p^3 - q^3$, if $p - q = \frac{10}{9}$ and $pq = \frac{5}{3}$

(a) $\frac{5050}{729}$ (b) $\frac{5050}{8}$ (c) $\frac{5051}{729}$ (d) $\frac{4050}{729}$

**37.** If $25x^2 - 30x + k$ is a perfect square, then $k$ is equal to

(a) 25 (b) 9
(c) 16 (d) 10

**38.** Find the number of conical *CAP* 1.5 cm in diameter and 0.2 cm height to be melted to form a right circular cone of height 5 cm and diameter 4.5 cm.

(a) 225 (b) 175
(c) 215 (d)275

**39.** The side $BC$ of the $\Delta ABC$ is extended to $D$. If $\angle ACD = 120°$, $\angle ABC = \frac{2}{3}\angle CAB$, then what is the value of $\angle BAC$?

(a) 60° (b) 45°
(c) 30° (d) 72°

**40.** Volume of a hemisphere is 19404 $cm^3$. The total surface area is

(a) 2772 sq.cm (b) 4158 sq.cm
(c) 5544 sq.cm (d) 1386 sq.cm

## 2 Marks Questions

**41. Assertion** (A) $P$ is a point on the side $BC$ of a $\Delta ABC$ such that $AB = AP$. Through $A$ and $C$ lines are drawn parallel to $BC$ and $PA$, respectively, so as to intersect at $D$. Then, $ABCD$ is a cyclic quadrilateral.

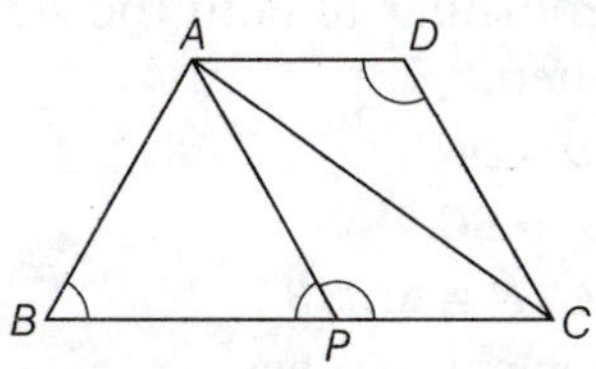


**Reason** (R) The sum of either pair of opposite angles of a cyclic quadrilateral is 180°.

Which of the following is true?

(a) (A) is true and (R) is correct explanation of (A)
(b) (A) is false and (R) is correct explanation of (A)
(c) (A) is true and (R) is false
(d) Both (A) and (R) are false

**42. Assertion** (A) A rectangle and an equilateral triangle have equal perimeters. If length of the rectangle is 7 cm more than its breadth and diagonal equal to 13 cm. Then, area of equilateral triangle is 289 $cm^2$.

**Reason** (R) If $a$, $b$ and $c$ denote the lengths of sides of a triangle, then

Area $= \frac{1}{2} \times a \times b \times c$

Which of the following is true?
(a) If (A) is true and (R) is the correct explanation of (A)
(b) If (A) is false and (R) is the correct explanation of (A)
(c) If (A) is true and (R) is false
(d) If both (A) and (R) are false

**43.** If $2^{-m} \times \frac{1}{2^m} = \frac{1}{4}$, then

$\frac{1}{14}\left[(4^m)^{\frac{1}{2}} + \left(\frac{1}{5^m}\right)^{-1}\right]$ is equal to

(a) $\frac{1}{2}$ (b) 2 (c) 4 (d) $\frac{-1}{4}$

**44.** Area of the figure is

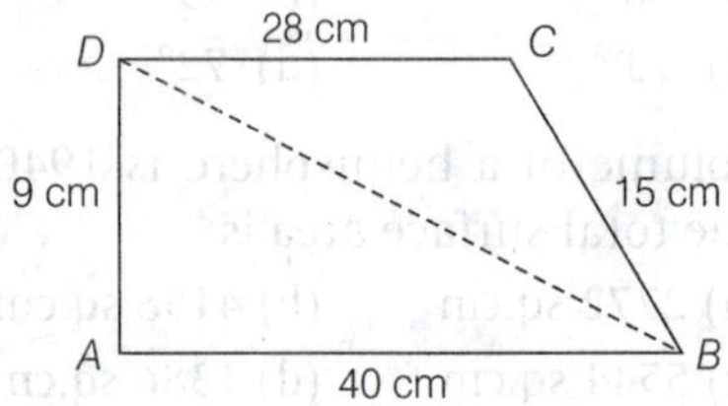


(a) $216 \text{ m}^2$ (b) $316 \text{ m}^2$
(c) $306 \text{ m}^2$ (d) $206 \text{ m}^2$

**45.** *P* is the point (– 5, 3) and *Q* is the point (–5, *m*). If sum of abscissas and ordinates of both points is equal, then the possible value of *m* is
(a) –5 (b) –13
(c) –10 (d) 3

**46.** *ABCD* is a parallelogram in which *BC* is produced to *E* such that $CE = BC$. *AE* interesects *CD* at *F*. If area $\Delta DFB = 3 \text{ cm}^2$, find area of parallelogram *ABCD* is
(a) $6 \text{ cm}^2$ (b) $12 \text{ cm}^2$
(c) $18 \text{ cm}^2$ (d) $9 \text{ cm}^2$

**47.** A spherical canon ball, 28 cm in diameter is melted and cast into a right circular mould, the base of which is 35 cm in diameter. The height of the cone, is
(a) 35.84 cm
(b) 39.76 cm
(c) 42.58 cm
(d) None of the above

**48.** *PQRS* is a rectangle inscribed in a quadrant of a circle of radius 13 cm. *A* is any point on *PQ*. If $PS = 5$ cm, then find ar ($\Delta ARS$).
(a) $15 \text{ cm}^2$ (b) $20 \text{ cm}^2$
(c) $25 \text{ cm}^2$ (d) $30 \text{ cm}^2$

**49.** $(\sqrt{x} + \sqrt{y})^2 = x + y + 2\sqrt{xy}$ and $\sqrt{x}\sqrt{y} = \sqrt{xy}$, where *x* and *y* are positive real numbers.

(i) If $x = 2\sqrt{5} + \sqrt{3}$ and $y = 2\sqrt{5} - \sqrt{3}$, then $x^4 + y^4 =$
(a) 1538 (b) 1200 (c) 1048 (d) 149

(ii) If $x = \sqrt{3} + 3\sqrt{2}$ and $y = \sqrt{3} - 3\sqrt{2}$, then $x^4 + y^4 - 8x^2y^2 =$
(a) 3914 (b) 3010
(c) –486 (d) –856

**50.** Line segment joining the mid-points *M* and *N* of parallel sides *AB* and *DC*, respectively of a trapezium *ABCD* is perpendicular to both the sides *AB* and *DC*. Then,
(a) $AD = DN$
(b) $AD = BC$
(c) $\Delta AMN \cong \Delta NMB$
(d) None of the above

# HINTS AND SOLUTIONS

## Chapter 1 : Number Systems

**1.** (*b*) False; e.g.
$(2+\sqrt{3})+(2-\sqrt{3})=4$ which is not an irrational number.

**2.** (*b*) The sum of a rational number and an irrational number is an irrational number e.g. $2+\sqrt{3}$ is an irrational number.

**3.** (*c*) Option (a) and (b) are not correct because 0 is only integer, neither positive nor negative.
Option (c) every natural number is a whole number (correct).
Option (d) $\sqrt{2}$ is an irrational number (not correct).

**4.** (*b*) We know that, product of any number with its reciprocal is always 1. This is called multiplicative inverse.

i.e. $\quad a\times\frac{1}{a}=1$

**5.** (*c*) $\dfrac{2-\sqrt{5}+3+2\sqrt{5}-4-\sqrt{5}}{4}$

$$=p+q\sqrt{5}$$

$$\Rightarrow \quad \frac{1+0}{4}=p+q\sqrt{5}$$

i.e. $\quad p=\frac{1}{4}, q=0$ [on comparing]

**6.** (*a*) Let $x=1.\overline{37}$

$\Rightarrow \quad x=1.3737.......$ ...(i)

(multiply both sides by 100)

$\Rightarrow \quad 100x=137.37$ ...(ii)

Subtract Eq. (i) from Eq. (ii), we get

$$99x=136 \quad \Rightarrow x=\frac{136}{99}$$

**7.** (*b*) $\because \quad x=1.242424...$ ...(i)

$\Rightarrow 100x=124.24$ ...(ii)

On subtracting Eq. (i) from Eq. (ii), we get

$99x=123$ ...(i)

$$\Rightarrow \quad x=\frac{123}{99}\Rightarrow x=\frac{41}{33}=\frac{p}{q}$$

$\therefore \quad p=41$ and $q=33$

Now, $p+q=41+33=74$

**8.** (*b*) An irrational number between $a$ and $b=\sqrt{ab}$

$\therefore$ An irrational number between $\frac{3}{7}$ and $\frac{5}{7}$

$$=\sqrt{\frac{3}{7}\times\frac{5}{7}}=\frac{\sqrt{15}}{7}$$

**9.** (*d*) Rational number between $a$ and $b=\frac{1}{2}(a+b)$

From option (d), rational number between −8 and −15

$$=\frac{1}{2}(-8-15)=\frac{-23}{2}$$

**10.** (*b*) $\sqrt{32-x\sqrt{15}}=\sqrt{27}+\sqrt{5}$

Squaring both sides, we get

$$32-x\sqrt{15}=(\sqrt{27})^2+(\sqrt{5})^2+2\sqrt{27\times5}$$

$$\Rightarrow \quad 32-x\sqrt{15}=27+5+2\sqrt{3\times3\times3\times5}$$

$$\Rightarrow \quad 32-x\sqrt{15}=32+6\sqrt{15}$$

$$\Rightarrow \quad x=-6$$

[on comparing]

**11.** (*c*) $\dfrac{3}{5-\sqrt{3}}+\dfrac{2}{5+\sqrt{3}}$

$$=\frac{3(5+\sqrt{3})+2(5-\sqrt{3})}{(5-\sqrt{3})(5+\sqrt{3})}$$

$$=\frac{15+3\sqrt{3}+10-2\sqrt{3}}{25-3}$$

$$=\frac{25+\sqrt{3}}{22}$$

**12.** (*d*) Given, $x=\sqrt{6}+\sqrt{5}$

$$\therefore \quad \frac{1}{x}=\frac{1}{\sqrt{6}+\sqrt{5}}$$

$$=\frac{1}{\sqrt{6}+\sqrt{5}}\times\frac{\sqrt{6}-\sqrt{5}}{\sqrt{6}-\sqrt{5}}$$

$$=\frac{\sqrt{6}-\sqrt{5}}{6-5}=\sqrt{6}-\sqrt{5}$$

Now,

$$x-\frac{1}{x}=\sqrt{6}+\sqrt{5}-\sqrt{6}+\sqrt{5}$$

$$=2\sqrt{5}$$

$$\therefore x^2+\frac{1}{x^2}-2=\left(x-\frac{1}{x}\right)^2$$

$$=(2\sqrt{5})^2=20$$

**13.** (*b*) We have,

$$a+\frac{1}{a}=\frac{1}{\sqrt{3}-1}\times\frac{\sqrt{3}+1}{(\sqrt{3}+1)}$$

$$=\frac{\sqrt{3}+1}{(\sqrt{3})^2-(1)^2}=\frac{\sqrt{3}+1}{3-1}=\frac{\sqrt{3}+1}{2}$$

$$\Rightarrow \quad a+\frac{1}{a}=\frac{\sqrt{3}+1}{2}$$

Squaring both sides, we get

$$a^2+\frac{1}{a^2}+2=\frac{3+1+2\sqrt{3}}{4}$$

$$\Rightarrow \quad a^2+\frac{1}{a^2}+2=1+\frac{\sqrt{3}}{2}$$

$$\Rightarrow \quad a^2+\frac{1}{a^2}=-1+\frac{\sqrt{3}}{2}$$

**14.** (*b*) $\{\sqrt[m]{(\sqrt[n]{a})}\}^{mn}=\left\{(a)^{\frac{1}{mn}}\right\}^{mn}=a$

**15.** (*b*) $25^{x-1}=5^{2x-1}-100$

$$\Rightarrow \quad 100=5^{2x-1}-25^{x-1}$$

$$\Rightarrow \quad 100=5^{2x-1}-(5^2)^{x-1}$$

$$\Rightarrow \quad 100=5^{2x-1}-5^{2x-2}$$

$$\Rightarrow \quad 100=5^{2x-2}(5-1)$$

$$\Rightarrow \quad \frac{100}{4}=5^{2x-2} \Rightarrow 25=5^{2x-2}$$

$$\Rightarrow \quad 5^2=5^{2x-2} \Rightarrow 2x-2=2$$

$$\Rightarrow \quad 2x=4 \quad \Rightarrow x=2$$

**16.** (*b*) $\because \sqrt{2^n}=1024$ [given]

$$\Rightarrow \quad (2^n)^{1/2}=2^{10} \Rightarrow 2^{n/2}=2^{10}$$

$$\Rightarrow \quad \frac{n}{2}=10 \text{ [by comparing]}$$

$$\Rightarrow \quad n=20$$

$$\therefore \quad 3^{2\left(\frac{n}{4}-4\right)}=3^{2\left(\frac{20}{4}-4\right)}=3^{2(5-4)}$$

$$=3^2=9$$

**17.** (*b*) Since, $\sqrt[7]{a^4b^3c^5}\times\sqrt[7]{a^3b^4c^2}$

$$=\sqrt[7]{a^{4+3}b^{3+4}c^{5+2}}$$

$$=\sqrt[7]{a^7b^7c^7}=abc$$

$\therefore$ Rationalising factor

$$=\sqrt[7]{a^3b^4c^2}$$

**18.** (*c*) Given,

$$(x^{1/3})^2-5(x^{1/3})+6=0$$

Let $y=x^{1/3}$, then

$$y^2-5y+6=0$$

$\Rightarrow \quad (y-2)(y-3)=0$

$\therefore \quad y = 2, 3$

When $y = 2$, then

$x^{1/3} = 2$

$\Rightarrow \quad x = 2^3 = 8$

When $y = 3$, then $x^{1/3} = 3$

$\Rightarrow \quad x = 3^3 = 27$

**19.** (b) $(\sqrt[6]{15-2\sqrt{56}})(\sqrt[3]{\sqrt{7}+2\sqrt{2}})$

$= (\sqrt[6]{(\sqrt{8})^2+(\sqrt{7})^2-2\sqrt{7\times 8}})(\sqrt[3]{\sqrt{7}+2\sqrt{2}})$

$= (\sqrt[6]{(\sqrt{8}-\sqrt{7})^2})(\sqrt[3]{2\sqrt{2}+\sqrt{7}})$

$= (\sqrt{8}-\sqrt{7})^{2/6}(2\sqrt{2}+\sqrt{7})^{1/3}$

$= (2\sqrt{2}-\sqrt{7})^{1/3}(2\sqrt{2}+\sqrt{7})^{1/3}$

$= [(2\sqrt{2})^2-(\sqrt{7})^2]^{1/3}$

$= (8-7)^{1/3} = 1$

**20.** (b)

$\left(\frac{x^a}{x^b}\right)^{a+b} \cdot \left(\frac{x^b}{x^c}\right)^{b+c} \cdot \left(\frac{x^c}{x^a}\right)^{c+a}$

$= x^{(a-b)(a+b)} \cdot x^{(b-c)(b+c)} \cdot x^{(c-a)(c+a)}$

$= x^{a^2-b^2+b^2-c^2+c^2-a^2}$

$= x^0 = 1$

**21.** (a) Given, $a^x = c^q = b \Rightarrow a^x = b$

$\Rightarrow \quad a = b^{1/x} \quad$ ...(i)

and $\quad c^q = b$

$\Rightarrow \quad c = b^{1/q} \quad$ ...(ii)

Also given, $c^y = a^z = d$

$\Rightarrow \quad c^y = d$

$\Rightarrow \quad c = d^{1/y} \quad$ ...(iii)

and $\quad a^z = d$

$\Rightarrow \quad a = d^{1/z} \quad$ ...(iv)

From Eqs. (i) and (iv), we get

$b^{1/x} = d^{1/z} \Rightarrow b = d^{x/z} \quad$ ...(v)

From Eqs. (ii) and (iii), we get

$b^{1/q} = d^{1/y} \Rightarrow b = d^{q/y} \quad$ ...(vi)

From Eqs. (v) and (vi), we get

$d^{x/z} = d^{q/y}$

$\therefore \quad \frac{x}{z} = \frac{q}{y} \Rightarrow xy = qz$

**22.** (a) Given surds are in the form $2^{1/2}, 3^{1/6}, 4^{1/3}$ and $5^{1/4}$.

So, LCM of 2, 6, 3 and 4 is 12.

$\therefore 2^{1/2} = (2^6)^{1/12} = (64)^{1/12}$

$3^{1/6} = (3^2)^{1/12} = (9)^{1/12}$

$4^{1/3} = (4^4)^{1/12} = (256)^{1/12}$

$5^{1/4} = (5^3)^{1/12} = (125)^{1/12}$

Clearly, greatest surd $(256)^{1/12}$

$= \sqrt[3]{4}$

**23.** (d) Given, $x = \frac{\sqrt{5}+\sqrt{3}}{\sqrt{5}-\sqrt{3}}$,

$y = \frac{\sqrt{5}-\sqrt{3}}{\sqrt{5}+\sqrt{3}}$

Now,

$x + y = \frac{(\sqrt{5}+\sqrt{3})^2+(\sqrt{5}-\sqrt{3})^2}{(\sqrt{5})^2-(\sqrt{3})^2}$

$[\because (a+b)^2+(a-b)^2 = 2(a^2+b^2)]$

$= \frac{2(5+3)}{2} = \frac{2\times 8}{2} = 8$

$xy = \left(\frac{\sqrt{5}+\sqrt{3}}{\sqrt{5}-\sqrt{3}}\right)\left(\frac{\sqrt{5}-\sqrt{3}}{\sqrt{5}+\sqrt{3}}\right) = 1$

$\therefore \quad x^2+y^2+xy = (x+y)^2 - xy$

$= 8^2 - 1 = 63$

$[\because xy = 1]$

**24.** (b) Consider $\frac{\sqrt{15+4\sqrt{11}}}{\sqrt{31+8\sqrt{15}}}$

$= \frac{\sqrt{4+11+4\sqrt{11}}}{\sqrt{15+16+8\sqrt{15}}}$

$= \frac{\sqrt{(2)^2+(\sqrt{11})^2+2\cdot 2\sqrt{11}}}{\sqrt{(15)^2+(4)^2+2\cdot\sqrt{15}\cdot 4}}$

$= \frac{\sqrt{(2+\sqrt{11})^2}}{\sqrt{(\sqrt{15}+4)^2}} = \frac{\sqrt{11}+2}{4+\sqrt{15}}$

On rationalising, we get

$\frac{\sqrt{11}+2}{4+\sqrt{15}} = \left(\frac{\sqrt{11}+2}{4+\sqrt{15}}\right)\left(\frac{4-\sqrt{15}}{4-\sqrt{15}}\right)$

$= \frac{4\sqrt{11}-\sqrt{165}+8-2\sqrt{15}}{1}$

$= 8+4\sqrt{11}-\sqrt{165}-2\sqrt{15}$

$\therefore$ Given expression

$= [8+4\sqrt{11}-\sqrt{165}-2\sqrt{15}]$

$\times \frac{1}{8+4\sqrt{11}-\sqrt{165}-2\sqrt{15}} = 1$

**25.** (b) A. $\left(\sqrt[m]{\sqrt[n]{\frac{1}{a}}}\right)^{mn} = \left(\frac{1}{a}\right)^{\frac{mn}{mn}} = \frac{1}{a}$

B. $\frac{2^{m+n}}{2^{n-m}} = 16$

$\Rightarrow 2^{(m+n-n+m)} = 2^4$

$\left[\because \frac{a^m}{a^n} = a^{m-n}\right]$

$\Rightarrow \quad 2^{2m} = 2^4 \Rightarrow 2m = 4$

$[\because a^m = a^n \Rightarrow m = n]$

$\Rightarrow \quad m = 2$

C. $\left(\frac{100}{9}\right)^{-3/2} = \left(\left(\frac{10}{3}\right)^2\right)^{-3/2}$

$= \left(\frac{10}{3}\right)^{2\times\frac{-3}{2}} = \left(\frac{10}{3}\right)^{-3}$

$\left[\because (a^m)^n = a^{mn}, a^{-n} = \frac{1}{a^n}\right]$

$= \left(\frac{3}{10}\right)^3 = \frac{3}{10}\times\frac{3}{10}\times\frac{3}{10}$

D. $(x^{-1}+y^{-1})^{-1} = \left(\frac{1}{x}+\frac{1}{y}\right)^{-1}$

$= \left(\frac{y+x}{xy}\right)^{-1} = \frac{xy}{x+y}$

**26.** (b) Option (a) $\sqrt[3]{2}\times\sqrt[4]{3}$

$= \sqrt[12]{2^4}\times\sqrt[12]{3^3} = (16\times 27)^{\frac{1}{12}}$

$= (432)^{\frac{1}{12}}$ (correct)

Option (b) The rational factor of $(\sqrt{a}+\sqrt{b}) = \sqrt{a}-\sqrt{b}$ (not correct).

Option (c)

$(5+\sqrt{5})(5-\sqrt{5}) = 25-5 = 20$

(correct)

Option (d)

$\sqrt{10}\times\sqrt{15} = \sqrt{150} = 5\sqrt{6}$

(correct)

**27.** (b) A. $\frac{2}{\sqrt{7}} = \frac{a\sqrt{7}}{7}$

$\Rightarrow \quad 2\times 7 = a\sqrt{7}\times\sqrt{7} \Rightarrow a = 2$

B. $\left(\sqrt[6]{27}-\sqrt{6\frac{3}{4}}\right)^2$

$= \left(\sqrt[6]{27}-\sqrt{\frac{27}{4}}\right)^2$

$= \sqrt[3]{27} + \frac{27}{4} - 2 \times \sqrt[6]{27} \times \sqrt{\frac{27}{4}}$

$= 3 + \frac{27}{4} - \frac{2}{2} \times (27)^{\frac{1}{6}+\frac{1}{2}}$

$= \frac{39}{4} - (27)^{\frac{2}{3}} = \frac{39}{4} - 9 = \frac{3}{4}$

C. $\frac{\sqrt{3}+1}{2-\sqrt{3}} = \frac{(\sqrt{3}+1)(2+\sqrt{3})}{4-3}$

$= 2\sqrt{3} + 2 + 3 + \sqrt{3} = 5 + 3\sqrt{3}$

$\therefore$ Rationalising factor $= 5 - 3\sqrt{3}$

D. LCM of $(9, 6, 3) = 18$

Then $\sqrt[9]{4}, \sqrt[6]{3}, \sqrt[3]{2}$

$= (4^2)^{\frac{1}{18}}, (3^3)^{\frac{1}{18}}, (2^6)^{\frac{1}{18}}$

$= (16)^{\frac{1}{18}}, (27)^{\frac{1}{18}}, (64)^{\frac{1}{18}}$

$\therefore \sqrt[3]{2}$ is the greatest.

**28.** (c) $\frac{1}{1+\sqrt{2}} + \frac{1}{\sqrt{2}+\sqrt{3}} + \dots + \frac{1}{\sqrt{8}+\sqrt{9}}$

Consider, $\frac{1}{1+\sqrt{2}} = \frac{1-\sqrt{2}}{1-2}$

$= \sqrt{2} - 1$

[rationalisation]

Similarly, $\frac{1}{\sqrt{2}+\sqrt{3}} = \sqrt{3} - \sqrt{2}$

[rationalisation]

$\frac{1}{\sqrt{3}+\sqrt{4}} = \sqrt{4} - \sqrt{3}, \dots\dots$

$\frac{1}{\sqrt{8}+\sqrt{9}} = \sqrt{9} - \sqrt{8}$

$\therefore$ Value of given expression is

$\sqrt{9} - 1 = 3 - 1 = 2$

**29.** (c) Given, $x = 2 - \sqrt{3}$

Now, $\frac{1}{x} = \frac{1}{2-\sqrt{3}} \times \frac{2+\sqrt{3}}{2+\sqrt{3}}$

$= \frac{2+\sqrt{3}}{(2)^2 - (\sqrt{3})^2} = \frac{2+\sqrt{3}}{4-3} = 2 + \sqrt{3}$

$\therefore \quad x + \frac{1}{x} = 2 - \sqrt{3} + 2 + \sqrt{3}$

$x + \frac{1}{x} = 4$

and $x - \frac{1}{x} = 2 - \sqrt{3} - (2 + \sqrt{3})$

$= -2\sqrt{3}$

Now,

$x^2 - \frac{1}{x^2} = \left(x - \frac{1}{x}\right)\left(x + \frac{1}{x}\right)$

$= (-2\sqrt{3})(4) = -8\sqrt{3}$

and $\left(x + \frac{1}{x}\right)^2 = 4^2$

$\Rightarrow x^2 + \left(\frac{1}{x}\right)^2 + 2 = 16$

$\Rightarrow \quad x^2 + \frac{1}{x^2} = 14$

**30.** (c) Now, $\frac{3+2\sqrt{5}}{3-2\sqrt{5}} \times \frac{3+2\sqrt{5}}{3+2\sqrt{5}}$

$= \frac{(3+2\sqrt{5})^2}{(3)^2 - (2\sqrt{5})^2}$

$= \frac{9+20+12\sqrt{5}}{9-20} = \frac{29+12\sqrt{5}}{-11}$

Then, $-\frac{29}{11} - \frac{12}{11}\sqrt{5} = p + q\sqrt{5}$

On comparing both sides, we get

$p = -\frac{29}{11}$ and $q = \frac{-12}{11}$

$\therefore \quad 22(p-q) = 22\left(\frac{-29}{11} + \frac{12}{11}\right)$

$= 22 \times \frac{(-17)}{11} = 2 \times (-17) = -34$

## Chapter 2 : Polynomials

**1.** (b) Expression

$= (x^3 - y^3) - (x - y)$

Hence, degree is 3.

**2.** (b) Let $p(x) = 2x^2 + 2kx - 12$

$x = \frac{5}{2}$ is a zero of $p(x)$.

Then, $p\left(\frac{5}{2}\right) = 0$

$\Rightarrow 2\left(\frac{5}{2}\right)^2 + 2k \times \frac{5}{2} - 12 = 0$

$\Rightarrow \quad \frac{25}{2} + 5k - 12 = 0$

$\Rightarrow \quad \frac{25-24}{2} + 5k = 0$

$\Rightarrow \quad \frac{1}{2} + 5k = 0$

$\Rightarrow \quad k = -\frac{1}{10}$

**3.** (a) Given,

$p(x) = x^2 - 2\sqrt{2}x + 1$

Now, $p(2\sqrt{2}) = (2\sqrt{2})^2 - 2\sqrt{2}(2\sqrt{2}) + 1$

$= 8 - 8 + 1 = 1$

**4.** (c) Here, $P(x) = x^3 - x^2 + x + 1$

$P(1) = 1 - 1 + 1 + 1 = 2$

$P(-1) = -1 - 1 - 1 + 1 = -2$

$\frac{P(1) + P(-1)}{2} = \frac{2 + (-2)}{2} = 0$

**5.** (c) Let $p(x) = 2x^3 - 8x^2 + ax + b$

Since, $x = 3$ is a zero of the polynomial.

$\therefore p(3) = 0$

$\Rightarrow 2(3)^3 - 8(3)^2 + a \times 3 + b = 0$

$\Rightarrow 2 \times 27 - 8 \times 9 + 3a + b = 0$

$\Rightarrow \quad 54 - 72 + 3a + b = 0$

$\Rightarrow \quad -18 + 3a + b = 0$

$\Rightarrow \quad 3a + b = 18 \quad \dots(i)$

Also, $x = 0$ is a zero of the polynomial.

$\therefore \quad p(0) = 0$

$\Rightarrow 2(0)^3 - 8(0)^2 + a \times 0 + b = 0$

$\Rightarrow \quad 0 - 0 + 0 + b = 0$

$\Rightarrow \quad b = 0 \quad \dots(ii)$

On putting $b = 0$ in Eq. (i), we get

$3a + 0 = 18 \Rightarrow 3a = 18$

$\therefore \quad a = \frac{18}{3} = 6$

$\therefore \quad a + b = 6 + 0 = 6$

**6.** (b) Let

$f(x) = x^3 + 10x^2 + ax + b$

According to the question,

$f(1) = 0$

$\Rightarrow 1 + 10 + a + b = 0$

$\Rightarrow \quad a + b = -11 \quad \dots(i)$

and $f(2) = 0$

$8 + 40 + 2a + b = 0$

$\Rightarrow \quad 48 + 2a + b = 0$

$\Rightarrow \quad 2a + b = -48 \dots(ii)$

From Eqs. (i) and (ii), we get

$a = -37$ and $b = 26$

**7.** (b) If $x + 2$ is a factor.

$\therefore$ On putting $x = -2$, we get

$(-2+1)^7 + (-6+k)^3 = 0$

$\Rightarrow (k-6)^3 = 1$

$\Rightarrow k-6 = 1$

$\Rightarrow k = 7$

**8.** (a) Since, $x+1$ is a factor of given expression.

$\therefore a-b+c-d+e=0$

$[\because f(-1)=0]$

$\Rightarrow a+c+e=b+d$

**9.** (b) Since, $(x-2)$ is a factor of $x^3-7x+6$.

Then, $x^3-7x+6$

$= x^2(x-2)+2x(x-2)-3(x-2)$

$=(x-2)(x^2+2x-3)$

$=(x-2)\{(x^2+3x-x-3)\}$

$=(x-2)\{x(x+3)-1(x+3)\}$

$=(x-2)(x+3)(x-1)$

$\therefore$ Other zeroes $= 1, -3$

**10.** (d) Let, $f(x)=x^2+px+q$

and $g(x)=x^2+lx+m$

$(x+a)$ is a common factor of $f(x)$ and $g(x)$ then $f(-a)=0$ and $g(-a)=0$

$\therefore (-a)^2+p(-a)+q=0$

$\Rightarrow a^2-pa+q=0$ ...(i)

Also, $a^2-la+m=0$ ...(ii)

On subtracting Eq. (ii) from Eq. (i), we get

$(l-p)a+q-m=0$

$\Rightarrow (l-p)a=m-q$

$\therefore a=\dfrac{m-q}{l-p}$

**11.** (c) $\because x^3+y^3+z^3=3xyz$

$\therefore x+y+z=0$

$\Rightarrow x+y=-z$

**12.** (d) $6x^2+17x+5$

$=6x^2+15x+2x+5$

$=3x(2x+5)+1(2x+5)$

$=(3x+1)(2x+5)$

**13.** (b) $(x-3)$ is a factor of $x^2+ax-4=0$ and $x^2-4x+b=0$.

Put, $x=3$, in polynomials.

$\therefore (3)^2+a\times 3-4=0$

$\Rightarrow 9+3a-4=0$

$\Rightarrow 3a+5=0$

$\Rightarrow a=-\dfrac{5}{3}$

and $(3)^2-4\times 3+b=0$

$\Rightarrow 9-12+b=0$

$\Rightarrow -3+b=0$

$\Rightarrow b=3$

Now, $2a-b=2\times\left(-\dfrac{5}{3}\right)-3$

$=\dfrac{-10}{3}-3=\dfrac{-10-9}{3}=\dfrac{-19}{3}$

**14.** (b) $a^5b-ab^5=(ab)(a^4-b^4)$

$=(ab)(a^2+b^2)(a^2-b^2)$

$=(ab)\times(a^2+b^2)(a+b)(a-b)$

**15.** (a) $\because a+b+c=9$ and $ab+bc+ca=23$

$\therefore a^3+b^3+c^3-3abc$

$=(a+b+c)(a^2+b^2+c^2-ab-bc-ca)$

$=(a+b+c)\{(a+b+c)^2-3(ab+bc+ca)\}$

$=9\times(81-3\times 23)$

$=9\times 12$

$=108$

**16.** (b) Given, $(p-q)^6-27r^3$

$=\{(p-q)^2\}^3-(3r)^3$

$=[\{(p-q)^2-3r\}\{(p-q)^4+9r^2+(p-q)^2 3r\}]$

**17.** (b) Here,

$xya^2=(x-y)^2(a+1)$

$\Rightarrow \dfrac{xy}{(x-y)^2}=\dfrac{a+1}{a^2}$

$\Rightarrow \dfrac{xy}{(x-y)^2}=\dfrac{1}{a}+\dfrac{1}{a^2}$

$\Rightarrow \dfrac{4xy}{(x-y)^2}=\dfrac{4}{a}+\dfrac{4}{a^2}$

So, $1+\dfrac{4}{a}+\dfrac{4}{a^2}=1+\dfrac{4xy}{(x-y)^2}$

$\Rightarrow 1+\dfrac{4}{a}+\dfrac{4}{a^2}=\dfrac{(x-y)^2+4xy}{(x-y)^2}$

$=\dfrac{x^2+y^2-2xy+4xy}{(x-y)^2}$

$=\dfrac{(x+y)^2}{(x-y)^2}$

**18.** (c) Given, $a-b=6$ ... (i)

and $a^2-b^2=222$

$(a+b)(a-b)=a^2-b^2$

$(a+b)\times 6=222$

$a+b=37$ ...(ii)

On solving Eqs. (i) and (ii), we get

$a=\dfrac{43}{2}$ and $b=\dfrac{31}{2}$

$\because a^3-b^3=\left(\dfrac{43}{2}\right)^3-\left(\dfrac{31}{2}\right)^3$

$=\dfrac{79507}{8}-\dfrac{29791}{8}$

$=6214$

**19.** (b) Area $=4a^2+4a-3$

[we know that area $= l\times b$]

$=4a^2+6a-2a-3$

$=2a(2a+3)-1(2a+3)$

$=(2a-1)(2a+3)$

$\therefore$ Possible length and breadth are $(2a-1)$ and $(2a+3)$.

**20.** (b)

$(x+y)(x-y)(x^2+xy+y^2)(x^2-xy+y^2)$

$=(x+y)(x^2+xy+y^2)(x-y)(x^2-xy+y^2)$

$=(x^3+y^3)(x^3-y^3)$

$=(x^3)^2-(y^3)^2=x^6-y^6$

**21.** (a) We have,

$\dfrac{a^2-19a-25}{a-7}=a-12+\dfrac{P}{a-7}$

$\Rightarrow \dfrac{a^2-19a-25}{a-7}=\dfrac{(a-12)(a-7)+P}{a-7}$

$\Rightarrow a^2-19a-25$

$=a^2-19a+84+P$

$\Rightarrow -84-25=P \Rightarrow P=-109$

**22.** (c) Volume of cuboidal tank

$=$ length $\times$ breadth $\times$ height

$=(2x-y)(2x+y)(4x^2+y^2)$

$=(4x^2-y^2)(4x^2+y^2)$

$=(16x^4-y^4)\text{m}^3$

**23.** (d) $\because \dfrac{a}{b}+\dfrac{b}{a}=1$

$\Rightarrow a^2+b^2=ab$

$\Rightarrow \quad a^2 - ab + b^2 = 0$

$\therefore a^3 + b^3$

$= (a+b)(a^2 - ab + b^2)$

$= 0$

**24.** (c) Given, $x^2 + 2x = 45$

Now, $x^4 + 4x^3 + 4x^2 - 13$

$= x^4 + 2 \times 2x \times x^2 + (2x)^2 - 13$

$= (x^2 + 2x)^2 - 13 = (45)^2 - 13$

$= 2025 - 13 = 2012$

**25.** (b) Given,

$a^2 + b^2 + c^2 + 3 = 2a - 2b + 2c$

$\Rightarrow a^2 + 1 - 2a + b^2 + 2b + 1 + c^2 - 2c + 1 = 0$

$\Rightarrow (a-1)^2 + (b+1)^2 + (c-1)^2 = 0$

$\Rightarrow \quad a = 1, b = -1, c = 1$

$\therefore (a + b - c)^3 = (1 - 1 - 1)^3 = -1$

**26.** (b) (A) Since, $(ax + b)$ is a factor of $p(x)$, then $p\left(-\frac{b}{a}\right) = 0$

(B) If $n$ is odd integer, then $(x + a)$ is a factor of $(x^n + a^n)$

(C) $a^3b - b^3a$

$ab(a^2 - b^2)$

$ab(a+b)(a-b)$

(D) For finding zeroes, put

$3x - 4 = 0$

$\Rightarrow \quad x = \frac{4}{3}$

**27.** (b) A. $98 \times 102 = (100 - 2)(100 + 2)$

$= (100)^2 - 4 = 10000 - 4$

$= 9996$

B. $\frac{1}{2}(a+b+c)$

$\{(a-b)^2 + (b-c)^2 + (c-a)^2\}$

$= \frac{1}{2}(a+b+c)$

$\{a^2 + b^2 - 2ab + b^2 + c^2 - 2bc + c^2 + a^2 - 2ca\}$

$= \frac{1}{2}(a+b+c)\{2a^2 + 2b^2 + 2c^2 - 2ab - 2bc - 2ca\}$

$= (a+b+c)$

$(a^2 + b^2 + c^2 - ab - bc - ca)$

$= (a^3 + b^3 + c^3 - 3abc)$

C. $a^{\frac{1}{3}} + b^{\frac{1}{3}} + c^{\frac{1}{3}} = 0$

$\Rightarrow \quad a^{\frac{1}{3}} + b^{\frac{1}{3}} = -c^{\frac{1}{3}}$

Cubing both sides

$a + b + 3a^{\frac{1}{3}}b^{\frac{1}{3}}(a^{\frac{1}{3}} + b^{\frac{1}{3}}) = -c$

$\Rightarrow \quad a + b + c = 3a^{\frac{1}{3}}b^{\frac{1}{3}}c^{\frac{1}{3}}$

$\Rightarrow (a+b+c)^3 = 27abc$

D. $(-1)^3 - (2)^3 + (3)^3$

$= (-1)^3 + (-2)^3 + (3)^3$

$\Rightarrow 3(-1)(-2)(3)$

[If $a + b + c = 0$, then $a^3 + b^3 + c^3 = 3abc$, here $-1 - 2 + 3 = 0$]

$= 18$

**28.** (a) Let $x = \frac{1}{a}, y = \frac{1}{b}$ and $z = \frac{1}{c}$, then

$\left(\frac{1}{x} + \frac{1}{y} + \frac{1}{z}\right)^2 - \left(\frac{2}{xy} + \frac{2}{yz} + \frac{2}{zx}\right)$

$= (a+b+c)^2 - (2ab + 2bc + 2ca)$

$= a^2 + b^2 + c^2$

**29.** (c) **Statement I** We have,

$\frac{(a^2 - b^2)^3 + (b^2 - c^2)^3 + (c^2 - a^2)^3}{(a+b)^3 + (b+c)^3 + (c+a)^3}$

$= \frac{3(a^2 - b^2)(b^2 - c^2)(c^2 - a^2)}{(a+b)^3 + (b+c)^3 + (c+a)^3}$

[$\because a^3 + b^3 + c^3 = 3abc$; if $a + b + c = 0$]

**Statement II** We have,

$a^2 + b^2 + c^2 - ab - bc - ac$

$= \frac{1}{2}\{2a^2 + 2b^2 + 2c^2 - 2ab - 2bc - 2ac\}$

$= \frac{1}{2}[(a-b)^2 + (b-c)^2 + (c-a)^2]$

**30.** (a) $x^4 - 81y^4 = (x^2)^2 - (9y^2)^2$

$= (x^2 - 9y^2)(x^2 + 9y^2)$

$= (x^2 - (3y)^2)(x^2 + 9y^2)$

$= (x - 3y)(x + 3y)(x^2 + 9y^2)$

**31.** (a) Now, $(x + y + z)^2$

$= x^2 + y^2 + z^2 + 2(xy + yz + zx)$

$\Rightarrow (1)^2 = x^2 + y^2 + z^2 + 2(-1)$

$\Rightarrow \quad x^2 + y^2 + z^2 = 3 \quad \ldots(i)$

Again, $x^3 + y^3 + z^3 - 3xyz$

$= (x + y + z)[x^2 + y^2 + z^2 - (xy + yz + zx)]$

$\Rightarrow x^3 + y^3 + z^3 - 3 \times (-1)$

$= (1)[3 - (-1)]$

$\Rightarrow \quad x^3 + y^3 + z^3 + 3 = 4$

$\Rightarrow \quad x^3 + y^3 + z^3 = 1$

## Chapter 3 : Linear Equations in Two Variables

**1.** (a) The given equation is

$3x^2 - 5x + 3 = x^2 + 7x - 1$

or $2x^2 - 12x + 4 = 0$

$x^2 - 6x + 2 = 0$

$\therefore$ It is not a linear equation.

Option (b)

The given equation is

$\frac{3 - x^2 + x}{2} = \frac{4x - 2x^2 + 5}{4}$

$\Rightarrow 12 - 4x^2 + 4x = 8x - 4x^2 + 10$

$4x = 2$

$\therefore$ It is a linear equation.

Option (c) The given equation is

$\frac{11x + 5}{13} - \frac{12x - 3}{4} = \frac{1}{5}$

$\Rightarrow 5(44x + 20 - 156x + 39) = 52$

$\Rightarrow \quad 5(59 - 112x) = 52$

$\Rightarrow \quad 295 - 560x = 52$

$\Rightarrow \quad 560x = 243$

It is a linear equation.

Option (d)

$\frac{4x^2 + 2x^3 + 5}{4} = \frac{x^3 + 2x^2 + x}{2}$

$8x^2 + 4x^3 + 10 = 4x^3 + 8x^2 + 4x$

$4x = 10$

It is a linear equation.

**2.** (c) $ax + by + c = 0$ represents a linear equation in two variables, if $a \neq 0, b \neq 0$, i.e. coefficients of $x$ and $y$ should not be equal to 0.

**3.** (b) Here, the coefficient of '$y$' in the given equation $x = 7$ is 0. So, the equation can be written as

$1 \cdot x + 0 \cdot y = 7$

Hence, the required equation is

$1 \cdot x + 0 \cdot y = 7$

**4.** *(d)* Since, (2, 0) is a solution of $3x + 2y = k/2$

$\therefore \quad 3 \times 2 + 2 \times 0 = k/2$

$\Rightarrow \quad k = 6 \times 2 = 12$

**5.** *(b)* By observing the values for $y = 2x - 1$.

If $x = -1$, then

$y = -2 - 1 = -3$

If $x = 0$, then $y = -1$

If $x = 1$, then $y = 1$

If $x = 2$, then $y = 3$

**6.** *(a)* Given, $2x + cy = 8 \quad \ldots(i)$

and $\quad x = y \quad \ldots(ii)$

From Eqs. (i) and (ii),

$2x + cx = 8$

$\Rightarrow \quad (2 + c)x = 8$

$\Rightarrow \quad 2 + c = 8 \quad [\because x = 1]$

$\therefore \quad c = 6$

**7.** *(b)* The given equation is

$2x + 0 \cdot y = 9$

So, $x = \frac{9}{2}$ and value of $y$ is real number.

**8.** *(c)* Since $x = -2$ and $y = 3$ is a solution of the equation

$3x + 5y = a^2$

$\therefore x = -2$ and $y = 3$ satisfies the given equation.

$\therefore \quad 3(-2) + 5(3) = a^2$

$\Rightarrow \quad -6 + 15 = a^2$

$\Rightarrow \quad 9 = a^2$

$\therefore \quad a = \pm 3$

**9.** *(d)* Since $(a + b, a - b)$ is a solution of equation

$3x + 2y = 20$

$\therefore \quad 3(a + b) + 2(a - b) = 20$

$\Rightarrow \quad 3a + 3b + 2a - 2b = 20$

$5a + b = 20 \ldots(i)$

Similarly, $(a + b, a - b)$ is a solution of equation

$4x - 5y = 42$

$\therefore 4(a + b) - 5(a - b) = 42$

$\Rightarrow 4a + 4b - 5a + 5b = 42$

$-a + 9b = 42 \ldots(ii)$

From Eqs. (i) and (ii), we get

$5(9b - 42) + b = 20$

$\Rightarrow 45b - 210 + b = 20$

$\Rightarrow \quad 46b = 230$

$\Rightarrow \quad b = 5$

**10.** *(a)* $(-2, 2)$ is a solution of

$2x + ky = 6$

$\therefore 2(-2) + k(2) = 6$

$-4 + 2k = 6$

$\Rightarrow \quad 2k = 6 + 4$

$k = \frac{10}{2} = 5$

**11.** *(d)* Here, $y = 3x + 5n$

It can be seen that $x$ can have infinite values and for infinite values of $x$, there can be infinite values of $y$.

So, $y = 3x + 5n$ has infinite possible solutions.

**12.** *(c)* Here point (4,1), then

$x = 4, \; y = 1$

Check option (a),

$x + 2y = 5$

$4 + 2 \times 1 = 5$

$6 = 5$

Option (a) is not correct

For option (b),

$2x + y = -6$

$2 \times 4 + 1 = -6$

$8 + 1 = -6$

$9 = -6$

Option (b) is not correct

For option (c),

$x + 2y = 6$

$4 + 2 \times 1 = 6$

$6 = 6$

Option (c) is correct answer.

**13.** *(b)* Total distance covered $= x$ km

Total taxi fare = ₹ $y$

Fare for first km = ₹ 8

$\therefore$ Remaining distance $= (x - 1)$ km

$\therefore$ Fare for $(x - 1)$ km = ₹ $5(x - 1)$

According to the question,

$8 + 5(x - 1) = y$

$\Rightarrow \quad 8 + 5x - 5 = y$

$\therefore \quad 5x - y + 3 = 0$

**14.** *(b)* In right angled isosceles triangle, the angles are 90°, $x°$ and $y°$.

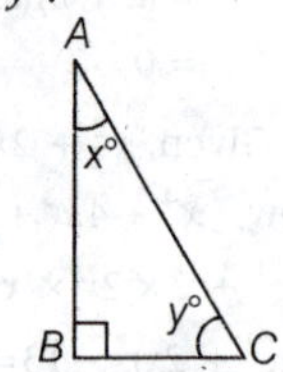


$x + y + 90° = 180°$

[$\because$ sum of all angles of a triangle is 180°]

$\therefore \quad x + y = 90°$

**15.** *(b)* Point (0, 0) satisfying the equation $y = mx$.

**16.** *(b)* Given amount earned by school by selling tickets for a play = ₹ 5100

Cost of each ticket = ₹ 12

Number of tickets sold = $t$

Cost of $t$ tickets = $12t$

$\therefore$ The equation used to determine the number of tickets were sold, $12t = 5100$

**17.** *(b)* Let fraction be $\frac{x}{y}$.

According to the question,

$\frac{x + 2}{y + 2} = \frac{9}{11}$

$\Rightarrow \quad 11x + 22 = 9y + 18$

$\Rightarrow \quad 11x - 9y = -4 \quad \ldots(i)$

and $\quad \frac{x + 3}{y + 3} = \frac{5}{6}$

$\Rightarrow \quad 6x + 18 = 5y + 15$

$\Rightarrow \quad 6x - 5y = -3$

**18.** *(a)* Let the numerator be $x$ and denominator be $y$ of the fraction.

According to the question,

$\frac{x + 2}{y} = \frac{1}{3}$

$\Rightarrow \quad 3x + 6 = y$

$\Rightarrow \quad 3x - y + 6 = 0$

**19.** *(b)* The cost of a pen be ₹ $x$ and the cost of a pencil be ₹ $y$.

According to the question,

$x = 2y + 3$

**20.** (c) 5 yr ago, age of Raju
$= (x - 5)$ yr
and age of Rita $= (y - 5)$ yr
According to the question,
$$x - 5 = (y - 5) + 10$$
$$\Rightarrow \quad x - 5 = y + 5$$
$$\Rightarrow \quad x - y - 10 = 0$$
$$\Rightarrow \quad x - y = 10$$

**21.** (c) Let number of cars and motorbikes be $C$ and $M$ respectively, then
$$10\,C = 4M \Rightarrow C = \frac{2}{5}M$$
and $C + M = 140$
$$\therefore \quad \frac{2M}{5} + M = 140$$
$$\Rightarrow \quad 7M = 140 \times 5$$
$$\Rightarrow \quad M = 20 \times 5 = 100$$
$$\therefore \quad C = 40$$

**22.** (b) Let the cost of 1 chair and 1 table be $x$ and $y$ respectively. Then, we get the following two equations $9x + 3y = 306$
When $x = 25$, then
$$9 \times 25 + 3y = 306$$
$$\Rightarrow \quad 3y = 306 - 225$$
$$\Rightarrow \quad 3y = 81 \Rightarrow y = ₹27$$

**23.** (c) Let cost of potato be ₹ $x$ per kg and cost of tomato be ₹ $y$ per kg.
According to the question,
$$3x = 2y$$
$$\Rightarrow \quad y = 3x/2$$
Given, $3x = 50$
$\therefore$ $50 = 2y \Rightarrow y =$ ₹ 25

**24.** (d) Let the present ages of father and son be $x$ yr and $y$ yr, respectively.
According to the question,
Age of father after 2 yr
= 3(Age of son after 2 yr) + 8
$$\Rightarrow \quad x + 2 = 3(y + 2) + 8$$
$$\Rightarrow \quad x + 2 = 3y + 6 + 8$$
$$\Rightarrow \quad x - 3y - 12 = 0$$
which is linear equation in two variables.
When son's age is 10 yr.
i.e put $y = 10$, then
$$x - 3 \times 10 - 12 = 0 \Rightarrow x = 42\text{ yr}$$

**25.** (a) Given $x = 2$ and $y = 1$
A. Given linear equation is $2x + 5y = 9$.
On putting $x = 2$ and $y = 1$ in LHS, we get
$$\text{LHS} = 2x + 5y = 2(2) + 5(1)$$
$$= 4 + 5 = 9 = \text{RHS}$$
So, $x = 2$ and $y = 1$ is a solution of given equation.
B. Given linear equation is
$$\frac{5}{2}x + 3y = 14$$
On putting $x = 2$ and $y = 1$ in LHS, we get
$$\text{LHS} = \frac{5}{2}x + 3y = \frac{5}{2}(2) + 3(1)$$
$$= 5 + 3 = 8 \neq 14$$
$\Rightarrow$ LHS $\neq$ RHS
So, $x = 2$ and $y = 1$ is not a solution of given equation.

**26.** (b) A : The degree of a linear equation is 1.
B : $x + 2y - 500$
C : A linear equation $ax + by + c = 0$ have infinite solutions.
D : The cost of book $= 2\times$ the cost of pen
$$\Rightarrow \quad x = 2y \Rightarrow x - 2y = 0$$

**27.** (c) **Assertion** (A) Since $\left(-\frac{3}{2}, k\right)$ is a solution of $2x + 3 = 0$
$$\therefore \quad 2\left(-\frac{3}{2}\right) + 3 = 0$$
$$\Rightarrow \quad 0 = 0$$
Hence, $\left(-\frac{3}{2}, k\right)$ is a solution of $2x + 3 = 0$ for all values of $k$, so it is correct.
**Reason** (R) Also $ax + b = 0$ can be expressed in linear equation in two variables as $ax + 0 \cdot y + b = 0$.
Hence, reason is not correct.

**28.** (b) A : $4x + 3y = 24$
put $x = 3$, $y = 4$ in equation,
$$12 + 12 = 24$$
$$\Rightarrow \quad 24 = 24$$
$\therefore (3, 4)$ is a solution of equation.
B : $\frac{x}{2} - \frac{y}{3} = 2$
put $x = 2$, $y = -3$ in equation,
$$\frac{2}{2} - \frac{-3}{3} = 2$$
$$\Rightarrow \quad 2 = 2$$
$\therefore (2, -3)$ is a solution of equation.
C : $3x + 5y = 15$
put $x = 3$, $y = \frac{6}{5}$ in equation,
$$3 \times 3 + 5 \times \frac{6}{5} = 15$$
$$\Rightarrow \quad 15 = 15$$
$\therefore \left(3, \frac{6}{5}\right)$ is a solution of equation.
D : $\frac{x - 2}{3} = y - 3$
put $x = 2$, $y = 3$ in equation
$$\frac{2 - 2}{3} = 3 - 3 \Rightarrow 0 = 0$$
$\therefore (2, 3)$ is a solution of equation.

**29.** (a) A : $8y = 9$, when written as an equation in two variable is $0 \cdot x + 8y = 9$
B. The linear equation $3x = 2y$, when expressed in two form $ax + by + c = 0$, then $a = 3$, $b = -2$ and $c = 0$.
C. Let the age of father be $x$ years and age of son is $y$ years.
According to the question,
$$x = 3y + 7$$
$$\Rightarrow x - 3y - 7 = 0$$
D. Put the value of $x = \lambda$ and $y = \frac{5}{2}$ in this equation $x + 4y - 7 = 0$, then we get

$\because -\lambda + 4\left(\frac{5}{2}\right) - 7 = 0$

$\Rightarrow \lambda = 10 - 7 \Rightarrow \lambda = 3$

**30.** (c) Let the age of Y's sister i.e, Z be x yrs.
$\therefore$ Age of Y be 2x yr's, age of X be (2x + 5) yr's.
and age of X's father i.e, M be $2(2x) + 8 = 4x + 8$ yrs.
According to the statement of the question, we have

$$4x + 8 = 48$$
$$\Rightarrow 4x = 48 - 8 = 40$$
$$\Rightarrow x = \frac{40}{4} = 10$$

$\therefore$ Age of Z = 10 yr
Age of X = (2x + 5) yr
$(2\times10 + 5)$ yr = 25 yr
Age of Y = $2\times10$ yr = 20 yr

**31.** (a) Total charge = ₹ y
Number of days = x
Then, according to the given condition,

$$y = 5 + (x-1)\times2$$
$$\Rightarrow y = 2x + 3$$

When x = 5, then
$$y = 10 + 3 = ₹13$$

**32.** (b) A: $x + y = 0$
On putting $x = 1$, $y = -1$ in equation,
$$1 + (-1) = 0 \Rightarrow 0 = 0$$
$\therefore (1, -1)$ is a solution of equation.
B : $y - 2x = 0$
On putting $x = \frac{3}{2}$, $y = 3$ in equation
$$3 - 2\times\frac{3}{2} = 0 \Rightarrow 0 = 0$$
$\therefore \left(\frac{3}{2}, 3\right)$ is a solution of equation.
C : $3x + 5y = 0$
On putting $x = -5$ and $y = 3$ in equation
$$3(-5) + 5(3) = 0$$
$$\Rightarrow -15 + 15 = 0 \Rightarrow 0 = 0$$
$\therefore (-5, 3)$ is a solution of equation.
D : $2x - y = 12$
On putting $x = 5$ and $y = -2$ in equation
$$\Rightarrow 2(5) - (-2) = 12$$
$$\Rightarrow 10 - (-2) = 10 \Rightarrow 12 = 12$$
$\therefore (5, 2)$ is a solution of equation.

**33.** (a) $35° = \frac{5F - 160°}{9}$
$$315° = 5F - 160°$$
$$5F = 475$$
$$F = 95°$$

**34.** (b) Since, C = F
$$\because C = \frac{5F - 160}{9}$$
$$\Rightarrow 9C - 5F = -160$$
$$\Rightarrow 4F = -160 \quad [C = F]$$
$$\Rightarrow F = -40$$

## Chapter 4 : Coordinate Geometry

**1.** (b) Given, coordinates of $P = (-5, 3)$ and $Q = (-5, m)$
According to the question,
$$m + 3 = -5 - 5$$
$$\Rightarrow m + 3 = -10$$
$$\Rightarrow m = -10 - 3 = -13$$

**2.** (d) According to the question,

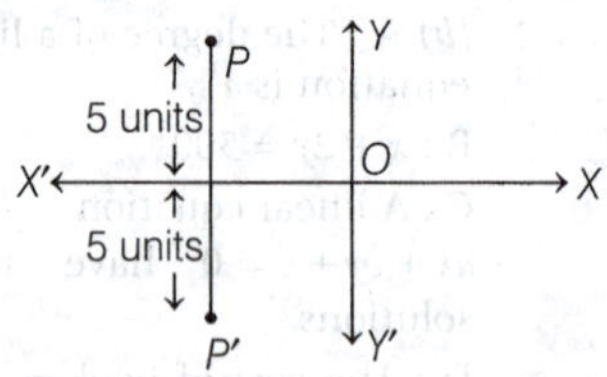


$\therefore$ For point P, y coordinate = 5 or −5

**3.** (c) According to the question,
$$y = x + 4 \Rightarrow -8 = x + 4$$
$$x = -8 - 4 = -12$$

**4.** (c) According to the question,

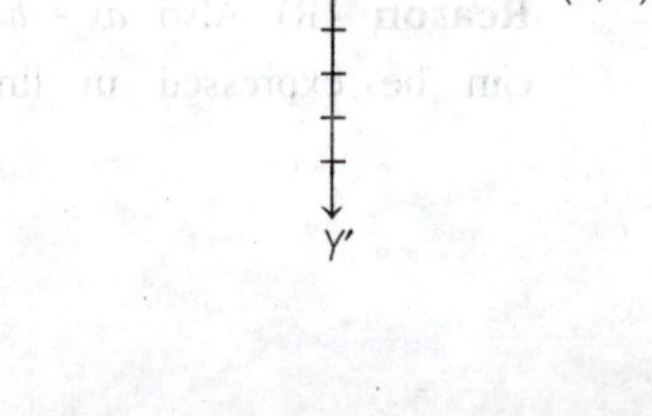


$$QP = \sqrt{QR^2 + PR^2}$$
$$= \sqrt{(4)^2 + (3)^2} = \sqrt{16 + 9}$$
$$= \sqrt{25} = 5 \text{ units}$$

**5.** (c) The sign of any point in IIIrd quadrant is (−, −).

**6.** (b) The form of sign of the point (−4, 2) is (−, +). So, the point lies in IInd quadrant.

**7.** (a) According to the question,
$x + 11 = 6 \Rightarrow x = -5$
and $5 = 7 + y \Rightarrow y = -2$

**8.** (d) We have, $x + y = 2$
if $x = 0$, $y = 2$ i.e, point (0, 2)
If $y = 0$, $x = 2$ i.e, point (2, 0)
$\therefore$ Line passes through Ist, 2nd and IVth quadrants.

**9.** (a) Since the x-coordinate of point P (a, b) is positive and y-coordinate is negative. So, the point P lies in IV quadrant.

**10.** (d) In IV quadrant, sign of the point (+, −). So option (d) point (−2, 4) does not lie in IV quadrant.

**11.** (c) The angle between the coordinate axes is 90°.

**12.** (d) Coordinates of point L are (−3, −2).

**13.** (b) Ordinate of point M = 1
Ordinate of point N = 3
$\therefore$ Required sum = 1 + 3 = 4

**14.** (b) Coordinates of point N are (1, 3) which represents the abscissa is 2 less than the ordinate.

**15.** (c) Abscissa of P = 2; Abscissa of N = 1
$\therefore$ Required difference = 2 − 1 = 1

**16.** (b) Since, point B lies on the Y-axis at a distance of 8 units from origin. Therefore, coordinates of B are (0, 8).
Radius of a circle is r = 8.
$\therefore$ Area of circle
$$= \pi r^2 = 3.14 \times (8)^2$$
$$= 200.96 \text{ sq units}$$

**17.** (*b*) $x$-coordinates of $A = 10$
$y$-coordinates of $B = -4$
$\therefore$ ($x$-coordinates of $A$) $-$ ($y$-coordinates of $B$)
$= 10 - (-4) = 10 + 4 = 14$

**18.** (*b*) From figure, $OQ = OR$ and $OP \perp QR$
$\therefore \Delta PQR$ is an equilateral triangle.
$\therefore \quad OP = \frac{\sqrt{3}}{2} \times QR$
$= \frac{\sqrt{3}}{2} \times (4 + 4)$
$= 4\sqrt{3}$
So, coordinates of $P = (4\sqrt{3}, 0)$.

**19.** (*b*) A : Ordinate $\to y$
B : Abscissa $\to x$
C : Ordered pair $\to (x, y)$
D : Coordinate of origin is (0, 0)

**20.** (*c*) A : Point $Q(3, -2)$ lies in IV quadrant.
B : Distance of a point $R(-2, 0)$ from origin is 2
C : Dimension of the rectangle $3 \times 2$
$\therefore$ Area of rectangle $= 3 \times 2 = 6$.
D : Point $T(3, 0)$ on $Y$-axis.

**21.** (*a*) We know that, the diagonals of a rhombus bisects to each-other.
$\therefore OA = OC = \frac{AC}{2} = \frac{16}{2} = 8$ cm
and $OB = OD = \frac{BD}{2} = \frac{8}{2} = 4$ cm
So, $A = (-8, 0)$; $B = (0, 4)$;
$C = (8, 0)$; $D = (0, -4)$

**22.** (*a*) $PQRS$ is a rhombus, then
$OP = OR = \frac{12}{2} = 6$
$OQ = OS = \frac{6}{2} = 3,$
coordinates of point $T$ are (5, 5).
(i) Abscissa of $P = -6$
Abscissa of $T = 5$
$\therefore$ Required sum $= -6 + 5 = -1$.
(ii) Ordinate of $Q = -3$
Ordinate of $R = 0$
Ordinate of $T = 5$
$\therefore$ Required sum
$= -3 + 0 + 5 = 2$

## Chapter 5 : Lines and Angles

**1.** (*c*) Here, point $R$ lies in the interior of $PQ$.

So, $PR + QR = PQ$
$\Rightarrow PR + QR = 12$ cm
Now,
$PR^2 + QR^2 + 2PR \cdot QR = 144$ cm

**2.** (*a*) Since, $C$ is mid-point of the line segment $AB$.
$\therefore \quad AB = AC + CB$ [by Euclid's axiom]
$\Rightarrow AB = AC + AC \quad [\because AC = CB]$
$\Rightarrow AC = \frac{1}{2} AB \quad$ ...(i)
Similarly as, $P$ is mid-point of line segment $AC$.
$\therefore \quad AP = \frac{1}{2} AC \quad$ ...(ii)
From Eqs. (i) and (ii), we get
$AP = \frac{1}{2}\left\{\frac{1}{2} AB\right\} = \frac{1}{4} AB$

**3.** (*c*) From figure,
$\angle ABC = \angle 1 + \angle 4$
$\angle ACB = \angle 2 + \angle 3$
$\because \quad \angle ABC = \angle ACB$
$\therefore \quad \angle 1 + \angle 4 = \angle 2 + \angle 3$
$\angle 1 + \angle 3 = \angle 2 + \angle 3$
$[\because \angle 4 = \angle 3]$
$\Rightarrow \quad \angle 1 = \angle 2$

**4.** (*d*) $\because \angle 1 = \angle 3$ and $\angle 3 = \angle 4$
$\therefore \quad \angle 1 = \angle 4$ and $\angle 2 = \angle 4$
So, $\quad \angle 1 = \angle 2$

**5.** (*d*) We have,
$\angle 1 = \angle 2$ [given]
$\angle 2 = \angle 3$ [given]
Hence, $\angle 1 = \angle 3$

**6.** (*d*) We know that, angle made on the straight line is 180°.
$\therefore \quad 5x° + 6x° + x° = 180°$
$\Rightarrow \quad 12x° = 180°$
$\therefore \quad x° = 15°$
$\therefore \angle AOB = 6x° = 6 \times 15° = 90°$
$\Rightarrow \angle EOD = \angle AOB = 90°$
[vertically opposite angles]

**7.** (*a*) Let one angle be $\angle x$.
$\therefore \quad$ Other angle $= \frac{3}{2} \angle x$
$\because$ Sum of two complementary angles = 90°
$\Rightarrow \angle x + \frac{3}{2} \angle x = 90°$
$\Rightarrow \quad \frac{5}{2} \angle x = 90° \Rightarrow \angle x = 36°$
So, the smallest angle is 36°.

**8.** (*d*) Let $\angle BOD = 2x°$
and $\quad \angle AOC = 3x°$
$\because \angle AOC + \angle COD + \angle DOB = 180°$
$\therefore 3x° + 2x° + 90° = 180°$
$\Rightarrow \quad 5x° = 90°$
$\Rightarrow \quad x° = 18°$
$\therefore \angle BOD = 2x° = 36°$

**9.** (*b*) Let one angle $A$ be $x°$.
$\therefore$ Other supplementary angle $B = (180° - x°)$
According to the question,
$(180° - x°) - x° = 30°$
$\Rightarrow \quad 180° - 2x° = 30°$
$\Rightarrow \quad 2x° = 150°$
$\Rightarrow \quad x° = 75°$
$\therefore$ Other angle
$= 180° - 75°$
$= 105°$

**10.** (*b*) We know that, angle made on the straight line is 180°.
$\therefore \quad 3x° + 4x° + 2x° = 180°$
$\Rightarrow \quad 9x° = 180°$
$\Rightarrow \quad x° = 20°$
$\therefore \angle AOF = 3x° = 60°$
As, $\angle DOC = \angle AOF$
[vertically opposite angles]
$\therefore \angle DOC = 60°$

**11.** (*d*) Let the angles be $7x°$ and $11x°$.

$\because$ The angles are complementary

$\therefore \quad 7x° + 11x° = 90°$

$\Rightarrow \quad 18x° = 90° \Rightarrow x° = 5°$

$\therefore$ First angle = 35°

and second angle = 55°

**12.** (*d*) Given, $\angle a$ and $\angle b$ forms a linear pair. Therefore,

$\angle a + \angle b = 180° \quad \ldots$(i)

Also given

$\angle a - 2\angle b = 30° \quad \ldots$(ii)

Solving Eqs. (i) and (ii), we get

$\angle a = 130°$ and $\angle b = 50°$

**13.** (*a*) Since, $\angle x$ and $\angle y$ forms a complementary pair.

Therefore, $\angle x + \angle y = 90°$

Now, $(\angle y + 35°) + (\angle x + 65°)$

$= \angle x + \angle y + 90°$

$= 90° + 90°$

$= 180°$

Hence, $(\angle y + 35°)$ and $(\angle x + 65°)$ form a supplementary pair.

**14.** (*c*) We know, that we are constructed the angles by using ruler and a pair of compasses which are multiples of $7\frac{1}{2}°$ or 15°.

$\therefore$ 70° can not be constructed by ruler and compass.

**15.** (*b*) If $\angle A$ is complementary to each other.

Then, $\angle A + \angle A = 90°$

$\Rightarrow \quad 2\angle A = 90°$

$\Rightarrow \quad \angle A = 45°$

Also, given $\angle B + \angle B = 180°$ [supplementary]

$\Rightarrow \quad 2\angle B = 180°$

$\Rightarrow \quad \angle B = 90°$

**16.** (*b*) In option (b), the angle between the bisectors of a linear pair of angles is a complementary angles itself.

Options (a), (c) are not correct.

**17.** (*d*) We know,

$\angle UOR = \angle SOT = 20°$

[vertically opposite angles]

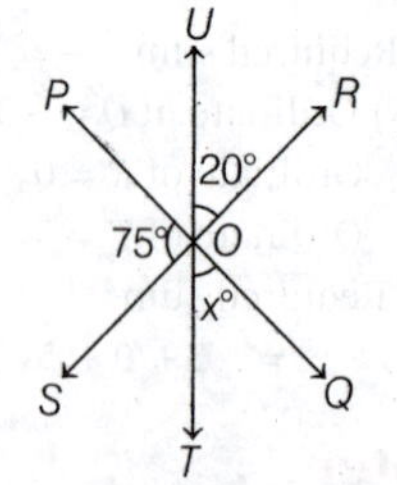


$\therefore \angle POS + \angle SOT + \angle TOQ = 180°$

[linear pair]

$\Rightarrow \quad 75° + 20° + x° = 180°$

$\Rightarrow \quad x° = 180° - 95° = 85°$

**18.** (*a*) Since, $AB$ is a straight line.

$\therefore \quad \angle AOB = 180°$

$\therefore \quad \angle x + \angle y = 180°$

and $\angle z + \angle w = 180°$

$\therefore \quad \angle x + \angle y = \angle z + \angle w$

**19.** (*b*) Since, $\angle a + \angle b = 90°$

$\Rightarrow \quad 2x + 3x = 90°$

$\therefore \quad x = 18°$

$\Rightarrow \quad \angle a = 36°$

Now, $\angle c = 180° - (90° - 36°)$

$= 126°$

**20.** (*b*) $\because \angle BOD = \angle AOC$

[vertically opposite angles]

$\Rightarrow \quad 2x° = y°$

$\therefore \angle COE + \angle EOB + \angle BOD = 180°$

$90° + x° + 2x° = 180°$

$\Rightarrow \quad 3x° = 90°$

$\Rightarrow \quad x° = 30°$

**21.** (*b*) Since, $AB$ is a straight line.

$\therefore \angle AOD + \angle DOC + \angle BOC = 180°$

$\Rightarrow x° + x° - 2 + 3x° - 3 = 180°$

$\Rightarrow \quad 5x° = 185°$

$\Rightarrow \quad x° = 37°$

$\therefore \quad \angle DOC = 37° - 2° = 35°$

$\therefore$ Reflex $\angle DOC = 360° - 35°$

$= 325°$

**22.** (*b*) From figure,

$\angle c = 50°$

(vertically opposite angles)

and $\angle c + \angle d = 180°$

(Co-interior angles)

$\Rightarrow \quad 50° + \angle d = 180°$

$\Rightarrow \quad d = 180° - 50° = 130°$

**23.** (*c*) $\angle x = \angle y$ (Given)

Therefore, $l \parallel m$

(corresponding angles) ...(i)

Also, $\angle a = \angle b$ (Given)

Therefore, $n \parallel m$

(corresponding angles) ...(ii)

From Eqs. (i) and (ii), $l \parallel n$

(Lines parallel to the same line)

**24.** (*d*) In the given figure, $AB \parallel DC$ and $AD \parallel BC$

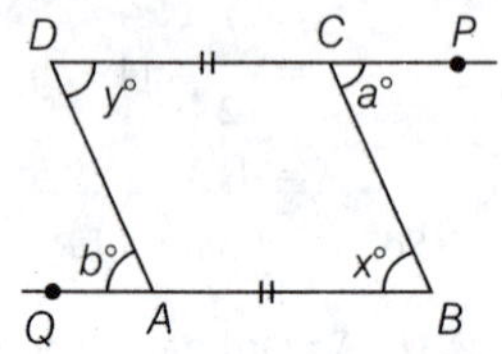


$\therefore \quad \angle a = \angle x \quad \ldots$(i)

[alternate interior angles]

and $\quad \angle b = \angle y \quad \ldots$(ii)

[alternate interior angles]

Adding Eqs. (i) and (ii), we get

$\angle a + \angle b = \angle x + \angle y$

**25.** (*b*) In the given figure, $AB \parallel CD$

$\Rightarrow \quad \angle PEB = \angle PGD = 80°$

(corresponding angles)

Now, $EGQ$ is a straight line.

$\therefore \angle EGD + \angle DGQ = 180°$

(linear pair)

$\Rightarrow \quad \angle DGQ = 100°$

Now, $\angle QHD = x° + \angle DGQ$

(exterior angle property)

$\Rightarrow \quad 120° = x° + 100°$

$\Rightarrow \quad x° = 20°$

**26.** (*b*) Since, $PQ \parallel RS$

$\therefore \quad \angle PQS + \angle RSQ = 180°$

(co-interior angles)

$\Rightarrow \quad 55° + \angle RSQ = 180°$

$\Rightarrow \quad \angle RSQ = 125°$

Now, $EF \parallel QS$

$\therefore \quad \angle RFE = \angle RSQ = 125°$

(corresponding angles)

**27.** (b)

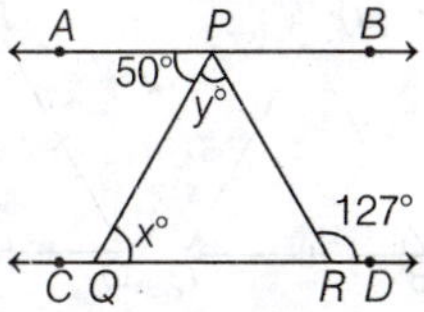


In $\Delta PQR$, an exterior angle is equal to the sum of the two non-adjacent interior angles.

$$\angle x + \angle y = 127°$$

**28.** (c) Draw $EO \parallel AB \parallel CD$

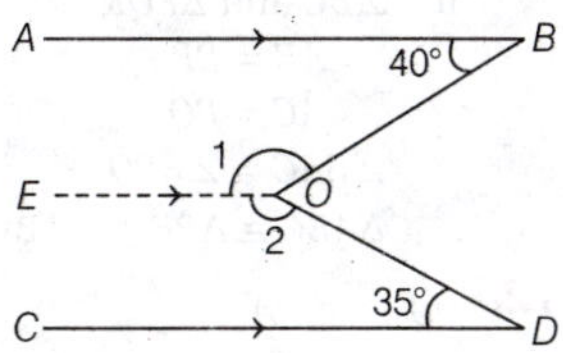


So, $\angle 1 + \angle 2 = x$

As, $EO \parallel AB$ and $OB$ is transversal.

$\therefore \angle 1 + \angle ABO = 180°$

(co-interior angles)

$\Rightarrow \angle 1 + 40° = 180° \Rightarrow \angle 1 = 140°$

Also, $EO \parallel CD$ and $DO$ is transversal.

$\therefore \angle 2 + \angle CDO = 180°$

(co-interior angles)

$\Rightarrow \angle 2 + 35° = 180° \Rightarrow \angle 2 = 145°$

$\therefore \angle 1 + \angle 2 = 140° + 145° = 285°$

$\therefore \angle x = 285°$

**29.** (c) Since, $OP \parallel RS$ and $RX$ is a transversal.

So, $\angle RXP = \angle XRS$

[alternate angles]

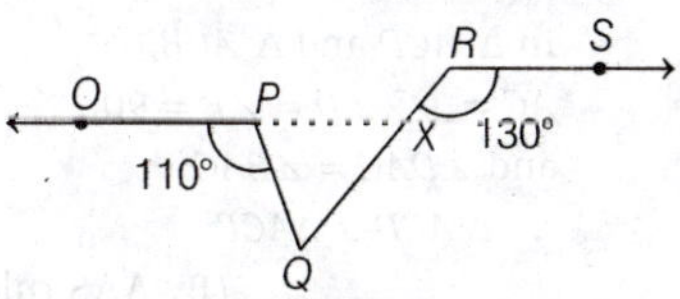


$\Rightarrow \angle RXP = 130°$ ... (i)

Now, $RQ$ is a line segment.

So, $\angle PXQ + \angle RXP = 180°$

[linear pair axiom]

$\Rightarrow \angle PXQ = 180° - \angle RXP$

$= 180° - 130°$

[from Eq. (i)]

$\Rightarrow \angle PXQ = 50°$

In $\Delta PQX$, $\angle OPQ$ is an exterior angle.

$\therefore \angle OPQ = \angle PXQ + \angle PQX$

$\Rightarrow 110° = 50° + \angle PQX$

$\therefore \angle PQR = 60°$

$[\because \angle PQX = \angle PQR]$

**30.** (b) We know that,

$\angle x + \angle y = 180°$ ...(i)

[since, angles on same side of transversal are supplementary]

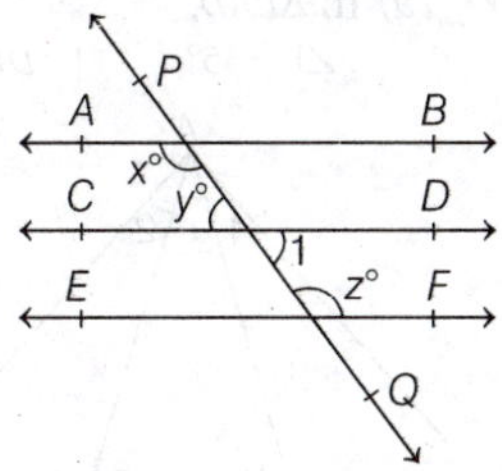


Now, $\angle 1 = \angle y$

[vertically opposite angles]

Also, $\angle 1 + \angle z = 180$

$\Rightarrow \angle y + \angle z = 180°$

Here, $y : z = 3 : 7$ [given]

$$\therefore \quad \angle y = \frac{3}{3+7} \times 180° = 54°$$

$$\text{and} \quad \angle z = \frac{7}{3+7} \times 180° = 126°$$

From Eq. (i),

$\angle x + \angle y = 180°$

$\therefore \angle x = 180° - 54°$

$= 126°$

$\therefore \angle x + \angle z = 126° + 126°$

$= 252°$

**31.** (a) $AB \parallel CD$

$\Rightarrow \angle 1 = \angle BLM$

[vertically opposite angles]

$\Rightarrow \angle BLM = 95°$

$\therefore \angle 2 = \angle BLM = 95°$

[corresponding angles]

**32.** (b) Given, $PQ \parallel RS$

$\therefore \angle PQC = \angle BRS = 60°$

and $\angle DQR = \angle QRA = 25°$

$\therefore \angle QRS = \angle QRA + \angle ARS$

$= \angle QRA + (180° - \angle BRS)$

$= 25° + 180° - 60° = 145°$

**33.** (d) $\because AB \parallel CF$

$\therefore \angle ABC = \angle BCF$

[Alternate interior angles]

$\Rightarrow \angle BCF = 40°$

Also,

$\angle ACB + \angle BCF + \angle FCD = 180°$

[Linear pair]

$\Rightarrow 65° + 40° + \angle FCD = 180°$

$\Rightarrow \angle FCD = 180° - 105°$

$\Rightarrow \angle FCD = 75°$

Since, $CD \parallel EF$

$\therefore x = \angle FCD = 75°$

**34.** (a) I. False, Angles forming a linear pair are supplementary.

II. False, If two lines are perpendicular to the third line, then those two lines are parallel to each other.

III. False, from figure $\angle a$ and $\angle f$ are corresponding angles

$\therefore \angle f = \angle a = 50°$

IV. False, The angle formed is complete angle.

**35.** (b) A : $\angle 3 + \angle 6 = 180°$

(Co-interior angles)

and $\angle 4 + \angle 5 = 180°$

$\therefore \angle 3 + \angle 6 = \angle 4 + \angle 5$

B : Correspond angles pairs $\angle 3$ and $\angle 7$

(other pairs are $\angle 2$ and $\angle 6$, $\angle 1$ and $\angle 5$, $\angle 4$ and $\angle 8$)

C : Vertically opposite angles in pair $\angle 5$ and $\angle 7$

(other pairs are $\angle 2$ and $\angle 4$, $\angle 1$ and $\angle 3$, $\angle 6$ and $\angle 8$)

D : Alternate angles $\angle 2$ and $\angle 8$

## Chapter 6 : Triangles

**1.** (d) In triangle,

I: $AB = AC = 6$ cm

II: $A'B' = B'C' = 5$ cm

III: $\angle PQR = 90°$, $\angle PRQ = 45°$,

then $\angle RPQ = 45°$

$\therefore PQ = QR$

Hence, triangles I, II and III are isosceles triangles.

**2.** (b)

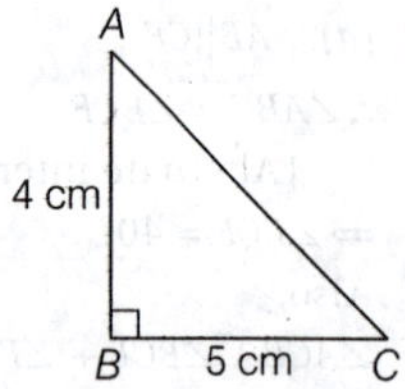


In a right angled triangle, hypotenuse ($AC$) is the largest side.

**3.** (b) In $\Delta ADB$ and $\Delta ADC$,

$BD = DC$

[since, $AD$ divides $BC$]

$\angle ADB = \angle ADC$ [each 90°]

$AD = AD$ [common]

$\therefore \Delta ADB \cong \Delta ADC$

[by SAS criterion]

$\Rightarrow AB = AC$ [by CPCT]

$\therefore \Delta ABC$ is an isosceles triangle.

**4.** (a) $\because 135° + \theta = 180°$

[angle on a straight line is 180°]

$\therefore \theta = 45°$

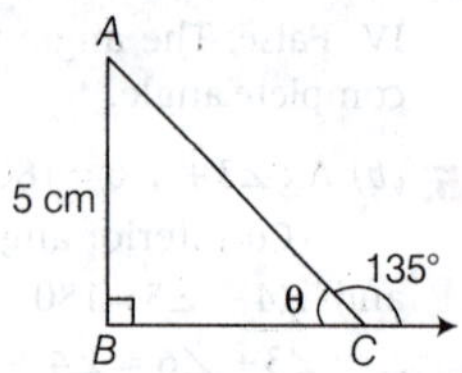


In $\Delta ABC$, $90° + 45° + \angle A = 180°$

$\therefore \angle A = 45°$

i.e. isosceles triangle.

Now, $BC = 5\,\text{cm}$

$\therefore AC = \sqrt{5^2 + 5^2} = 5\sqrt{2}\,\text{cm}$

**5.** (a) In triangle I, $3^2 + 4^2 = 5^2$

So, I is right angled triangle.

In triangle II, $5^2 + 6^2 \neq 7^2$

$\therefore$ II is not right angled triangle.

**6.** (a) Since, $BD$ is the bisector of $\angle B$.

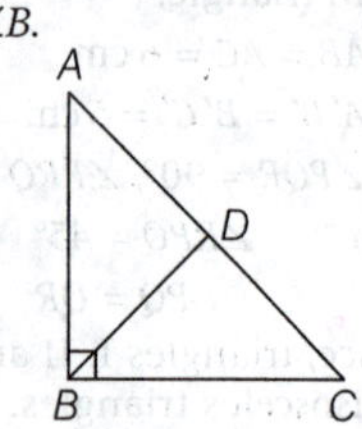


$\therefore \angle ABD = \angle DBC$

Given, $AB = BC$

i.e. $\angle C = \angle A = 45°$

[angles opposite to equal sides are equal]

$\because \angle B = 90°$

$\Rightarrow \angle BDC = 180° - (45° + 45°) = 90°$

Since, side opposite to a greatest angle is larger.

Hence, $BC$ is longest side.

**7.** (b) In $\Delta BAD$,

$\angle 1 = 35°$ [$\because DB = AB$]

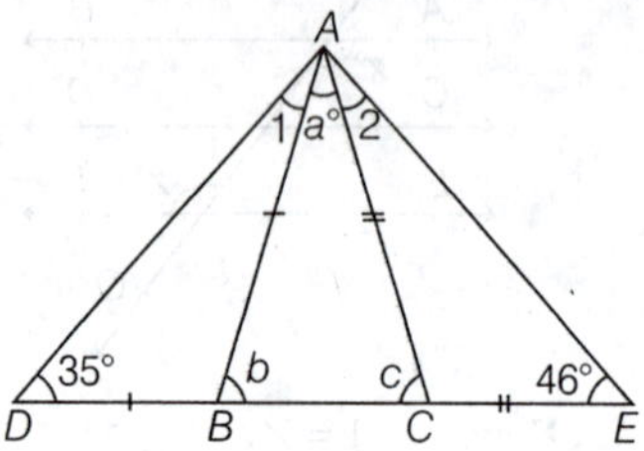


In $\Delta CAE$, $\angle 2 = 46°$

[$\because AC = CE$]

$\angle b = 35° + 35° = 70°$

and $\angle c = 46° + 46° = 92°$

In $\Delta ABC$,

$\angle A + \angle B + \angle C = 180°$

$\angle a = 180° - (162°) = 18°$

**8.** (d) Join $AD$ and $AE$.

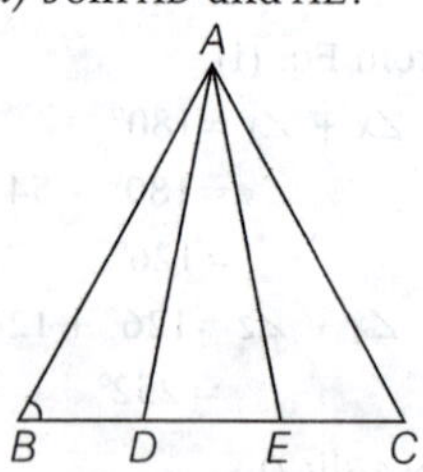


In $\Delta ABC$, $AB = AC$

$\Rightarrow \angle B = \angle C$ ...(i)

In $\Delta ABE$ and $\Delta ACD$

$AB = AC$ [Given]

$BE = CD$ [Given]

$\angle B = \angle C$ [from Eq. (i)]

$\therefore \Delta ABE \cong \Delta ACD$

[By congruency criterion]

$\Rightarrow AE = AD$ [By CPCT]

**9.** (b) We know that, the sum of exterior angles of a polygon is 360°.

**10.** (a)

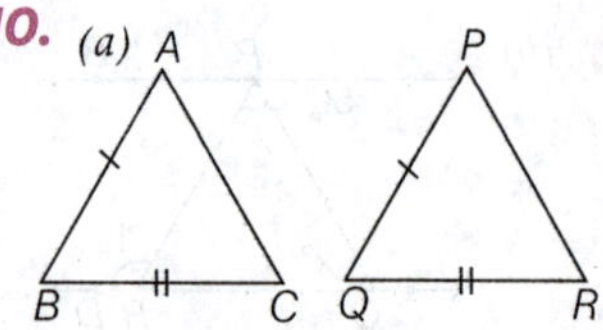


$\because \Delta ABC \cong \Delta PQR$ [given]

$\therefore \angle A = \angle P$

$\angle B = \angle Q$

$\Rightarrow \angle C = \angle R$

**11.** (c) According to the question, in $\Delta ABC$ and $\Delta PQR$

$AB = RP$

$AC = PQ$

$\angle BAC = \angle RPQ$

$\therefore \Delta ABC \cong \Delta PRQ$ [By SAS]

**12.** (b)

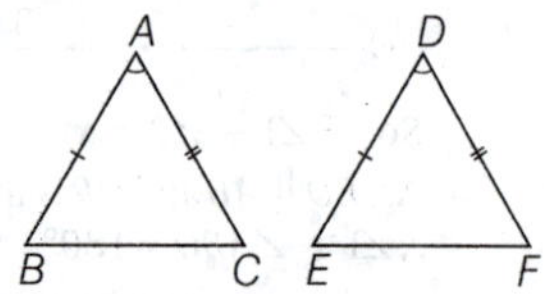


In $\Delta ABC$ and $\Delta DEF$,

$AB = DE$

$\angle A = \angle D$

if $AC = DF$,

then $\Delta ABC \cong \Delta DEF$

(By SAS)

**13.** (c) In the given figure, $\Delta ABC$ and $\Delta ADC$ are right angled triangles.

In $\Delta ACD$,

$AC = 5\,\text{cm}$, $AD = 3\,\text{cm}$

$\therefore CD = \sqrt{5^2 - 3^2} = \sqrt{16} = 4\,\text{cm}$

In $\Delta ACD$ and $\Delta ACB$,

$AC = AC$, $\angle D = \angle B = 90°$

and $\angle DAC = \angle BAC$

$\therefore \Delta ACD \cong \Delta ACB$

(By AAS rule)

Now, $BC = CD = 4\,\text{cm}$

$\therefore BC + CD = 8\,\text{cm}$

**14.** (c) In $\Delta ADB$ and $\Delta ADC$

$\angle BAD = \angle CAD$

($\because AD$ bisects $\angle A$)

$\angle ADB = \angle ADC$ ($\because$ each 90°)

$AD = AD$ (common side)

$\Delta ADB \cong \Delta ADC$

(By ASA congruency rule)

$\therefore \quad AB = AC$ (by CPCT)

$\therefore \Delta ABC$ is an isosceles triangle.

**15.** (b) In $\Delta PDC$ and $\Delta PAB$

$\angle CPD = \angle BPA$ (vertically opposite angles)

$CP = BP$ (given)

$PD = PA$ (given)

$\therefore \quad \Delta PDC \cong \Delta PAB$

(By SAS congruency)

**16.** (a) In $\Delta DEF$, $DE = DF$. So, $\Delta DEF$ is an isosceles.

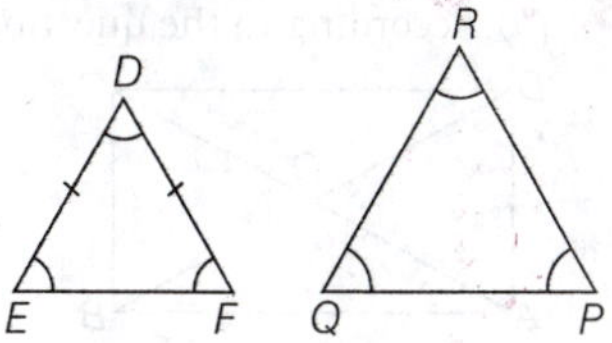


$\therefore \quad \angle F = \angle E$ ...(i)

Also, $\angle F = \angle P$

and $\angle E = \angle Q$ ...(ii)

From Eqs. (i) and (ii), we get

$\angle P = \angle Q$

Now, in $\Delta PQR$, $\angle P = \angle Q$

$\Rightarrow \quad RQ = PR$

So, $\Delta PQR$ is an isosceles.

Hence, $\Delta DEF$ and $\Delta PQR$ are isosceles but not necessarily congruent.

**17.** (d) We can not calculate $DF$ because other side (either $AB$ or $DE$) must be given.

**18.** (b) In $\Delta ABC$ and $\Delta ABD$, we see that

$AC = AD$

$BC = BD$

$AB = AB$ [common]

$\therefore \quad \Delta ABC \cong \Delta ABD$

[by SSS criterion]

**19.** (a) In $\Delta AFE$ and $\Delta DBC$,

$AB = CF$

$\Rightarrow AB + BF = CF + BF$

$\Rightarrow \quad AF = BC$

$EF = BD$ and $\angle AFE = \angle DBC$

$\therefore \Delta AFE \cong \Delta CBD$

[by SAS criterion]

**20.** (b) In $\Delta ABD$ and $\Delta FEC$

$AB = FE$ [given]

$BD = CE$ ($\because BC = DE$)

$\angle ABD = \angle CEF$ (each 90°)

$\therefore \quad \Delta ABD \cong \Delta FEC$

(By SAS congruency rule)

**21.** (b) We have, $AE = AD$

and $CE = BD$

$\Rightarrow \quad AE + CE = AD + BD$

$\Rightarrow \quad AC = AB$ ... (i)

Now, in $\Delta AEB$ and $\Delta ADC$, we have

$AE = AD$ (given)

$\angle EAB = \angle DAC$ (common angle)

$AB = AC$ [From Eq. (i)]

$\therefore \quad \Delta AEB \cong \Delta ADC$

(By SAS Congruency rule)

**22.** (d) In $\Delta ABE$ and $\Delta ACF$,

$BE = CF$

$\angle CFA = \angle BEA = 90°$

$\angle A = \angle A$

Hence, $\Delta ABE \cong \Delta ACF$

[By AAS Criterion]

**23.** (a) In $\Delta ACB$ and $\Delta ADB$

$AC = AD$ (given)

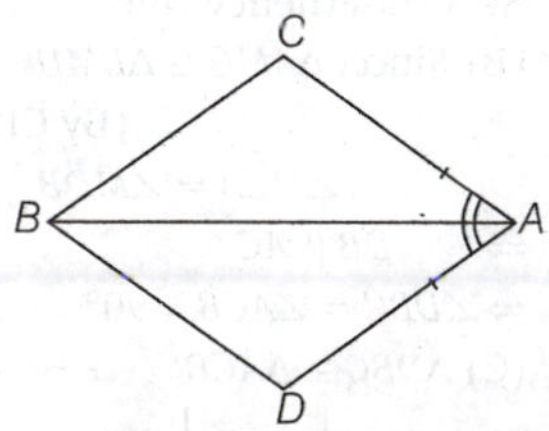


$\angle CAB = \angle DAB$ ($AB$ bisects $\angle A$)

and $AB = AB$ (common side)

$\therefore \quad \Delta ACB \cong \Delta ADB$

(by SAS rule of congruency)

**24.** (c) We have, $AB = 30$ cm, $BC = 29$ cm, $AC = 21$ cm

$\therefore \quad AR = \frac{AB}{2} = \frac{30}{2} = 15$ cm,

$AQ = \frac{AC}{2} = \frac{21}{2}$ cm

$P$ and $R$ are mid-points of sides $BC$ and $AB$ respectively.

$\therefore \quad PR \parallel AC$

and $PR = \frac{1}{2} AC = \frac{21}{2}$ cm

Similarly, $PQ \parallel AB$

and $PQ = \frac{1}{2} AB = \frac{30}{2} = 15$ cm

$\therefore$ Perimeter of quadrilateral

$ARPQ = AR + RP + PQ + AQ$

$= 15 + \frac{21}{2} + 15 + \frac{21}{2}$

$= 30 + 21 = 51$ cm

**25.** (a) We have,

$OA = OB = OC$ (radii of circle)

$\therefore \Delta AOB$ and $\Delta AOC$ are isosceles triangle.

[We know that angles opposite to equal sides of an isosceles triangles are equal.]

$\therefore \quad \angle OAB = \angle OBA = 35°$

and $\angle OCB = \angle OBC = 45°$

So, $\quad x = 2 \times 35° + 2 \times 45°$

$= 70° + 90° = 160°$

**26.** (b) We have, $\angle ADF = \angle BCG$

$\Rightarrow 180° - \angle ADF = 180° - \angle BCG$

$\Rightarrow \quad \angle ADE = \angle BCE$

In $\Delta EDA$ and $\Delta ECB$,

$\angle ADE = \angle BCE$

$ED = EC$ [Given]

$\therefore \quad \angle AED = \angle BEC$ [vertically opposite angle]

$\therefore \quad \Delta EDA \cong \Delta ECB$ [By ASA congruence property]

$\therefore AD = BC$ and $AE = BE$

[by CPCT]

Thus, $\Delta AEB$ is an isosceles triangle.

**27.** (b) In $\Delta AOE$ and $COD$,

we have $\angle A = \angle C$ [Given]

and $\angle AOE = \angle COD$

[vertically opposite angle]

$\therefore \quad \angle A + \angle AOE = \angle C + \angle COD$

$\Rightarrow 180° - \angle AEO = 180° - \angle CDO$

$\Rightarrow \quad \angle AEO = \angle CDO$

Now, $\angle AEO + \angle OEB = 180°$

[linear pair]

and $\angle CDO + \angle ODB = 180°$

[Linear pair]

$\therefore \angle AEO + \angle OEB$

$= \angle CDO + \angle ODB$

$\Rightarrow \angle OEB = \angle ODB$

[Using Eq. (i)]

$\Rightarrow \angle CEB = \angle ADB$ ...(ii)

Now, in $\Delta ABD$ and $\Delta CBE$,

we have

$\angle A = \angle C$

$\angle ADB = \angle CEB$ [from Eq. (ii)]

and $AB = BC$

$\therefore \Delta ABD \cong \Delta CBE$

[By SAS criterion of congruence]

**28.** (c) Since, $KD \perp BC$

and $KD \perp DE$

$\therefore BC || DE$

Extend $DE$ to point $G$ on $BF$ so that $BC || GE$.

$\therefore \angle DGZ = \angle CBG = 35°$

[Corresponding angles]

Now, $x = \angle DGF + \angle DFG°$

$= 35° + 25° = 60°$

[Exterior angle property]

**29.** (b) I. True,

[By SSS congruency rule]

II. True

III. False

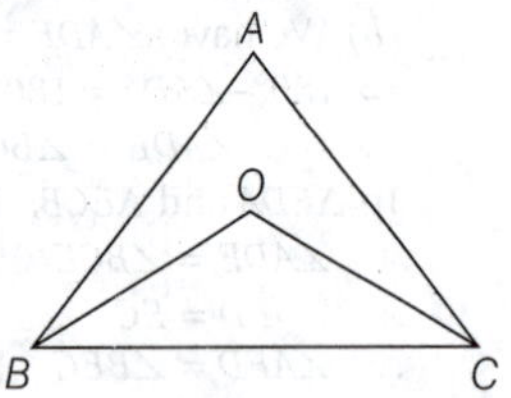

$\angle BOC = 180° - (\angle OBC + \angle OCB)$

IV. True

**30.** (a) A : Equilateral triangle is an acute angled triangle.

B: In $\Delta ABM$ and $\Delta ACM$

$AB = AC = 7$ cm

$AM = AM$ [common side]

$\angle AMB = \angle AMC$ [Each 90°]

$\Rightarrow \Delta AMB \cong \Delta AMC$

[By RHS rule]

C. In $\Delta AMB$ and $\Delta AMC$

$AB = AC$ [Given]

$BM = CM$ [Given]

$AM = AM$ [Common]

$\Rightarrow \Delta AMB \cong \Delta AMC$

[By SSS Congruence]

D : In a triangle one angle is 90° and other two sides are equal, then the triangle is the right isosceles triangle.

**31.** (b) A : $\angle x = 80° + 40° = 120°$

$\angle y = 70° + 40° = 110°$

[$\because \angle BOD = \angle AOC = 40°$, vertically opposite angles]

B : $\angle y = 180° - 125° = 55°$ (Linear pair)

Since, $\Delta ABC \cong \Delta EFG$,

$\therefore \angle B = \angle F = 55°$

In $\Delta EFG$,

$\angle x + \angle y + \angle F = 180°$

$\Rightarrow \angle x + 55° + 55° = 180°$

$\Rightarrow \angle x = 70°$

(from $\Delta ABC$ and $\Delta FEG$)

C : $\angle QSR + 28° = 65°$

$\Rightarrow \angle QSR = 37°$

$\therefore \angle y = 90° - 37° = 53°$

and $\angle x = 90° - 53° = 37°$

**32.** (c) A : In an equilateral triangle, all angles are equal

B : $\angle x = 90° - 35° = 55°$

C : A right angled isosceles triangle, other angles equal to 45°

D : Sum of interaior angles of a pentagon

$= (n - 2) \times 180°$

$= (5 - 2) \times 180° = 540°$

[$\because n = 5$]

**33.** (d) (A) $\Delta AMC \cong \Delta BMD$ [by SAS congruency rule

(B) Since, $\Delta AMC \cong \Delta BMD$

[By CPCT]

$\angle MCA = \angle MDB$

$\Rightarrow DB || AC$

$\Rightarrow \angle DBC = \angle ACB = 90°$

(C) $\Delta DBC \cong \Delta ACB$

(D) $CM = \frac{1}{2}CD = \frac{1}{2}(AB)$

## Chapter 7 : Quadrilaterals

**1.** (b) Let $ABCD$ be the given trapezium.

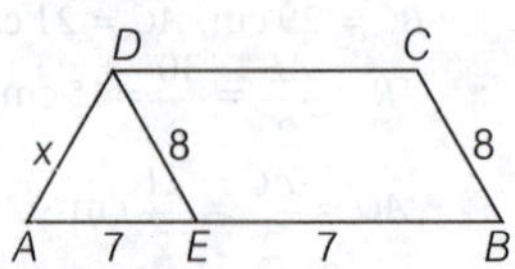

Draw $DE || CB$

Now, $CD || AB$

$\therefore EDCB$ is a parallelogram.

$\therefore DE = CB = 8$

$AE = 14 - EB$

$\Rightarrow AE = 14 - 7 \Rightarrow AE = 7$

In $\Delta ADE$, $8 - 7 \angle x \angle 8 + 7$

$\Rightarrow 1 < x < 15$

$\therefore x$ can take values 2, 3, 4, ......, 14.

So, possible values 2, 3, 4, ........., 14.

So, number of possible integral values of $x$ is 13.

**2.** (b) In a concave quadrilateral, 1 angle is more than 180°.

**3.** (b) According to the question,

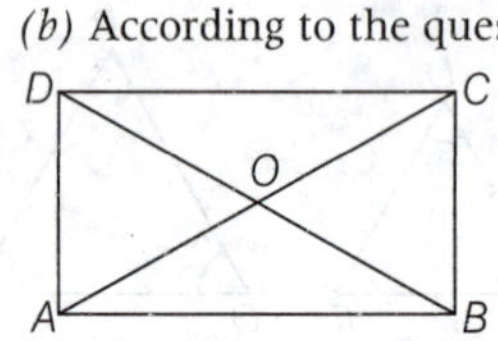

$AC$ and $BD$ bisect each other at $O$, then $ABCD$ is a parallelogram.

**4.** (b) $\angle OAB = \angle OBA$

Using exterior angle property, we get

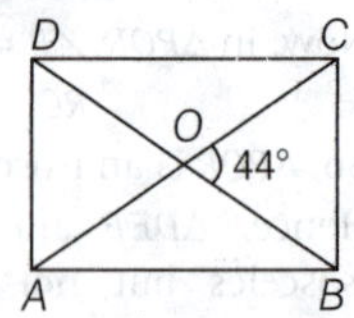

$\angle OAB + \angle OBA = 44°$

$\Rightarrow \angle OAB = 22°$

$\Rightarrow \angle OAD = 90° - \angle OAB$

$= 90° - 22$

$\therefore \angle OAD = 68°$

**5.** (a) $\because \angle C = 90°$

$\therefore \angle D = 180° - 90°$

$= 90° = \angle B$

[adjacent angles]

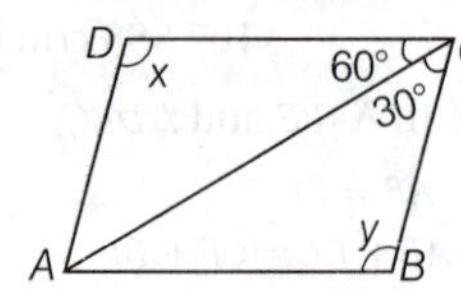

$\therefore \angle B = 90° = \angle A$

$\therefore \angle x = \angle y = 90°$

**6.** (c) Let $ABCD$ be the rhombus in which $AC = 40$ cm and $BD = 30$ cm

Since the diagonals of a rhombus are perpendicular bisector of each other.

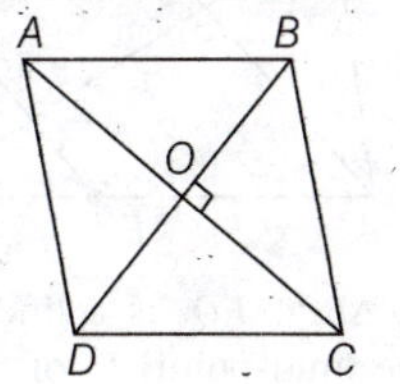


$\therefore \quad OB = \frac{1}{2} \times BD = \frac{30}{2} = 15\,\text{cm}$

and $OC = \frac{1}{2} \times AC = \frac{40}{2} = 20$ cm

In $\Delta BOC$, $BC^2 = OB^2 + OC^2$

[bY Pythagoras theorem]

$BC^2 = 15^2 + 20^2 = 625$

$BC = 25\,\text{cm}$

**7.** (c)

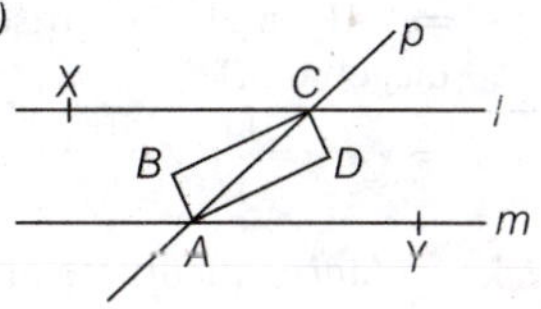


Given, $l \| m$

$\therefore \angle XCA = \angle YAC$

[Alternate interior angle]

$\Rightarrow \frac{1}{2}\angle XCA = \frac{1}{2}\angle YAC$

$\Rightarrow \quad \angle ACB = \angle CAD$

$\Rightarrow \quad CB \| DA$

Similarly, $AB \| DC$.

Therefore, $ABCD$ is a parallelogram.

**8.** (a) $\because$ Interior angle $= \frac{(n-2) \times 180°}{n}$

and exterior angle $= \frac{360°}{n}$

Now, $\frac{(n-2) \times 180°}{n} - \frac{360°}{n} = 0$

$\Rightarrow \quad 180°n - 360° - 360° = 0$

$\Rightarrow \quad n = \frac{720}{180} = 4$

**9.** (c)

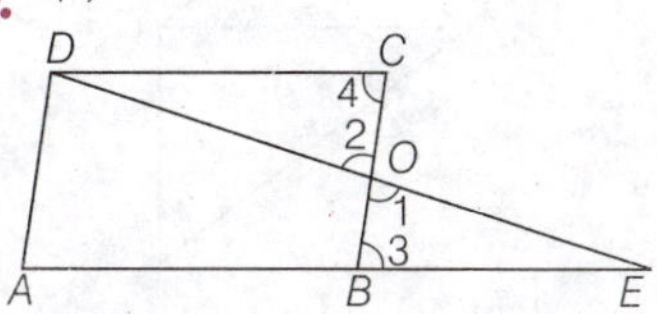


In $\Delta OBE$ and $\Delta OCD$,

$\angle 1 = \angle 2$

[vertically opposite angles]

$\angle 3 = \angle 4$

[alternate interior angles]

$OB = OC$ [given]

$\therefore \quad \Delta OBE \cong \Delta OCD$

(By ASA congruency rule)

$\Rightarrow \quad BE = CD$ [By CPCT]

Also, $AB = CD$

($\because ABCD$ is parallelogram)

$\therefore \quad AB = BE$

**10.** (d) Since, diagonals of a parallelogram bisect each other.

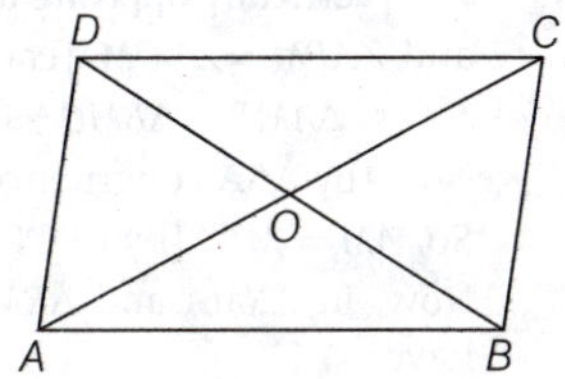


Thus, $OC = \frac{1}{2} \times AC = \frac{1}{2} \times 14$

$= 7\,\text{cm}$

$OD = \frac{1}{2} \times BD = \frac{1}{2} \times 17$

$= 8.5\,\text{cm}$

**11.** (d) In $\Delta ABD$,

$\angle ABD + \angle ADB = \angle b \quad \ldots\text{(i)}$

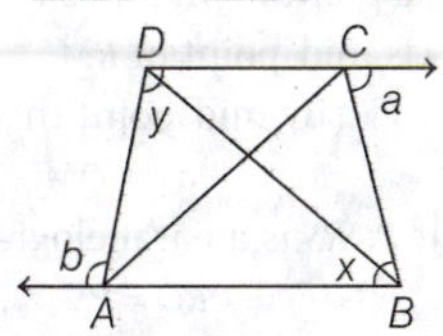


In $\Delta CBD$,

$\angle CBD + \angle CDB = \angle a \quad \ldots\text{(ii)}$

On adding Eqs. (i) and (ii), we get $(\angle ABD + \angle CBD)$

$+ (\angle ADB + \angle CDB) = \angle a + \angle b$

$\Rightarrow \quad \angle x + \angle y = \angle a + \angle b$

**12.** (d)

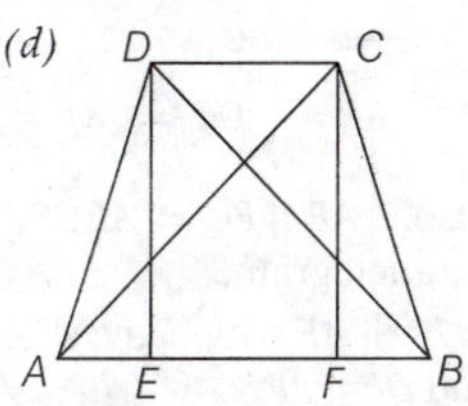


In $\Delta ABC$, $\angle B$ is acute.

$\therefore AC^2 = BC^2 + AB^2 - 2AB \cdot BF \quad \ldots\text{(i)}$

In $\Delta ABD$, $\angle A$ is acute.

$\therefore \quad BD^2 = AD^2 + AB^2 - 2AB \cdot AE \quad \ldots\text{(ii)}$

From Eqs. (i) and (ii), we get

$(AC^2 + BD^2)$

$= (BC^2 + AD^2) + 2AB\,(AB - BF - AE)$

$= BC^2 + AD^2 + 2AB \cdot EF$

$= BC^2 + AD^2 + 2AB \cdot CD$

**13.** (c) $\angle ECD + \angle DCA = 180°$.

[Linear pair]

$\Rightarrow \quad \angle DCA = 180° - 146° = 34°$

Also, $\angle DCA = \angle CAB = 34°$

[Alternate interior angle]

Since, diagonals of a rectangle are equal and bisect each other.

$\therefore \quad OA = OB$

$\Rightarrow \angle OAB = \angle OBA = 34°$

In $\Delta AOB$,

$\angle OAB + \angle OBA + \angle AOB = 180°$

$\Rightarrow \angle AOB = 180° - 2 \times 34° = 112°$

**14.** (d) $ABCD$ is a parallelogram and $AR, BP, CP, DR$ are bisectors of $\angle A, \angle B, \angle C$ and $\angle D$ respectively.

In $\Delta ARD$,

$\angle 1 + \angle 2 + \angle 3 = 180°$

$\angle 1 + \angle 2 = 90°$

as $\quad \angle A + \angle B = 180°$

$\Rightarrow \quad \angle 3 = 90°$

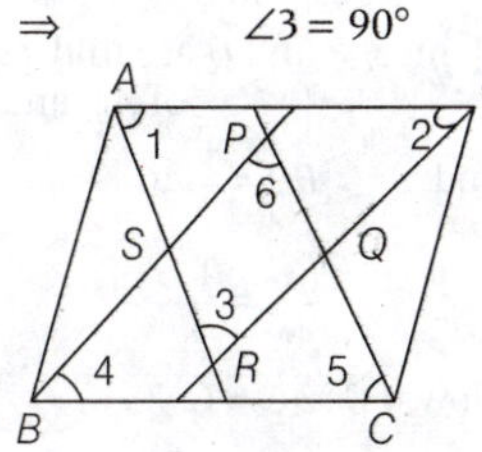


Similarly, in

$\Delta BPC$, $\angle 4 + \angle 5 = 90°$

$\Rightarrow \quad \angle 6 = 90°$

Hence, $PQRS$ is a parallelogram with $\angle 3 = \angle 6 = 90°$

Hence, $PQRS$ is a rectangle.

**15.** (a) In $\Delta AOP$ and $\Delta COQ$, we have

$AP = CQ$ [Given]

$\angle 1 = \angle 2$

[$\because$ alternate interior angles are equal]

$\angle 3 = \angle 4$

[vertically opposite anlges]

$\therefore$ $\Delta AOP \cong \Delta COQ$

[by AAS congruence rule]

$\therefore OA = OC$ and $OP = OQ$ [CPCT]

Hence, $AC$ and $PQ$ bisect each other.

**16.** (c) Here, $D$ and $E$ are mid-points of $AB$ and $AC$ respectively.

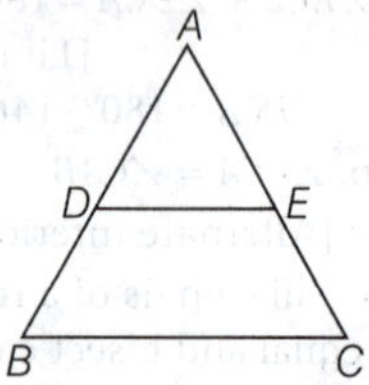


According to the mid-point theorem,

$DE \parallel BC$ and $DE = \frac{1}{2}BC$

Hence, $BCED$ formed a trapezium.

**17.** (c) Since $SR \parallel PQ$

$\therefore \angle PSR + \angle SPQ = 180°$

$\Rightarrow 2x + 3x = 180°$

$\Rightarrow 5x = 180°$

$\Rightarrow x = 36°$

**18.** (b) According to the mid-point theorem,

In $\Delta ACD$,

$PQ \parallel AC$

[since, $P$ and $Q$ are mid-points of $AD$ and $DC$]

and $PQ = \frac{1}{2}AC$

$\therefore \frac{PQ}{AC} = \frac{1}{2}$

Now, $PQ : AC = 1 : 2$

**19.** (c) Since, diagonals of a rhombus bisect each other at right angle, therefore, $y = 90°$

Now, $y + \angle QSR = 152°$

[exterior angle is equal to sum of interior opposite angles]

$\Rightarrow \angle QSR = 152° - 90°$

$\Rightarrow \angle QSR = 62°$

Since, $SR \parallel PQ$

$\therefore \angle QRP = \angle SQP = 62°$

[Alternate angle]

$\Rightarrow x = 62°$

Also, $\angle SRP + \angle SRT = 180°$

$\angle SRP = 180° - 152° = 28°$

and $SP = SR$

$\Rightarrow \angle SRP = \angle SPR = 28°$

$\Rightarrow z = 28°$

**20.** (b) In $\Delta AMP$ and $\Delta BMQ$, we have

$PM = MQ$ [given]

$\angle AMP = \angle BMQ$

[vertically opposite angles]

and $\angle APM = \angle BQM$ [each 90°]

$\therefore \Delta AMP \cong \Delta BMQ$

[by ASA congruence rule]

So, $AM = MB$ [by CPCT] ...(i)

Now, in $\Delta RMA$ and $\Delta RMB$, we have

$\angle AMR = \angle BMR = 90°$ [given]

$RM = RM$ [common side]

and $AM = MB$ [from Eq. (i)]

$\therefore \Delta RMA \cong \Delta RMB$

[by SAS congruence rule]

So, $RA = RB$ [by CPCT]

**21.** (b) Consider $\Delta SRM$, $L$ is mid-point of $SR$ and $SM \parallel LQ$

$\therefore Q$ is mid-point of $RM$.

(By mid-point theorem)

$\Rightarrow RQ = QM$ ...(i)

But $PQRS$ is a parallelogram.

$\Rightarrow RQ = PS$ ...(ii)

From Eqs. (i) and (ii), we get

$PS = RM - RQ$

**22.** (b) Here, $ABCD$ is a parallelogram.

So, $AB \parallel DC$ and $AB = DC$

Also, $E$ and $F$ are mid-points of $AB$ and $CD$.

Now, $AB = DC$

$\Rightarrow \frac{1}{2}AB = \frac{1}{2}DC \Rightarrow AE = FC$

Also, $AE \parallel FC \Rightarrow AECF$ is a parallelogram.

$\Rightarrow EC \parallel AF$ which gives $EQ \parallel AP$ and $QC \parallel PF$.

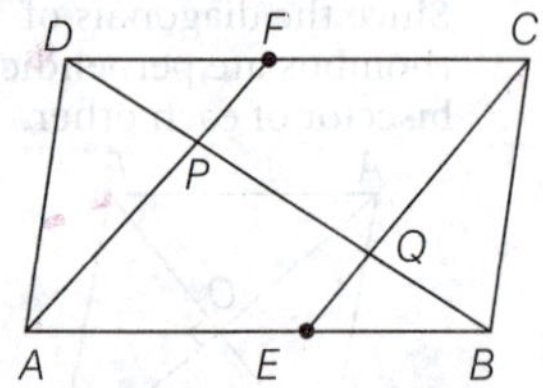


In $\Delta BPA$, $EQ$ is a line joining the mid-point $E$ of $AB$ and parallel to $PA$.

Then, by converse of mid-point theorem, $Q$ bisects $BP$.

$\Rightarrow BQ = QP$ ...(i)

Similarly by taking $\Delta CQD$,

$DP = QP$ ...(ii)

From Eqs. (i) and (ii),

$BQ = QP = DP$

$\Rightarrow AF$ and $CE$ trisect the diagonal $BD$

$\Rightarrow PQ = \frac{1}{3}BD = \frac{1}{3} \times 12 = 4$ cm

**23.** (c) Since, quadrilateral $AXYZ$ is a square.

$\therefore YZ = AZ = 2$cm

Now, $DZ = DY + YZ = 3 + 2$cm $= 5$cm

In right angled $\Delta AZD$,

$AD^2 = AZ^2 + DZ^2$

$= 4 + 25 = 29\text{cm}^2$

Since, $ABCD$ is a square,

$\therefore AB = AD$

$\Rightarrow AB^2 = AD^2 = 29 \text{ cm}^2$

In right angled $\Delta BAX$,

$AB^2 = AX^2 + BX^2$

$29 = 4 + BX^2$

$\Rightarrow BX = 5$cm

Since, $AXYZ$ is a square

$\therefore XY = AZ = 2$cm

Now, $BY = BX + XY$

$= 5 + 2 = 7$ cm

**24.** (d)

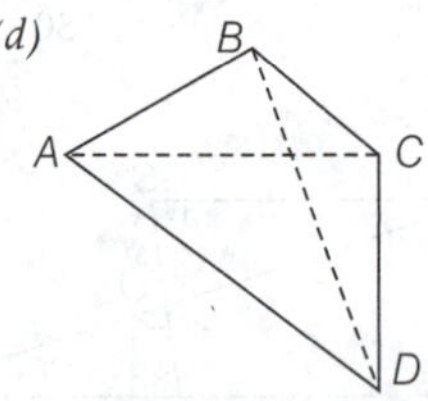


Join $AC$ and $BD$.

In any triangle, sum of any two sides is always greater than the third side.

$\therefore$ In $\Delta ABC$, $AB + BC > AC$ ...(i)

$\therefore$ In $\Delta ADC$, $AD + DC > AC$ ...(ii)

Taking $BD$ as diagonal.

In $\Delta BAD$, $AB + AD > BD$ ...(iii)

In $\Delta BCD$, $BC + CD > BD$ ...(iv)

Adding Eqs. (i), (ii), (iii), (iv),

$2(AB + BC + CD + AD) > 2(AC + BD)$

$AB + BC + CD + AD > AC + BD$

**25.** (a) $ABCD$ is a rhombus in which altitude $DL$ from $D$ to side $BC$ is drawn. $DL$ bisects $BC$.

In $\Delta DCL$ and $\Delta DBL$, we have

$CL = BL$ [$\because DL$ bisects $BC$]

$\angle CLD = \angle BLD$ [$\because$ each = 90°]

$DL = DL$ [common side]

$\therefore \Delta DCL \cong \Delta DBL$ [by SAS congruence rule]

$\therefore$ $CD = DB$ [by CPCT]

Also, $CD = BC$ [$\because$ sides of a rhombus are equal]

$\therefore$ $CD = DB = BC$

So, $\Delta BCD$ is an equilateral triangle.

Now, $\angle C = 60°$ [angle of an equilateral triangle]

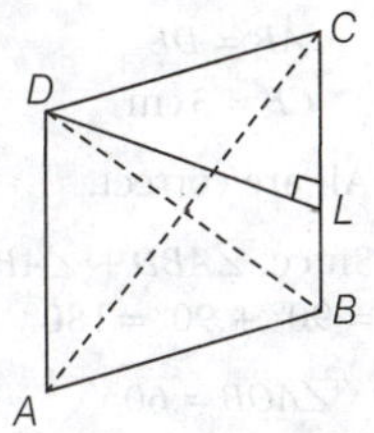


Since, sum of adjacent interior angles of a rhombus is 180°.

Now, $\angle ABC + \angle C = 180°$

$\Rightarrow$ $\angle ABC + 60° = 180°$

$\Rightarrow \angle ABC = 180° - 60° = 120°$,

i.e. $\angle B = 120°$

Since, every rhombus is a parallelogram, therefore, its opposite angles are equal.

Hence, $\angle A = \angle C = 60°$,

$\angle B = \angle D = 120°$

**26.** (b) A : Square having all angles and sides equal.

B : Trapezium having one pair of parallel sides.

C : Rhombus having all sides equal.

D : Opposite sides and opposite angles are equal of a rectangle.

**27.** (c) I. True

II. True

III. False, because the sum of all interior angles of a quadrilateral is 360°.

IV. False, A rhombus is a quadrilateral, whose all sides are equal.

**28.** (c) We have produced $DE$ to $F$ such that

$DE = EF$ ... (i)

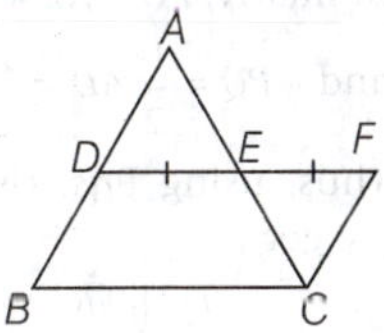


In $\Delta ADE$ and $\Delta CFE$,

$AE = CE$ [$\because E$ is the mid-point of $AC$]

$\angle AED = \angle CEF$ [vertically opposite angles]

$DE = FE$ [By Eq. (i)]

$\therefore$ $\Delta ADE \cong \Delta CFE$ [by SAS congruency rule]

$\therefore$ $AD = CF$

and $\angle ADE = \angle CFE$ [By CPCT]

This shows that alternate interior angles are equal.

Thus, $AD \parallel CF$

Therefore, the additional information which we need is $DE = EF$

**29.** (b) I. True

Let smallest angle be $\angle x$.

$\therefore$ Other angle $= 2\angle x - 60°$

Now, $\angle x + \angle x + (2\angle x - 60°) + (2\angle x - 60°) = 360°$

[since, angle sum property and opposite angles are equal]

$\Rightarrow$ $6\angle x = 480°$

$\therefore$ $\angle x = 80°$

II. False

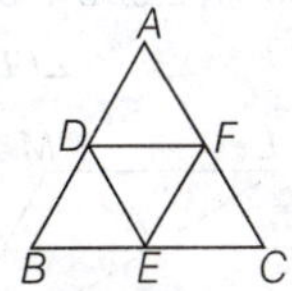


It divides it into four equal triangles.

III. True

$\because \angle BAC = \angle CAD = 35°$

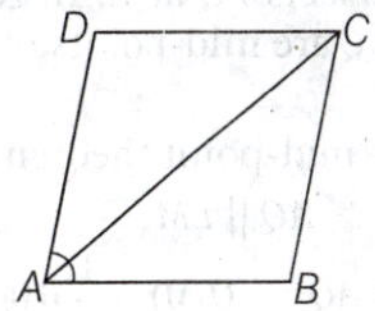


$\therefore$ $\angle DAB = 70°$

Now, $\angle ABC = 180° - 70° = 110°$

**30.** (a) I.

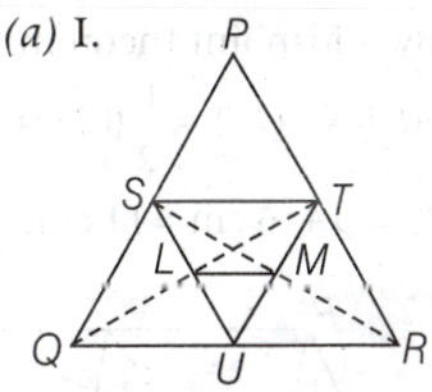


In $\Delta PQR$, $S$ and $T$ are mid-points of $PQ$ and $PR$, respectively.

$\therefore ST \parallel QR$ and $ST = \frac{1}{2}QR = QU$

$\because ST \parallel QU$ and $SQ = TU$

So, $STUQ$ is a parallelogram whose diagonals $QT$ and $SU$ intersect at $L$, therefore $L$ is the mid-point of $SU$.

Similarly, $M$ is the mid-point of $TU$.

$\therefore LM = \frac{1}{4}QR = \frac{1}{4} \times 6 = 1.5\,\text{cm}$

II. $\because$ $\angle PAB = \angle APD$ [alternate interior angles]

As, $AB \parallel CD$ and $PA$ is transversal.

$\therefore$ $\angle APD = \angle PAD$

$\Rightarrow$ $AD = PD$

Similarly,

$PC = BC = 4\,\text{cm}$

III. $\because \angle A = 60° = \angle C$

[opposite angles are equal]

In $\Delta BCD$,

$$\angle C + \angle CDB + \angle DBC = 180°$$

$$\Rightarrow \quad 60° + \angle CDB + 80° = 180°$$

$$\therefore \quad \angle CDB = 40°$$

**31.** (c)

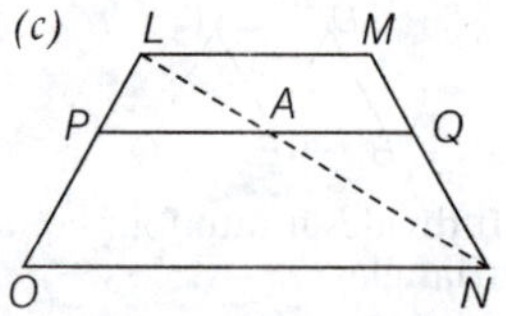


Join $PQ$ and $LN$, where $LN$ intersects $PQ$ at $A$. In $\Delta LMN$, $A$ and $Q$ are mid-points of $LN$ and $MQ$.

$\therefore$ By mid-point theorem,

$$AQ \parallel LM$$

and $AQ = \frac{1}{2}(LM) = \frac{1}{2}(10) = 5\,\text{cm}$

In $\Delta LON$, $P$ and $A$ are mid-point of $LO$ and $LN$

$\therefore$ By mid-point theorem,

$$AP = \frac{1}{2}(ON) = \frac{1}{2}(12) = 6\text{ cm}$$

$\therefore PQ = 5 + 6\text{ cm} = 11\text{ cm}.$

**32.** (a)

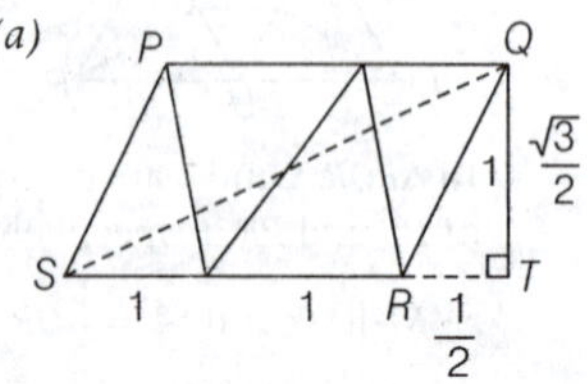


$RT = \frac{1}{2}$ unit,

$SR = 1 + 1 = 2$ units

$ST = \left(2 + \frac{1}{2}\right)$ units $= \frac{5}{2}$ units

$$QT = \sqrt{QR^2 - RT^2} = \sqrt{1^2 - \left(\frac{1}{2}\right)^2}$$

$$= \frac{\sqrt{3}}{2}\text{ unit.}$$

Now, is $\Delta SQT$,

$SQ$ is the hypotenuse.

So, $SQ = \sqrt{ST^2 + QT^2}$

$$= \sqrt{\left(\frac{5}{2}\right)^2 + \left(\frac{\sqrt{3}}{2}\right)^2}$$

$$= \sqrt{7}\text{ units}$$

Therefore, the length of the diagonal $SQ$ is $\sqrt{7}$ units.

**33.** (c) Since, $PS \parallel BC$

and $PS = \frac{1}{2}BC$ ...(i)

[using mid-point theorem]

Similarly, $QR \parallel BC$

and $QR = \frac{1}{2}BC$ ...(ii)

Now, from Eqs. (i) and (ii), we get

$$PS \parallel QR$$

and $PS = QR$ ...(iii)

Further, in $\Delta ACD$, $S$ and $R$ are respectively the mid-point of $AC$ and $CD$.

$\therefore$ $SR \parallel AD$

and $SR = \frac{1}{2}AD = \frac{1}{2}BC$ ...(iv)

Similarly, $PQ \parallel AD$

and $PQ = \frac{1}{2}AD = \frac{1}{2}BC$ ...(v)

Thus, using Eqs. (iv) and (v), we get

$$PQ \parallel SR$$

and $PQ = SR$ ...(vi)

From Eqs. (i), (ii), (iii) and (iv), we get

$$PS = QR = SR = PQ$$

and from Eqs. (iii) and (vi), we get

$$PQ \parallel SR \text{ and } PS \parallel QR.$$

Hence, $PQRS$ is a rhombus.

## Chapter 8 : Circle

**1.** (a)

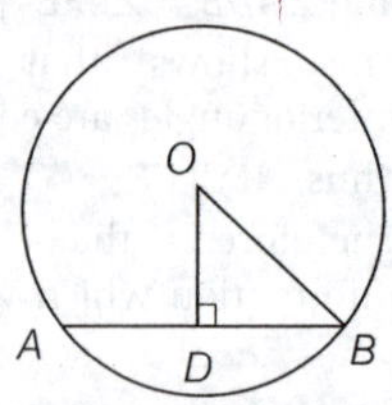


Since, $OD$ is perpendicular line drawn from centre to the chord. Therefore it bisects the chord.

Thus, $AD = BD = \frac{24}{2} = 12\,\text{cm}$

$\therefore \quad OD = \sqrt{13^2 - 12^2}$

[by Pythagoras theorem]

$= \sqrt{169 - 144}$

$= \sqrt{25}\,\text{cm} = 5\,\text{cm}$

**2.** (d) Given, $AB = 10$ cm and $OM = ON = 4$ cm

Since, equal chords are equidistant form the centre.

$\therefore \quad CD = 10\,\text{cm}$

**3.** (a) Given, $DE = 8$ cm and $CG \perp DE$

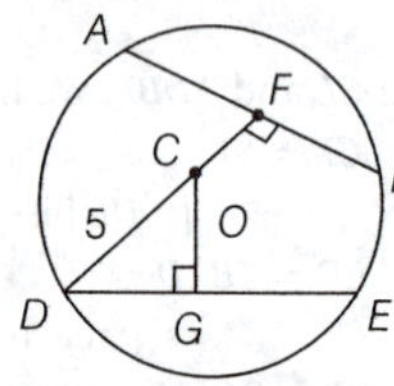


$\Rightarrow \quad DG = GE$

[since, perpendicular from the centre to the chord bisects the chord in equal part]

$\Rightarrow \quad DG = \frac{1}{2}DE = 4\text{ cm}$

In $\Delta CGD$,

$$CD^2 = CG^2 + DG^2$$

$$\Rightarrow \quad 5^2 = CG^2 + 4^2$$

$$\Rightarrow \quad CG^2 = 3^2 \Rightarrow CG = 3\text{ cm}$$

Also, $CG = CF$

As, $AB = DE$

$\therefore \quad CF = 3\,\text{cm}$

**4.** (d) All are correct.

**5.** (c) Since, $\angle ABD + \angle ABC$

$= 90° + 90° = 180°$

**6.** (c) $\because \angle AOB = 60°$ [given]

$\therefore \quad OA = OB$ [radii of circle]

$\therefore \angle OAB + \angle OBA + \angle AOB = 180°$

$\Rightarrow \angle OAB + \angle OBA + 60° = 180°$

$\Rightarrow \angle OAB + \angle OBA = 120°$

$\Rightarrow \angle OAB = \angle OBA = 60°$

Hence, $\Delta OAB$ is an equilateral triangle.

$\therefore \quad AB = 5\text{ cm}$

**7.** (b) If they lie on same side of centre.

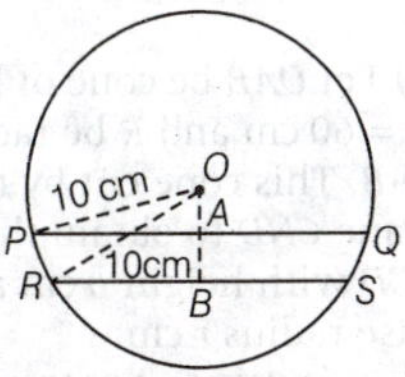


From the above figure,

$PQ = 16\text{ cm}$

$RS = 12\text{ cm}$

So, in $\Delta OAP$, $AO = \sqrt{10^2 - 8^2}$

$= 6\text{ cm}$

In $\Delta ORB$,

$OB = \sqrt{10^2 - 6^2} = 8\text{ cm}$

$\therefore$ Distance between chords

$AB = 8 - 6 = 2\text{ cm}$

**8.** (a) $O$ is the centre of circle. $M$ and $L$ are mid-points of chords $AB$ and $CD$ respectively.

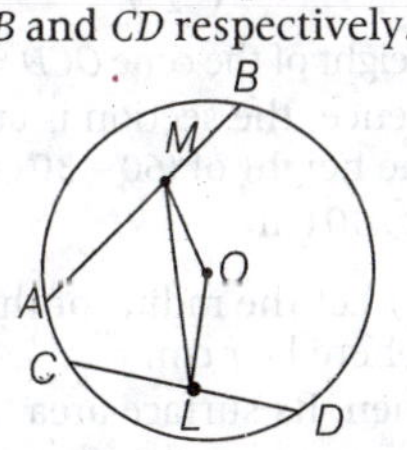


$\therefore \quad OM \perp AB$ and $OL \perp CD$

As $\quad AB = CD$

$\therefore \quad OM = OL$

[Equal chords are equidistant from centre]

So, $\Delta OML$ is an isosceles.

$\therefore \angle OML = \angle OLM = 25°$ [given]

Therefore,

$\angle LMB = \angle OML + \angle OMB$

$= 35° + 90° = 125°$

**9.** (b) Given that, $AB = 12\text{ cm}$, $r_1 = 10\text{ cm}$, $r_2 = 8\text{ cm}$, $OO' = ?$ and $AT = BT = 6\text{ cm}$

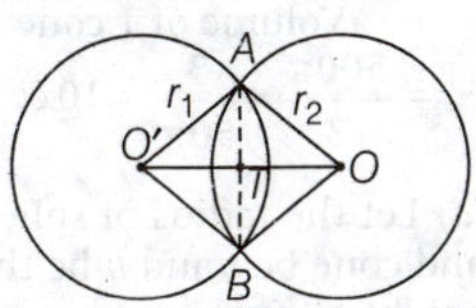


In $\Delta O'AT$,

$O'T = \sqrt{10^2 - 6^2} = 8\text{ cm}$

Now, in $\Delta ATO$, $OT = \sqrt{8^2 - 6^2}$

$= \sqrt{64 - 36} = \sqrt{28}\text{ cm}$

$\therefore OO' = O'T + OT$

$= (8 + \sqrt{28})\text{ cm}$

**10.** (b) Given, $PQRS$ is a cyclic quadrilateral.

$\therefore \angle PSR + \angle PQR$

$= \angle QPS + \angle QRS = 180°$

$\Rightarrow \quad 2y + 3y = 2x + 4x$

$\Rightarrow \quad 5y = 6x \Rightarrow \dfrac{x}{y} = \dfrac{5}{6}$

$\Rightarrow \quad x : y = 5 : 6$

**11.** (c) In $\Delta OAB$,

$\angle OAB = \angle OBA$

$[\because OB = OA = \text{radii}]$

$\therefore \angle OBA = 40°$

Now, in $\Delta BOC$,

$\angle OCB = \angle OBC - 30°$

$\therefore \quad \angle ABC = 40° + 30° = 70°$

$\therefore \quad \angle AOC = 2\angle ABC = 140°$

[since, angle made at centre by a chord is twice the angle made at any other point on circumference]

**12.** (c) In $\Delta CDE$,

$\angle D + \angle C = 130°$

[Theorem of exterior angle triangle]

$\angle D + 20° = 130° \Rightarrow \angle D = 110°$

$\therefore \ \angle BAC = 110°$

ame segment angles]

**13.** (c) Given, $\angle BAC = 64°$

Since, angles in same segment are equal.

$\therefore \angle BAC = \angle BDC = 64°$

**14.** (a) In $\Delta BDE$,

$\angle ABD = 180° - (120° + 45°)$

$[\because \angle A = \angle D = 45°]$

$= 15°$

**15.** (c) $\because \dfrac{\text{arc } AXB}{\text{arc } BYC} = \dfrac{1}{3}$

$\Rightarrow \quad \dfrac{\angle AOB}{\angle BOC} = \dfrac{1}{3}$

$\Rightarrow \angle AOB + \angle BOC = 180°$

[by Linear Pair Axiom]

$\Rightarrow \angle AOB + 3\angle AOB = 180°$

$\therefore \quad \angle AOB = 45°$

$\therefore \angle BOC = 3 \times 45° = 135°$

**16.** (d) Since, $\angle 4 = 35°$

[as angle opposite to equal sides are equal]

$\therefore \angle 5 = 180° - 35° - 35° = 110°$

and $\angle 6 = \dfrac{1}{2}\angle 5 = 55°$

**17.** (d) Since, $ABCD$ is a cyclic quadrilateral.

$\therefore \quad x + z = 180° \quad \text{...(i)}$

and $\quad \angle E = \angle D = 45°$

$\Rightarrow \quad z = 45°$

$\therefore \ x = 180° - 45° = 135°$

Also, $\quad y = 2z$

[since, angle at the centre is twice the angle at remaining part of circle]

$\therefore \ x + y - z = x + 2z - z = x + z$

$= 180°$

**18.** (b) Since, $ABCD$ is a cyclic quadrilateral.

$\therefore \quad x + 3x = 180°$

$\Rightarrow \quad 4x = 180°$

$\Rightarrow \quad x = 45°$

Now, $\quad \angle BOD = 2\angle BAD$

[$\because$ angle subtended by an arc at the centre is double the angle subtended by it at any point on the remaining part of the circle]

$\therefore \quad y = 2x = 2 \times 45° = 90°$

Similarly,

$z = 2(3x) = 6 \times 45° = 270°$

**19.** (b) Since, $102° + \angle y = 180°$

[by cyclic quadrilateral]

$\therefore \ \angle y = 78°$

$\Rightarrow \angle x = 2\angle y = 2 \times 78° = 156°$

[central angle]

**20.** (c) We know that the angle subtended by an arc of a circle at the centre of the circle is double the angle subtended by it at any point on the circle.

So, $\angle AOP = 2\angle AQP$

$\Rightarrow \angle AQP = \frac{1}{2}\angle AOP$

$= \frac{1}{2} \times 70° = 35°$

**21.** (b) A : $r_1 + r_2 = AB$ [circles touches externally]

B : $r_1 = r_2$ [radii of circles]

C : $r_1 + r_2 > AB$ [circles intersect]

D : $r_1 < r_2$ [$\angle OBA < \angle AOB$]

**22.** (c) I. $x = 2 \times 45° = 90°$

II. supplementary

III. centre

IV. quadrant of circle

**23.** (b) I. False, Each three equal arcs make angle 120°, but major arc makes an angle 180°.

II. False, the sum of a pair of opposite angles of a cyclic quadrilateral is 180°.

III. True IV. True

**24.** (a) Since, angle subtended by an arc of a circle at the centre is twice the angle subtended by it at any point of the remaining part of the circle.

$\therefore \angle EBF = \frac{1}{2}\angle EOF = \frac{1}{2}\angle z$

$\therefore \angle ABF = \pi - \frac{1}{2}\angle z$

[Linear Pair Axiom] ...(i)

Similarly,

$\angle EDF = \frac{1}{2}\angle EOF = \frac{1}{2}\angle z$

$\therefore \angle ADE = \pi - \frac{1}{2}\angle z$

[Linear Pair Axiom] ...(ii)

$\angle BCD = \angle ECF = \angle y$

[Vertically Opposite Angles]

Now, in quadrilateral $ABCD$

$\angle ABC + \angle BCD + \angle CDA + \angle BAD = 2\pi$

(Angle sum property of a quadrilateral)

$\Rightarrow \pi - \frac{1}{2}\angle z + \angle y$

$\pi - \frac{1}{2}z + \angle x = 2\pi$

$\Rightarrow \angle x + \angle y = \angle z$

**25.** (b) $\because \angle ACB = \frac{1}{2}\angle APB$

$= \frac{120°}{2} = 60°$

[since, angle at centre is twice of the angle made at other point on remaining part of circle]

So, $ACD$ is a straight line.

Now, $\angle ACB + \angle BCD = 180°$

$\Rightarrow 60° + \angle BCD = 180°$

$\Rightarrow \angle BCD = 120°$

Now, in the second circle,

$\angle BCD = \frac{1}{2}$ reflex $\angle BQD$

$\Rightarrow 120° = \frac{1}{2}(360° - x)$

$\therefore x = 120°$

**26.** (a) Given that, $CD \parallel AB$ and $\angle BAD = 40°$

$\because AOB$ is the diameter.

$\therefore \angle ADB = 90°$

[angle in a semi-circle]

Now, In $\Delta ADB$,

$\angle DAB + \angle ADB + \angle ABD = 180°$

$40° + 90° + \angle ABD = 180°$

$\Rightarrow \angle ABD = 50°$

In cyclic quadrilateral $ABDC$, we have

$\angle ABD + \angle ACD = 180°$

$\Rightarrow 50° + \angle ACD = 180°$

$\Rightarrow \angle ACD = 130°$

Also, $\angle CDA = 40° = \angle DAB$

[alternate angles]

In $\Delta CAD$,

$\angle CAD + \angle CDA + \angle ACD = 180°$

$\Rightarrow \angle CAD + 40° + 130° = 180°$

$\Rightarrow \angle CAD = 10°$

## Chapter 9 : Surface Area of Solid Figures

**1.** (c) Let $OAB$ be cone of height; $H = 60$ cm and $R$ be radius of $OAB$. This cone cut by the plane $CND$ to obtain the cone $OCD$ with height $h$ cm and base radius $r$ cm.

Then, $\Delta OND \sim \Delta OMB$

So, $\frac{ND}{MB} = \frac{ON}{OM} \Rightarrow \frac{r}{R} = \frac{h}{60}$ ...(i)

Volume of cone, $OCD = \frac{1}{8} \times$ Volume of cone $OAB$

$\Rightarrow \frac{1}{3}\pi r^2 h = \frac{1}{8} \times \frac{1}{3}\pi R^2 \times 60$

$\Rightarrow \frac{r^2}{R^2} = \frac{60}{8h} \Rightarrow \left(\frac{h}{60}\right)^2 = \frac{60}{8h}$

$\Rightarrow h^3 = \frac{60 \times 60 \times 60}{8}$

$\Rightarrow h^3 = \left(\frac{60}{2}\right)^3 \Rightarrow h = 30$

Height of the cone $OCD = 30$ cm.

Hence, the section is cut at the height of $(60 - 30)$cm, i.e, 30 cm

**2.** (b) Let the radius of the sphere be $r$ cm.

Then, its surface area

$= 4\pi r^2$ cm$^2$

$\therefore 4\pi r^2 = 314 \Rightarrow r^2 = \frac{314}{4 \times 3.14}$

$\Rightarrow r^2 = 25 \Rightarrow r = 5$cm

Now, volume of the sphere

$= \frac{4}{3}\pi \times 5^3 = \frac{500}{3}\pi$ cm$^3$

and volume of a cone

$= \frac{1}{3}\pi R^2 h = \frac{1}{3}\pi \times (2.5)^2 \times 8$

$= \frac{50}{3}\pi$ cm$^3$

$\therefore$ Number of cone recast

$= \frac{\text{Volume of the sphere}}{\text{Volume of 1 cone}}$

$= \frac{500\pi}{3} \times \frac{3}{50\pi} = 10$ cone

**3.** (d) Let the radius of sphere and cone be $r$ and $h$ be the height of cone.

According to the question,
Volume of sphere = Volume of cone

$$\Rightarrow \frac{4}{3}\pi r^3 = \frac{1}{3}\pi r^2 h \Rightarrow r = h/4$$

Diameter of the cone $= \frac{h}{2}$

Difference between the diameter and height of the cone $= h - \frac{h}{2} = \frac{h}{2}$

$\therefore$ Percentage by which the height exceeds the diameter of cone $= \frac{h/2}{h/2} \times 100 = 100\%$

**4.** *(d)* Let $r$ be radius of the sphere

New radius $= (r + \frac{10}{100}r) = \frac{11r}{10}$

and original surface area of sphere $= 4\pi r^2$

and new surface area

$$= 4\pi\left(\frac{11r}{10}\right)^2 = 4\pi \times \frac{121r^2}{100}$$

$\therefore$ Percentage increase in surface area

$$= \frac{\text{Change in Area}}{\text{Original Surface Area}} \times 100$$

$$= \frac{\frac{121}{100} \times 4\pi r^2 - 4\pi r^2}{4\pi r^2} \times 100$$

$$= \frac{21}{100} \times 100 = 21\%$$

**5.** *(b)* Let the radii of two spheres be $r_1$ cm and $r_2$ cm respectively and their volumes be $V_1$ and $V_2$ respectively.

Then, $\frac{V_1}{V_2} = \frac{64}{27}$

$$\Rightarrow \frac{\frac{4}{3}\pi r_1^3}{\frac{4}{3}\pi r_2^3} = \frac{64}{27} \Rightarrow \frac{r_1}{r_2} = \frac{4}{3} \quad \ldots\text{(i)}$$

Also, given, $r_1 + r_2 = 7$ ...(ii)

On solving Eqs. (i) and (ii), we get $r_1 = 4\,\text{cm}$ and $r_2 = 3\,\text{cm}$

Now, $S_1 - S_2 = 4\pi r_1^2 - 4\pi r_2^2$

$$= 64\pi - 36\pi = 28\pi\ \text{cm}^2$$

$$= 28 \times \frac{22}{7} = 88\ \text{cm}^2$$

**6.** *(b)* Given, $r = 6$ m and $h = 8$ m

$$l = \sqrt{r^2 + h^2} = \sqrt{36 + 64} = \sqrt{100} = 10\ \text{m}$$

Curved surface area of conicaltent $= \pi rl$

$$= \frac{22}{7} \times 6 \times 8 = \frac{1056}{7}\ \text{m}^2$$

$\therefore$ Required length of cloth

$$= \frac{\text{CSA}}{\text{width of cloth}} = \frac{1056}{7 \times 12} = 12.57\ \text{m}$$

**7.** *(b)* Let $r_1$ and $h_1$ be the radius and height of first cone and $r_2$ and $h_2$ be the radius and height of second cone. Then,

$$\frac{2r_1}{2r_2} = \frac{4}{5} \Rightarrow \frac{r_1}{r_2} = \frac{4}{5}$$

Given that,

$$\frac{\text{Volumc of first cone}}{\text{Volume of second cone}} = \frac{1}{5}$$

$$\Rightarrow \frac{\frac{1}{3}\pi r_1^2 h_1}{\frac{1}{3}\pi r_2^2 h_2} = \frac{1}{5}$$

$$\Rightarrow \frac{h_1}{h_2} = \frac{1}{5} \times \left(\frac{r_2}{r_1}\right)^2$$

$$\Rightarrow \frac{h_1}{h_2} = \frac{1}{5} \times \frac{25}{16}$$

$$\therefore h_1 : h_2 = 5{:}16$$

**8.** *(a)* Let the radius of the common base be $r$. Let $h_1$ and $h_2$ be the heights of the cone and cylinder respectively. Then,

Volume of the cone $= \frac{1}{3}\pi r^2 h_1$,

Volume of cylinder $= \pi r^2 h_2$

It is given that the cone and the cylinder area of the same volume.

$$\therefore \frac{1}{3}\pi r^2 h_1 = \pi r^2 h_2$$

$$\Rightarrow \frac{1}{3}h_1 = h_2 \Rightarrow \frac{h_1}{h_2} = \frac{3}{1}$$

$$\Rightarrow h_1 : h_2 = 3:1$$

Hence, the ratio of the height of the cone and cylinder is 3:1.

**9.** *(a)* Here, toy is a combination of a hemisphere and a cone.

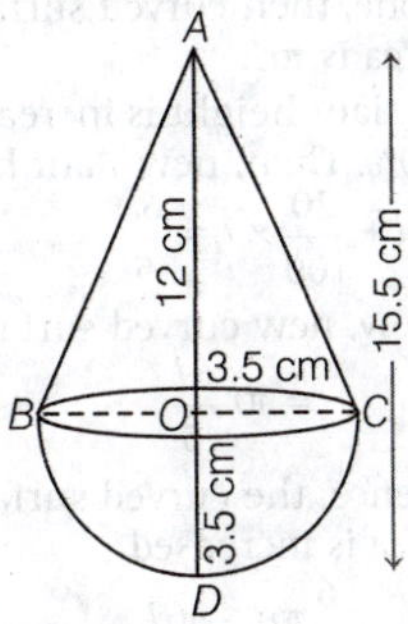


Given, total height of toy,

$$AD = 15.5\ \text{cm}$$

*For hemispherical portion,*
Radius, $OC = OD = OB = 3.5$ cm

*For conical portion,*
Height, $OA = AD - OD$
$= 15.5 - 3.5 = 12$ cm
and radius = 3.5 cm

Now, total surface area of the toy
= Curved surface area of cone + Curved surface area of hemisphere

$$= \pi rl + 2\pi r^2$$

$$= \pi r\sqrt{h^2 + r^2} + 2\pi r^2 \quad [\because l = \sqrt{h^2 + r^2}]$$

$$= \frac{22}{7} \times 3.5 \times \sqrt{(12)^2 + (3.5)^2} + 2 \times \frac{22}{7} \times (3.5)^2$$

$$= 11\sqrt{144 + 12.25} + 22 \times 3.5$$

$$= 11\sqrt{156.25} + 11 \times 7$$

$$= 11\,(12.5) + 77$$

$$= 137.5 + 77 = 214.5\ \text{cm}^2$$

**10.** *(d)* Number of cones

$$= \frac{\text{Volume of sphere}}{\text{Volume of one cone}}$$

$$= \frac{\frac{4}{3}\pi r^3}{\frac{1}{3}\pi r_1^2 h_1} = \frac{\frac{4}{3}\pi \times 3 \times 3 \times 3}{\frac{1}{3} \times \pi \times \frac{2}{10} \times \frac{2}{10} \times 3}$$

$$= \frac{3 \times 3 \times 3 \times 4 \times 10 \times 10}{2 \times 2 \times 3}$$

$$= 9 \times 100 = 900$$

**11.** (*b*) Let *l* be the slant height and *r* be the radius of the cone, then curved surface area is $\pi rl$.

If slant height is increased by 20%. Then, new slant height

$= l + \frac{20}{100} \times l = \frac{6l}{5}$

Now, new curved surface area

$= \pi r \frac{6l}{5}$

Hence, the curved surface area is increased

$= \frac{\frac{6}{5}\pi rl - \pi rl}{\pi rl} \times 100$

$= \frac{1}{5} \times 100 = 20\%$

**12.** (*d*) Let *h* m be the height, *r* m be the radius of base of the cone.

$\therefore$ Area of the base of cone

$= 14 \times 6 = 84\,m^2$

$[\because \text{area of base} = \pi r^2]$

$\Rightarrow \quad \pi r^2 = 84\,m^2 \quad \ldots(i)$

Volume of the cone

$= 14 \times 22 = 308\,m^3$

$\Rightarrow \quad \frac{1}{3}\pi r^2 h = 308\,m^3 \ldots(ii)$

On dividing Eq. (ii) by Eq. (i), we get

$\frac{\frac{1}{3}\pi r^2 h}{\pi r^2} = \frac{308}{84}$

$\Rightarrow h = \frac{308 \times 3}{84} = 11 \Rightarrow h = 11\,m$

**13.** (*b*) Let radius of base cone bet *r*.

$\because$ Circumference of base of the cone = Length of arc of given sector whose central angle is 120°.

$2\pi r = \frac{\theta}{360°} \times 2\pi r$

$\Rightarrow \quad 2\pi r = \frac{120°}{360°} \times 2\pi \times 12$

$\Rightarrow \quad r = \frac{1}{3} \times 12 = 4\,cm$

Now, volume of cone $= \frac{1}{3}\pi r^2 h$

$\because h = \sqrt{l^2 - r^2} = \sqrt{12^2 - 4^2}$

$= \sqrt{144 - 16} = \sqrt{128} = 16\sqrt{2}$

$\therefore V = \frac{1}{3}\pi (4)^2 \times 16\sqrt{2}$

$= \frac{256\sqrt{2}}{3}\pi\, cm^3$

**14.** (*d*) Radius of the hemisphere, $r = 3\,cm$

Volume of milk in the hemisphere $= \frac{2}{3}r^3 = \frac{2}{3}\pi \times 3^3$

$= \frac{22}{7} \times 2 \times 3^2\, cm^3$

$= \frac{22}{7} \times 2 \times 3^2 \times \frac{1}{1000}$ litre

Flow of liquid through the pipe

$= \frac{1}{14}$ litre per second.

Time taken to empty the tank

$= \frac{22}{7} \times 2 \times 3^2 \times \frac{1}{1000} \times 14$

$= \frac{396}{500}$ sec

$= 0.792$ sec

**15.** (*b*) The diameter of the largest sphere that can be carved out of a cube of a side 14 cm will be 14 cm.

$\therefore$ Radius of the sphere is

$r = \frac{14}{2} = 7\,cm$

$\therefore$ Volume of the sphere $= \frac{4}{3}\pi r^3$

$= \frac{4}{3} \times \frac{22}{7} \times (7)^3$

$= 1437.33\, cm^3$

**16.** (*c*) Given that radius of the cone is $\frac{2}{3}r$

and if *h* is the height of cone.

$\therefore \quad h = \frac{2}{3}r$ (given)

Now, Volume of the cone

$= \frac{1}{3}\pi R^2 h$

$= \frac{1}{3}\pi\left(\frac{2}{3}r\right)^2 \times \frac{2}{3}r$

$= \frac{1}{3}\pi \times \frac{4}{9}r^2 \times \frac{2}{3}r = \frac{8}{81}\pi r^3$

**17.** (*d*) Given that $r_1 = r_2$

and $\quad \frac{l_1}{l_2} = \frac{2}{3} \quad \ldots(i)$

Now, the ratio of their curved surface are

$= \frac{\text{Curved surface area of first cone}}{\text{Curved surface area of second cone}}$

$= \frac{\pi r_1 l_1}{\pi r_2 l_2} = \frac{r_1}{r_1} \times \left(\frac{l_1}{l_2}\right)$

$\therefore$ The ratio of their curved surface area is 2 : 3.

**18.** (*c*) Given, radius of the broadest end ($r$) = 2.1 cm and length ($h$) = 20 cm

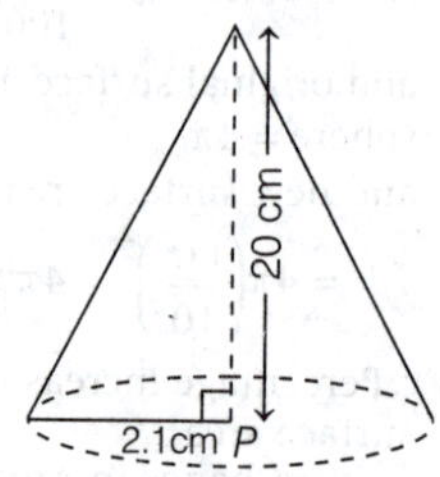


Let *l* be the slant height of the conical corn cob.

Then $l = \sqrt{r^2 + h^2}$

$= \sqrt{(2.1)^2 + (20)^2}$

$= \sqrt{4.41 + 400}$

$= \sqrt{404.41} = 20.11\,cm$

$\therefore$ Curved surface area of the corn cob $= \pi rl$

$= \frac{22}{7} \times 2.1 \times 20.11$

$= 132.726 = 132.73\, cm^2$

Total number of grains on the corn cob

= Curved surface area of the corn cob × Number of grains of corn on 1 $cm^2$

$= 132.73 \times 4$

$= 530.92 \approx 531$

**19.** (*a*) **Assertion** In semicircular sheet, Slant height of the conical cup $l = 14\,cm$,

Let $r$ cm be the radius and $h$ cm the height (depth) of the conical cup.

Then, circumference of the base of the conical cup

= circumference of the sheet

$\Rightarrow 2\pi r = \pi \times 14 \Rightarrow r = 7$ cm

Now, $l^2 = r^2 + h^2$

$\Rightarrow h = \sqrt{l^2 - r^2}$

$\Rightarrow h = \sqrt{(14)^2 - (7)^2}$

$= \sqrt{(7)^2 (2^2 - 1)} = 7\sqrt{3}$ cm

$\Rightarrow h = (7 \times 1.732) = 12.12$ cm

$\therefore$ Depth of the cup = 12.12 cm

Now, capacity of the cup

= Volume of the cup

Capacity of the cup $= \frac{1}{3}\pi r^2 h$

$= \frac{1}{3} \times \frac{22}{7} \times 7 \times 7 \times 1212$

$= 62226$ cm$^3$

Reason is also correct and it is correct explanation of Assertion.

**20.** *(c)* Whole surface area of solid formed

= CSA of cone $PQR$ + CSA of cone $UVR$ + Area of base

$= \pi r_1 l_1 + \pi r_2 l_2 + \pi(r_1^2 - r_2^2)$

$= \pi[6\sqrt{6^2 + (2\sqrt{7})^2}$

$+ 3\sqrt{3^2 + (\sqrt{7})^2} + (6^2 - 3^2)]$

$= \pi[6\sqrt{36 + 28} + 3\sqrt{9 + 7} + 27]$

$= \pi[6 \times 8 + 3 \times 4 + 27]$

$= \pi[48 + 12 + 27] = 87\pi$

**21.** *(a)* Let the external and internal radii of the hemispherical vessel be $R$ cm and $r$ cm respectively.

Then, $R = 12.5$ cm

and $r = 12$ cm

Now, Area of the outer surface $= 2\pi R^2$

Area of the inner surface

$= 2\pi r^2$

Area of the ring at the top

$= \pi R^2 - \pi r^2$

$\therefore$ Total area to be pointed

$= 2\pi R^2 + 2\pi r^2 + \pi R^2 - \pi r^2$

$= \pi(3R^2 + r^2)$

$= \frac{22}{7}[3 \times (12.5)^2 + (12)^2]$

$= \frac{22}{7} \times [468.75 + 144]$ cm$^2$

$= 1925.78$ cm$^2$

$\therefore$ Cost of painting

$= \frac{1925.78}{10} \times 0.2 =$ ₹ 38.5156

**22.** *(d)* Let $r$ be the radius and $S$ be the curved surface area.

Then, $S = 4\pi r^2$.

It is given that the diameter decreased by 20%.

$\therefore$ Decreased in diameter

$= 20\%$ of $2r = \left(\frac{20}{100} \times 2r\right) = \frac{2}{5}r$

Now, new diameter

$= 2r - \frac{2}{5}r = \frac{8}{5}r$

$\Rightarrow$ New radius $= \frac{4}{5}r$

Let $S_1$ be the new curved surface area. Then,

$S_1 = 4\pi\left(\frac{4r}{5}\right)^2 = \frac{64}{25}\pi r^2$

$\therefore$ Decrease in curved surface area $= 4\pi r^2 - \frac{64}{25}\pi r^2$

$= \frac{36}{25}\pi r^2$

So, percentage decrease in curved surface area is equal to

$= \frac{S - S_1}{S} \times 100\%$

$= \frac{\frac{36}{25}\pi r^2}{4\pi r^2} \times 100 = 36\%$

**23.** *(b)* (i) False, because sides containing the right angle.

(ii) False, Sphere has 1 face.

(iii) True, $l = \sqrt{r^2 + h^2} = \sqrt{4^2 + 3^2}$

$= \sqrt{16 + 9} = \sqrt{25} = 5$ cm

CSA of cone, $= \pi r l = \frac{22}{7} \times 4 \times 5$

$= \frac{440}{7}$ cm$^2$

**24.** *(c)* I. Total surface area of cone $= \pi r(l + r)$

II. Total surface area of sphere $= 4\pi r^2$

$\Rightarrow 4\pi r^2 = 88$

$\Rightarrow r^2 = 7$

$\therefore r = \sqrt{7}$ cm

III. Total surface area of cone

$= \pi r l + \pi r^2$

$= \frac{22}{7} \times 4 \times 7 + 50.28$

$\times \frac{22}{7} \times 4 \times 4$

$= 88 + 50.28$

$= 138.28$ cm$^2$

**25.** *(a)* **Statement I** Let diameter of sphere be $2r$.

Curved surface area of sphere $= 4\pi r^2$

New diameter

$= \left(2r - \frac{20}{100} \times 2r\right)$

$= \left(2r - \frac{2r}{5}\right) = \frac{8r}{5}$

$\therefore$ The new radius $= \frac{\frac{8r}{5}}{2} = \frac{4r}{5}$

New, curved surface area of sphere $= 4\pi\left(\frac{4r}{5}\right)^2$

$\therefore$ New, decreased in CSA

$= \frac{4\pi r^2 - 4\pi \times \left(\frac{4r}{5}\right)^2}{4\pi r^2} \times 100\%$

$= \frac{4\pi r^2 - \frac{64\pi r^2}{25}}{4\pi r^2} \times 100\%$

$= \frac{900}{25}\% = 36\%$

**Statement II** True

**26.** *(a)* (A) Total surface area of hemisphere

$= 3\pi r^2$

$= 3 \times \frac{22}{7} \times (10.5)^2 = 1039.5$ cm$^2$

(B) Total surface area of cone
$= \pi r(l + r)$
$= \frac{22}{7} \times 30 \times (30 + 40)$
$= \frac{22}{7} \times 30 \times 70 = 6600 \text{ cm}^2$

(C) Total surface area of hemisphere is given by $= 3\pi r^2$
$= 3 \times \frac{22}{7} \times 21 \times 21 \text{ cm}^2$
$= 4158 \text{ cm}^2$

(D) Total surface area of cone is given by
$= \pi rl + \pi r^2$
$= \pi r(l + r)$
$= \frac{22}{7} \times 5(\sqrt{r^2 + h^2} + r)$
$= \frac{22}{7} \times 5[\sqrt{5^2 + 12^2} + 5]$
$= \frac{22}{7} \times 5(13 + 5)$
$= 282.85 \text{ cm}^2$

**27.** *(b)* I : Volume of hemisphere
$= \frac{2}{3}\pi r^3 = \frac{2}{3}\pi \times (9)^3 = 486\pi \text{ cm}^3$

II : Let the internal radius of sphere is $r$ and external radius of sphere is $R$, then $r = 2$ cm and $R = 4$ cm

$\therefore$ Volume of solid part of hollow sphere
$= \frac{4}{3}\pi R^3 - \frac{4}{3}\pi r^3 \text{ cm}^3$
$= \frac{4}{3}\pi(R^3 - r^3) \text{ cm}^3$
$= \frac{4}{3}\pi(4^3 - 2^3) \text{ cm}^3$
$= \frac{4}{3}\pi \times 56 \text{ cm}^3$

Since, Volume of Solid part = Volume of cone

Here, radius of cone is 4 cm and let height is $h$.

Then, $\frac{1}{3}\pi r^2 h = \frac{4}{3}\pi \times 56$

$\Rightarrow h = \frac{4 \times 56}{16} = 14 \text{ cm}$

Hence, height of cone is 14 cm.

III : Let the radius of metallic sphere is $R$.

$\therefore R = 10.5$

Then, volume metallic sphere
$= \frac{4}{3}\pi R^3 = \frac{4}{3}\pi(10.5)^3$

and radius of small sphere is $r = 3.5$ cm

So, Volume of small sphere
$= \frac{4}{3}\pi r^3$
$= \frac{4}{3}\pi(3.5)^3$

Let $n$ be the number of small sphere recast from metallic sphere of radius $R$, then

$n \times$ volume of small sphere = Volume of metallic sphere of radius 10.5

$\Rightarrow n \times \frac{4}{3}\pi(3.5)^3 = \frac{4}{3}\pi(10.5)^3$

$\Rightarrow n = \left(\frac{10.5}{3.5}\right)^3 = 27$

IV : Radius, $r = \frac{6}{2} = 3$ cm

$h = 7$ cm

Volume of cone $= \frac{1}{3}\pi r^2 h$
$= \frac{1}{3} \times \pi \times (3)^2 \times 7$
$= 21\pi \text{ cm}^3$

**28.** *(c)* P : Let the radius of the base of the cone be $r$ cm and its heights be $h$ cm. Then, radius of the hemisphere
$= r$ cm

Now, volume of cone
= Volume of hemisphere

$\Rightarrow \frac{1}{3}\pi r^2 h = \frac{2}{3}\pi r^3$

$\Rightarrow h = 2r \Rightarrow h : r = 2 : 1$

[height of hemisphere is its radius]

Q : Let $r_1$ and $r_2$ be the radii of two cones and $V_1$ and $V_2$ be their volumes. Let $h$ be the height of the two cones. Then,

$V_1 = \frac{1}{3}\pi r_1^2 h$ and $V_2 = \frac{1}{3}\pi r_2^2 h$

$\therefore \frac{V_1}{V_2} = \frac{\frac{1}{3}\pi r_1^2 h}{\frac{1}{3}\pi r_2^2 h} = \frac{r_1^2}{r_2^2} = \frac{9}{25}$

$\left[\because \frac{r_1}{r_2} = \frac{3}{5} \text{ (Given)} \because \frac{r_1^2}{r_2^2} = \frac{9}{25}\right]$

So, the required ratio of the volumes of two cones is 9:25.

R : $V_{cone} = 2V_{hemisphere}$

($r$, $h$ is the radius and height of cone and $r$ be the radius of hemisphere)

$\frac{1}{3}\pi r^2 h = 2\left(\frac{2}{3}\pi r^3\right)$

$\Rightarrow \frac{h}{r} = \frac{4}{1} \Rightarrow h : r = 4 : 1$

(S) Volume of 8 solid spheres
= Volume of a solid sphere

$8 \times \left(\frac{4}{3}\pi r^3\right) = \frac{4}{3}\pi r'^3$

$\Rightarrow \frac{r'^3}{r^3} = 8 \quad \text{...(i)}$

and $S = 4\pi r^2$

$S' = 4\pi r'^2$

$\frac{S}{S'} = \left(\frac{r}{r'}\right)^2$

From Eq. (i),

$8 = \frac{r'^3}{r^3}$

$\Rightarrow \frac{r'}{r} = \frac{2}{1} \Rightarrow \frac{r}{r'} = \frac{1}{2}$

$\therefore \frac{S}{S'} = \frac{1}{2}$

**29.** *(b)* Let the radius of solid sphere; $R = 10$ cm

Then, volume of solid sphere
$= \frac{4}{3}\pi R^3 = \frac{4}{3}\pi(10)^3 \text{ cm}^3$

Now, let $r$ be the radius of solid balls.

Then, volume of one ball
$= \frac{4}{3}\pi r^3 \text{ cm}^3$

Since, number of balls moulded from sphere is 8,

$\therefore$ 8 × Volume of one ball
= Volume of solid sphere

$\Rightarrow 8 \times \frac{4}{3}\pi r^3 = \frac{4}{3}\pi 10^3$

$\Rightarrow r^3 = \left(\frac{10}{2}\right)^3$

$\Rightarrow r = 5$

Hence, surface area of one ball $= 4\pi r^2 = 4 \times \pi \times 25$
$= 100\pi \text{ cm}^2$

**30.** *(a)* We have, $VO' = 11.2\,cm$
$OA = OO' = 5.2\,cm$

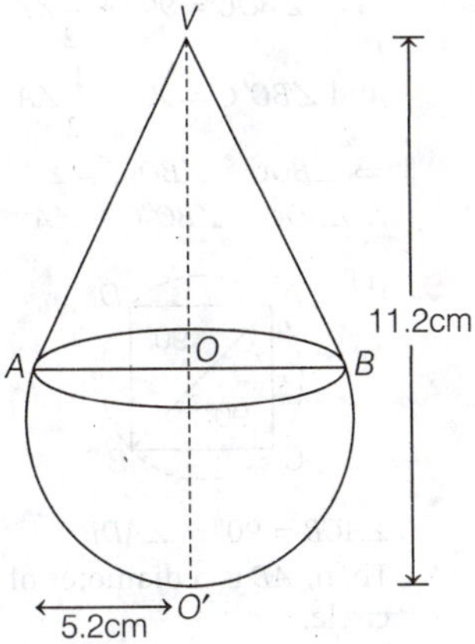


Let $r$ be the radius of the hemisphere and $h$ be the height of the conical part of the toy. Then, $r = OA = 5.2\,cm$,
$h = VO - OO' = (11.2 - 5.2) = 6\,cm$
Also radius of the base of the cone $= OA = 5.2\,cm$
$\therefore$ Volume of the wooden toy
= Volume of the conical part + Volume of the hemisphere part

$$= \frac{1}{3}\pi r^2 h + \frac{2}{3}\pi r^3$$
$$= \frac{\pi r^2}{3}(h + 2r)\,cm^3$$
$$= \frac{1}{3} \times \frac{22}{7} \times 5.2 \times 5.2 \times (6 + 2 \times 5.2)$$
$$= 464.57\,cm^3$$

## Chapter 10 : Statistics

**1.** *(c)* A frequency polygon is constructed by plotting frequency of the class interval and mid-value of the class.

**2.** *(c)* The frequency of a class may change for any class interval. But for a specific class, the class size will remain the same. Hence, the correct statement is that in a histogram, the area of each rectangle is proportional to the frequency of its class interval.

**3.** *(b)* In the less than type of ogive the cumulative frequency is plotted against the upper limit of the concerned class interval.

**4.** *(b)* In a histogram the class intervals or the groups are taken along the horizontal axis or X-axis.

**5.** *(d)* A histogram is a pictorial representation of the grouped data in which class interval and frequency are respectively taken along horizontal axis and vertical axis.

**6.** *(b)* In a histogram each class rectangle is constructed with base as class intervals.

**7.** *(d)* Total number of newspaper published in Hindi = 3700
Published in Punjabi = 200
Published in Urdu = 700
Published in Bengali = 1100
Published in English = 3400
Published in Tamil = 1000
Hence, overall total
$= 3700 + 200 + 700 + 1100 + 3400 + 1000$
$= 10100$

**8.** *(d)* From the given graph, we can observe Bengali and Gujarati are the required pair.

**9.** *(c)* Number of newspaper published in Marathi = 1400 and number of newspapers published in English = 3400
So, total newspaper published in Marathi and English
$= 1400 + 3400 = 4800$
Similarly,
Total number of newspaper published in Tamil and Hindi
$= 1000 + 3700 = 4700$
Hence, the number of newspaper published = Marathi and English is $4800 - 4700 = 100$ more than the total newspaper published in Tamil and Hindi.

**10.** *(d)* The adjusted frequency for the class 25- 45 is
$$= \frac{\text{Frequency of the class}}{\text{Class width}} \times \text{Minimum width}$$
$$= \frac{8}{20} \times 5 = 2$$

**11.** *(b)* Required mean
$$= \frac{10 + 18 + 11 + 20}{2}$$
$$= \frac{59}{2} = 29.5$$

**12.** *(c)* Since, the prime numbers between 1 and 20 are 2, 3, 5, 7, 11, 13, 17 and 19.
$\therefore$ Mean
$$= \frac{2 + 3 + 5 + 7 + 11 + 13 + 17 + 19}{8}$$
$$= \frac{77}{8} = 9.6$$

**13.** *(d)* Total production of wheat
$= 16 + 2 + 5 + 2 + 6 = 31$
Total production of rice
$= 8 + 10 + 5 + 4 + 3 = 30$
So, total combined production
$= 31 + 30 = 61$
Therefore, percentage of total production of wheat to the total combined production
$$= \frac{31}{61} \times 100 = 50.82\%$$

**14.** *(d)* Cumulative frequency distribution is not the graphical representation of statistical data.

**15.** *(c)* Cumulative frequency are graphical representation in a frequency distribution.

**16.** *(b)* Combined population of chennai and Mumbai
= 80 + 120 = 200 lakhs
and combined population of Delhi, Chennai and Kolkata
= 150 + 80 + 130 = 360 lakhs
Therefore, required ratio
= 200:360 = 5:9

**17.** *(c)* Average pass percentage of X class in 1994-95, 1997-98 and 1998-99 and average pass percentage of XII class in 1996-97 and 1997-98

$$= \frac{85+90}{2} = 87.5\%$$

**18.** (b) Total number of vehicles passing through a crossing during a particular day

$$= 300+400+250+250+150+100+200+325+375$$
$$= 2350$$

**19.** (b) **Statement I** number of students wearing shoe number $10 = 400$ and number of students wearing shoe number $9 = 100$ and $400 > (3\times100)$

Hence, statement I is false.

**Statement II** number of students wearing shoe number $4 = 500$ and number of students wearing shoe number $8 = 500$. Hence, statement Ii is true.

**20.** (b) We know that, If $\bar{x}$ is the mean of $x_1, x_2, \ldots\ldots, x_n$

$$\bar{x} = \frac{(x_1 + x_2 + x_3 + \ldots + x_n)}{n}$$

$$\Rightarrow x_1 + x_2 + x_3 + \ldots + x_n = n\bar{x}$$

Now mean

$$= \frac{[(ax_1 + ax_2 + ax_3 + \ldots + ax_n)] + \left(\frac{x_1}{a} + \frac{x_2}{a} + \ldots. + \frac{x_n}{a}\right)}{n+n}$$

$$= \frac{na\bar{x} + n\frac{\bar{x}}{a}}{2n} = \frac{n\bar{x}\left(a + \frac{1}{a}\right)}{2n}$$

$$= \frac{\bar{x}\left(a + \frac{1}{a}\right)}{2} = \left(a + \frac{1}{a}\right)\frac{\bar{x}}{2}$$

## Practice Set 1

**1.** (c) $2x + \sqrt{3}y - 4a = 0$ has solution,

$$x = 1, y = 0$$
$$\Rightarrow 2\times1 + \sqrt{3}\times0 - 4a = 0$$
$$\Rightarrow \quad 2 = 4a \Rightarrow a = \frac{1}{2}$$

**2.** (b) Given, $\quad AD = CD$

$$\Rightarrow \quad \angle ABD = \angle CBD$$
$$\Rightarrow \quad 2\angle x = \angle x + 40$$
$$\Rightarrow \quad \angle x = 40°$$

**3.** (d) Thursday had the highest laps driven.

**4.** (c) Since $y - 2p$ is a factor of $\frac{y^3}{4p^2} - 2y + lp$

So, on substituting $y = 2p$ into the given equation, we get

$$\frac{(2p)^3}{4p^2} - 2(2p) + lp = 0$$
$$\Rightarrow \quad \frac{8p^3}{4p^2} - 4p + lp = 0$$
$$\Rightarrow \quad 2p - 4p + lp = 0$$
$$\Rightarrow \quad -2p + lp = 0$$
$$\Rightarrow \quad lp = 2p$$
$$\Rightarrow \quad l = 2$$

**5.** (d) Number of zeroes of the zero polynomial is infinite.

**6.** (d) $\frac{7\sqrt{2}}{3+\sqrt{2}} = \frac{7\sqrt{2}(3-\sqrt{2})}{(3+\sqrt{2})(3-\sqrt{2})}$

$$= \frac{7\sqrt{2}(3-\sqrt{2})}{(3^2-2)}$$
$$= \frac{21\sqrt{2}-14}{7} = 3\sqrt{2} - 2$$

$$\frac{2\sqrt{5}}{\sqrt{6}+\sqrt{5}} = \frac{2\sqrt{5}(\sqrt{6}-\sqrt{5})}{(\sqrt{6}+\sqrt{5})(\sqrt{6}-\sqrt{5})}$$
$$= \frac{2\sqrt{5}(\sqrt{6}-\sqrt{5})}{(\sqrt{6})^2-(\sqrt{5})^2} = \frac{2\sqrt{30}-10}{6-5}$$
$$= 2\sqrt{30} - 10$$

$$\frac{3\sqrt{2}}{\sqrt{15}+3\sqrt{2}} = \frac{3\sqrt{2}(3\sqrt{2}-\sqrt{15})}{(3\sqrt{2}+\sqrt{15})(3\sqrt{2}-\sqrt{15})}$$
$$= \frac{3\sqrt{2}(3\sqrt{2}-\sqrt{15})}{18-15}$$
$$= \frac{3\sqrt{2}(3\sqrt{2}-\sqrt{15})}{3}$$
$$= \frac{18-3\sqrt{30}}{3} = 6 - \sqrt{30}$$

$$\therefore \frac{7\sqrt{2}}{3+\sqrt{2}} - \frac{2\sqrt{5}}{\sqrt{6}+\sqrt{5}} - \frac{3\sqrt{2}}{\sqrt{15}+3\sqrt{2}}$$
$$= 3\sqrt{2} - 2 - 2\sqrt{30} + 10 - 6 + \sqrt{30}$$
$$= 3\sqrt{2} - \sqrt{30} + 2$$

**7.** (a) Area swept by the minute hand $= \pi r^2 \times \frac{35}{60}$

$$= \frac{22}{7}\times\frac{x}{2}\times\frac{x}{2}\times\frac{35}{60} = \frac{11}{24}x^2$$

**8.** (a) We know that,

$$\angle BOC = 90° + \frac{1}{2}\angle A$$

and $\angle BO'C = 90° - \frac{1}{2}\angle A$

$$\Rightarrow \angle BOC - \angle BO'C = \angle A$$
$$\therefore \angle BOC = \angle BO'C + \angle A$$

**9.** (c)

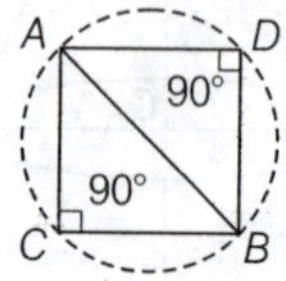


$\angle ACB = 90° = \angle ADB$

Then, $AB$ is a diameter of a circle.

So, $ABCD$ is a cyclic quadrilateral.

**10.** (b) Since, $\angle AOC' = \angle BOC$ [vertically opposite angles]

In $\Delta OBD$,

$$\angle BOD + \angle BDO + \angle OBD = 180°$$
$$\Rightarrow \angle x + 32° + \angle x + 14° + 90° = 180°$$
$$[\because \angle BOD = \angle BOC + \angle COD]$$
$$\Rightarrow \quad 2\angle x + 136° = 180°$$
$$\Rightarrow \quad 2\angle x = 44°$$
$$\therefore \quad \angle x = 22°$$

**11.** (c) Since, the equation intersect $X$-axis.

$$\therefore \quad y = 0 \Rightarrow 0 = 4x - 2$$
$$\Rightarrow \quad 2 = 4x \Rightarrow x = \frac{1}{2}$$

Hence, the required point is $\left(\frac{1}{2}, 0\right)$

**12.** (b) Volume of each bullet

$$= \frac{4}{3}\pi r^3 = \frac{4}{3}\pi \times 2^3$$
$$= \frac{4\times8\times\pi}{3}$$

Volume of cone $= \frac{1}{3}\pi r^2 h$

$$= \frac{1}{3}\pi\times12\times12\times44$$

$\therefore$ Numbers of bullets

$$= \frac{\frac{1}{3}\times\pi\times12\times12\times44}{\frac{4\times8\times\pi}{3}}$$

$$= 3\times3\times22 = 198$$

**13.** (*b*) Given,

$$\sqrt[5]{\sqrt[4]{(2^4)^3}} - 5\sqrt[5]{8} + 2\sqrt[5]{\sqrt[4]{(2^3)^4}}$$

$$= \sqrt[5]{(2^4)^{3/4}} - 5\sqrt[5]{8} + 2\sqrt[5]{2^3}$$

$$= \sqrt[5]{8} - 5\sqrt[5]{8} + 2\sqrt[5]{8} = -2(\sqrt[5]{8})$$

**14.** (*d*) In $\Delta ABC$, $AB = AC$

$\Rightarrow \quad \angle C = \angle B$

[since, angles opposite to equal sides are equal]

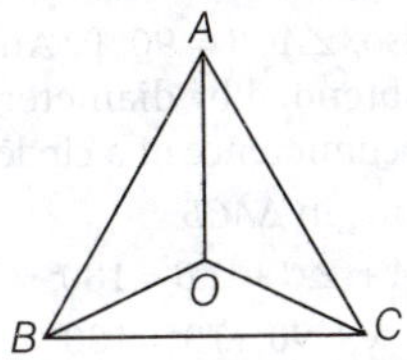


$\Rightarrow \quad \frac{1}{2}\angle B = \frac{1}{2}\angle C$

$\Rightarrow \quad \angle OBC = \angle OCB$

$\Rightarrow \quad OB = OC$

In $\Delta ABO$ and $\Delta ACO$,

$AB = AC$

$\angle OBA = \angle OCA$

and $\quad OB = OC$

$\Delta ABO \cong \Delta ACO$

[by SAS Congruency rule]

$\Rightarrow \angle BAO = \angle CAO$ [by CPCT]

Hence, $AO$ is the bisector of $\angle BAC$.

**15.** (*a*) $\because$ Total expenditure =
$6240 \times 3 + 6780 \times 4 + 7236 \times 5$
$= 18720 + 27120 + 36180$
$=$ ₹ 82020

and savings = ₹ 7080

Total income

$=$ ₹ $(82020 + 7080) =$ ₹ 89100

$\therefore$ Average monthly income

$= \frac{89100}{12} =$ ₹ 7425

**16.** (*c*) Given,

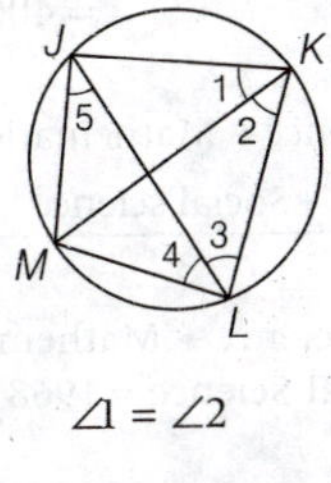


$\angle 1 = \angle 2 \quad$ ...(i)

[since, $MK$ bisects $\angle JKL$]

Also, $\angle 1 = \angle 4 \quad$ ...(ii)

[angles in same segment are equal]

and $\angle 2 = \angle 5$ [angle in same segments are equal] ...(iii)

From Eqs. (i), (ii) and (iii),

$\angle 4 = \angle 5$

$\Rightarrow \quad JM = ML$

[$\because$ sides opposite to equal angle are equal]

Hence, $\Delta JML$ is an isosceles triangle.

**17.** (*d*) Let side of square field be $a$ unit.

Distance covered by Edward

$= a + a = 2a$ sq. unit

Distance covered by Misha

$= \sqrt{a^2 + a^2} = \sqrt{2}a$ sq. unit

$\therefore$ Required percentage

$= \frac{2a}{\sqrt{2}a} \times 100$

$= \sqrt{2} \times 100 = 141\,\%$

**18.** (*b*) $p(x) = (40 - 4x^2)(x) - 15x$
$= 40x - 4x^3 - 15x$
$= -4x^3 + 25x$

**19.** (*a*) $(\sqrt{2} + \sqrt{3})(\sqrt{3} - \sqrt{2})$
$= (\sqrt{3} + \sqrt{2})(\sqrt{3} - \sqrt{2})$
$= (\sqrt{3})^2 - (\sqrt{2})^2$
$= 3 - 2$
$= 1 =$ Rational number

**20.** (*d*) Construct a line

$PX \parallel OP \parallel RS$

$\angle QRS = \angle QYX = 130°$

[corresponding angle]

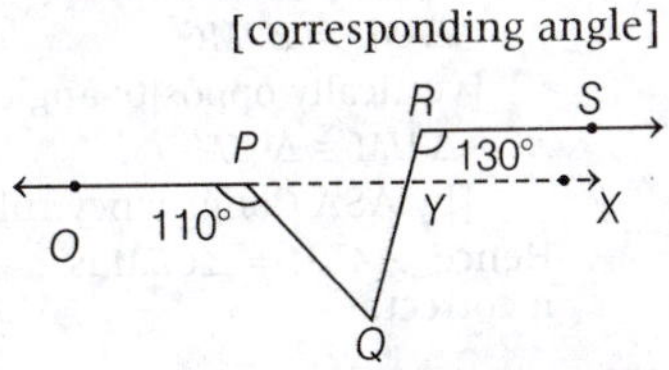


$\angle OPQ + \angle YPQ = 180°$

[Linear pair]

$\Rightarrow \angle YPQ = 180° - \angle OPQ$
$= 180° - 110° = 70°$

and $\angle PYQ = 180° - \angle QYX$
$= 180° - 130° = 50°$

$\therefore \angle PQR = 180° - (70° + 50°)$
$= 60°$

**21.** (*b*) We have,

$4x^3 + 2x^2 - 8x + 7$

On putting $x = \frac{\sqrt{3}+1}{2}$, we get

$$4\left(\frac{\sqrt{3}+1}{2}\right)^3 + 2\left(\frac{\sqrt{3}+1}{2}\right)^2 - 8\left(\frac{\sqrt{3}+1}{2}\right) + 7$$

$$= \frac{(\sqrt{3}+1)^3}{2} + \frac{(\sqrt{3}+1)^2}{2} - \frac{8(\sqrt{3}+1)}{2} + 7$$

$$= \frac{1}{2}[3\sqrt{3} + 1 + 3\sqrt{3}(\sqrt{3}+1) + 3 + 1 + 2\sqrt{3} - 8\sqrt{3} - 8 + 14]$$

$$= \frac{1}{2}(3\sqrt{3} + 1 + 9 + 3\sqrt{3} + 4 + 2\sqrt{3} - 8\sqrt{3} + 6)$$

$$= \frac{1}{2}(20) = 10$$

**22.** (*b*) $\frac{p}{q} + \frac{q}{p} = \frac{p^2 + q^2}{pq}$

$= \frac{p^2 + q^2 + 2pq - 2pq}{pq}$

$= \frac{(p+q)^2 - 2pq}{pq}$

$= \frac{(10)^2 - 2 \times 5}{5} = \frac{100 - 10}{5}$

$= \frac{90}{5} = 18$

**23.** (*d*) Let the side of an equilateral triangle be $a$ cm.

Then, area of triangle $= \frac{\sqrt{3}}{4}a^2$

Again, let new side of the triangle be $3a$.

Then, area $= \frac{\sqrt{3}}{4} \times (3a)(3a)$

$= \frac{9\sqrt{3}}{4}a^2$

Increase in area

$= \frac{9\sqrt{3}}{4}a^2 - \frac{\sqrt{3}}{4}a^2 = 2\sqrt{3}a^2$

$\therefore$ Percentage increase in area

$$= \frac{2\sqrt{3}a^2}{\frac{\sqrt{3}}{4}a^2} \times 100 = 800\%$$

**24.** (a) The number of times annual rainfall below 120 cm

$$= 6 + 5 = 11$$

The number of times the annual rainfall above 130 cm

$$= 2 + 9 = 11$$

The required percent

$$= \frac{11}{11} \times 100\% = 100\%$$

**25.** (d) The diagonals of a parallelogram bisect each other.

**26.** (b) In 1994 amount of manure manufactured by the company was maximum.

**27.** (c)

$$\frac{7 + 4\sqrt{5} + 4 - 2\sqrt{5} - 10 - 5\sqrt{5}}{6} = P + q\sqrt{5}$$

$$\Rightarrow \frac{1 - 3\sqrt{5}}{6} = p + q\sqrt{5}$$

$$\Rightarrow \frac{1}{6} - \frac{3}{6}\sqrt{5} = p + q\sqrt{5}$$

$$\Rightarrow p = \frac{1}{6} \text{ and } q = \frac{-3}{6}$$

[on comparing]

$$\therefore \sqrt{p - q} = \sqrt{\frac{1}{6} - \left(\frac{-3}{6}\right)} = \sqrt{\frac{1+3}{6}}$$

$$= \frac{2}{\sqrt{6}} = \frac{2\sqrt{6}}{6} = \frac{\sqrt{6}}{3}$$

**28.** (b)

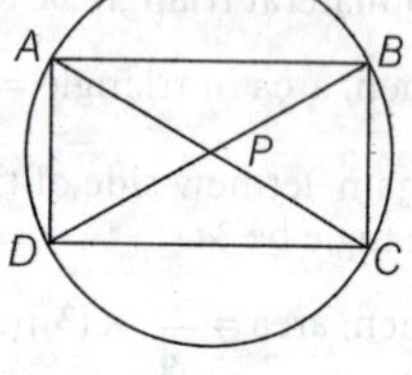


In the given figure, consider $\Delta PAB$ and $\Delta PDC$,

$AB = CD$ [given]

$\angle PAB = \angle PDC$

[angle in same segment]

and $\angle PBA = \angle PCD$

[angle in same segment]

$\therefore$ $\Delta PAB \cong \Delta PDC$

[by ASA congruence rule]

**29.** (b) Given, $ABCD$ is a rectangle.

$\therefore$ $\angle ADC = 90°$

Now,

$\angle CDE + \angle CDA + 260° = 360°$

$\Rightarrow \angle CDE = 10°$

Also, $BD = BE$

$\therefore$ $\angle BDE = \angle BED = 40°$

$\Rightarrow \angle BDC + \angle CDE = 40°$

$\Rightarrow \angle BDC = 30°$

**30.** (b) Since, $\Delta ABC$ is an isosceles triangle.

$\therefore$ $BA = BC$

Then, $\angle BAM = \angle BCN$

Now, $MA = MB$

Then, $\Delta AMB$ is an isosceles triangle.

Therefore, $\angle BAM = \angle ABM$

Similarly, $NC = NB$

$\Rightarrow$ $\angle CBN = \angle BCN$

In $\Delta BAN$ and $\Delta CNB$,

$AB = BC$

$\angle BAM = \angle BCN$

and $\angle ABM = \angle CBN$

$\therefore$ $\Delta AMB \cong \Delta CNB$

**31.** (d) Since, $M$ is the mid-point of $AC$, then $AM = MC$.

Also, $AI$ and $CJ$ are perpendicular to $BM$.

So, $AI$ is parallel to $CJ$ with $CA$ as the transversal.

$\therefore$ $\angle MAI = \angle MCJ$

[alternate angles]

$\angle AMI = \angle JMC$

[vertically opposite angles]

$\therefore$ $\Delta AIM \cong \Delta CJM$

[by ASA Congruency rule]

Hence, $\angle ABM = \angle CBM$ is incorrect.

**32.** (b)

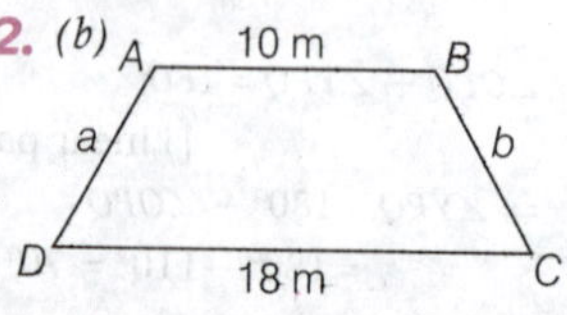


Area of trapezium

$$= \frac{1}{2}(10 + 18) \times 14$$

$$= \frac{1}{2} \times 28 \times 14 = 14 \times 14$$

$$= 196 \text{ m}^2$$

$\therefore$ Share of land each one gets

$$= \frac{196}{2} = 98 \text{ m}^2$$

**33.** (c) Here, $\angle OBC = \angle OCB = 70°$

[$\because OB = OC$ = radius of a circle]

Also, $\angle ACB = 90°$ [$\because$ Angle subtended by diameter on circumference of a circle is 90°]

Now, in $\Delta ACB$,

$\angle A + \angle C + \angle B = 180°$

$\Rightarrow x + 90° + 70° = 180°$

$\Rightarrow$ $x = 20°$

**34.** (b) Given, $x = \frac{\sqrt{3} + 2}{\sqrt{2}}$

$\Rightarrow$ $\sqrt{2}x = \sqrt{3} + 2$

$\Rightarrow$ $\sqrt{2}x - 2 = \sqrt{3}$

On squaring both sides, we get

$$(\sqrt{2}x - 2)^2 = (\sqrt{3})^2$$

$\Rightarrow$ $2x^2 + 4 - 4\sqrt{2}x = 3$

$\Rightarrow$ $2x^2 + 1 = 4\sqrt{2}x$

Again squaring both sides, we get

$$(2x^2 + 1)^2 = (4\sqrt{2}x)^2$$

$\Rightarrow$ $4x^4 + 1 + 4x^2 = 32x^2$

$\Rightarrow$ $4x^4 - 28x^2 + 1 = 0$

$\Rightarrow$ $4x^4 - 28x^2 + 4 = 3$

$\Rightarrow$ $x^4 - 7x^2 + 1 = 3/4$

**35.** (d) Given,

Average number of teachers $= 800$

and total subjects $= 5$

$\therefore$ Total teachers $= 800 \times 5$

$= 4000$

Also,

$$\frac{\text{Science} + \text{Mathematics} + \text{Social science}}{3} = 656$$

$\Rightarrow$ Science + Mathematics + Social Science = 1968

$\Rightarrow$ Hindi + English

$= 4000 - 1968 = 2032$

Now, the number of teachers teaching Hindi

$= \frac{20}{100} \times 4000 = 800$

$\therefore$ Number of teachers teaching English

$= 2032 - 800 = 1232$

**36.** (b) Cone and hemisphere have equal bases mean they have same radii $R$.

$\because$ Volume of Cone = Volume of hemisphere $\frac{1}{3}\pi R^2 h = \frac{2}{3}\pi R^3$

$h = 2R \Rightarrow \frac{h}{R} = \frac{2}{1}$

$\Rightarrow \quad h : R = 2 : 1$

**37.** (d)

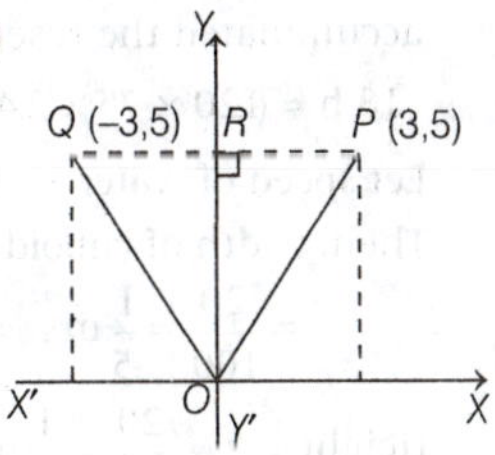


Coordinates of point $Q$

$\equiv (-3, 5)$

$\therefore$ Area of $\Delta POQ = \frac{1}{2} \times OR \times PQ$

$= \frac{1}{2} \times 5 \times 6$

$= 15$ sq units

**38.** (b) From the figure,

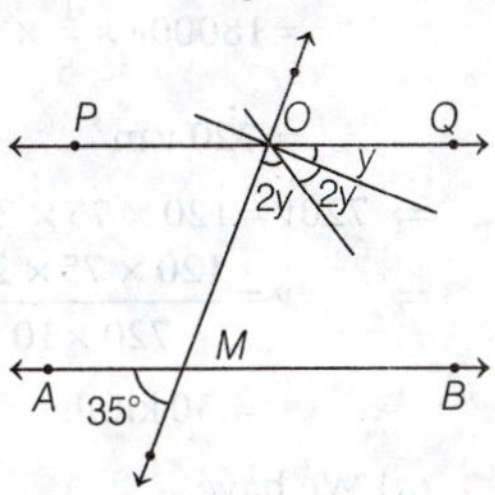


$\because \angle QOM + \angle OMB = 180°$

$(2\angle y + 2\angle y + \angle y) + 35° = 180°$

$(\because \angle M = 35°)$

$\Rightarrow \quad 5\angle y = 180° - 35°$

$\Rightarrow \quad \angle y = 36° - 7 = 29°$

**39.** (a)

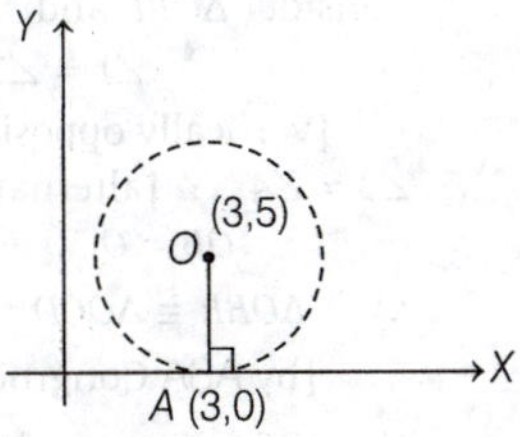


Radius of the circle

$= (5 - 0) = 5$ units

[$\because$ abscissa of $O$ and $A$ are same]

$\therefore$ Area of circle $= \pi(r)^2$

$= \pi(5)^2$

$= 25\pi$ sq units.

**40.** (c) $A(3, 5)$ and $B(1, 4)$ lie on the graph of line $ax + by = 7$

$\therefore \quad 3a + 5b = 7 \quad \ldots(i)$

$a + 4b = 7 \quad \ldots(ii)$

$\therefore$ From Eqs. (i) and (ii), we get

$b = 2, a = -1$

$\therefore \quad (a, b) = (-1, 2)$

**41.** (a) In $\Delta DCF$ and $\Delta GBF$

$CF = BF$

[$F$ is mid point of $BC$]

$\angle CFD = \angle BFG$

[vertically opposite angles]

$\angle DCF = \angle FBG$

[alternate angle]

$\therefore \quad \Delta DCF \cong \Delta GBF$, then

$DF = FG$

and $\quad DC = BG$

$\because \quad DF = FG$

**42.** (d) $\left(\frac{x^{1/a}}{x^{1/b}}\right)^{\frac{a^2b^2}{b-a}} \cdot \left(\frac{x^{1/b}}{x^{1/c}}\right)^{\frac{b^2c^2}{c-b}} \cdot \left(\frac{x^{1/c}}{x^{1/a}}\right)^{\frac{a^2c^2}{a-c}}$

$= \left(x^{\frac{1}{a}-\frac{1}{b}}\right)^{\frac{a^2b^2}{b-a}} \cdot \left(x^{\frac{1}{b}-\frac{1}{c}}\right)^{\frac{b^2c^2}{c-b}} \cdot \left(x^{\frac{1}{c}-\frac{1}{a}}\right)^{\frac{a^2c^2}{a-c}}$

$\left[\because \frac{a^m}{a^n} = a^{m-n}\right]$

$= \left(x^{\frac{b-a}{ab}}\right)^{\frac{a^2b^2}{b-a}} \cdot \left(x^{\frac{c-b}{bc}}\right)^{\frac{b^2c^2}{c-b}} \cdot \left(x^{\frac{a-c}{ac}}\right)^{\frac{a^2c^2}{a-c}}$

$= x^{ab} \cdot x^{bc} \cdot x^{ca}$

$= x^{ab + bc + ca}$

$[\because a^m \cdot a^n = a^{m+n}]$

**43.** (a) Since, $ABCD$ is a rhombus, so its all sides are equal.

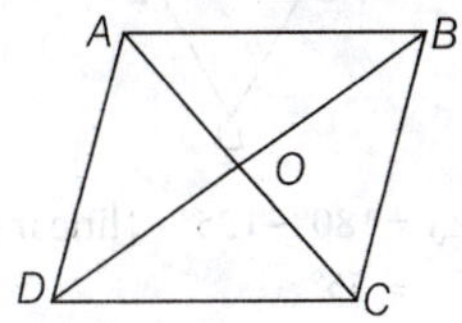


Therefore, $\quad BC = DC$

In $\Delta BDC$,

$\angle BDC = \angle DBC = x°$

Also, $\quad \angle BCD = 60°$ [given]

$\therefore \quad x° + x° + 60° = 180°$

$\Rightarrow \quad x° = 60°$

$\therefore \angle BDC = \angle DBC$

$= \angle BCD = 60°$

So, $\Delta BCD$ is an equilateral triangle.

$\therefore \quad BD = BC = a$

$AB^2 = OA^2 + OB^2$

[$\because$ diagonals of rhombus intersect each other at 90°]

$\Rightarrow OA^2 = AB^2 - OB^2$

$\Rightarrow OA^2 = a^2 - \left(\frac{a}{2}\right)^2$

$= a^2 - \frac{a^2}{4}$

$= \frac{3a^2}{4}$

$\therefore \quad OA = \frac{\sqrt{3}}{2}a$

Now, $AC = \left(2 \times \frac{\sqrt{3}}{2}a\right) = \sqrt{3}\,a$

$\therefore AC : BD = \sqrt{3}\,a : a = \sqrt{3} : 1$

**44.** (b) A.

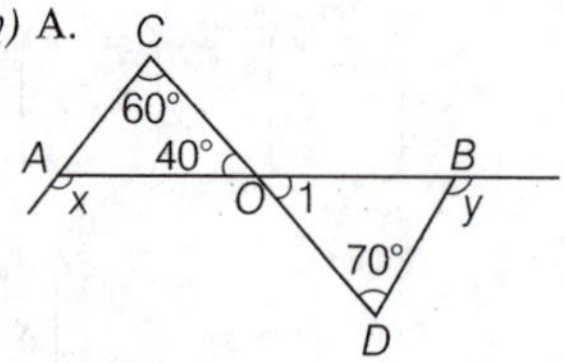

$\angle 1 = \angle COA = 40°$

$\therefore \quad \angle y = 40° + 70° = 110°$

Also, $\angle x = 60° + 40° = 100°$

B.

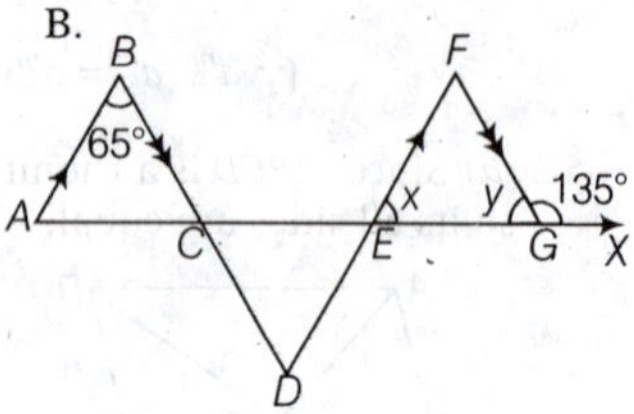

$\angle y = 180° - 125°$ [linear pair]

$= 55°$

Now, $FG \| BC$

$\therefore \angle BCE = \angle FGX = 135°$

[corresponding angle]

$\therefore \angle BAC = \angle BCE - \angle ABC$

$= 135° - 65° = 70°$

Now, $\angle x = \angle BAC = 70°$

[corresponding angle]

C. In $\Delta PQS$,

$\angle x + \angle y = 90°$ ...(i)

In $\Delta RQS$,

$\angle SRQ = 180° - 60° = 120°$

$\angle QSR = 180° - (42 + 120°) = 18°$

Since, $PQ \| ST$

$\therefore \quad \angle x = \angle QSR = 18°$

From Eq. (i), $18° + \angle y = 90°$

$\Rightarrow \quad \angle y = 72°$

**45.** (b)

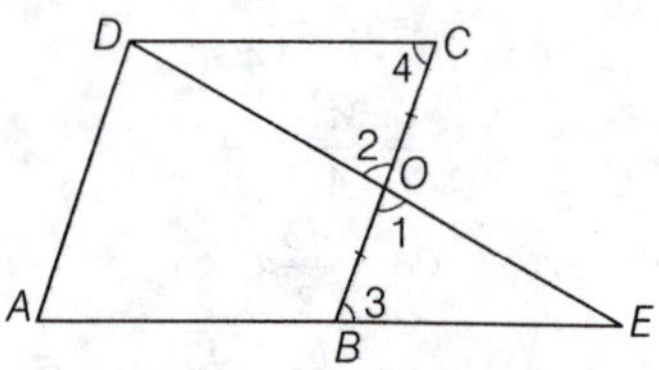

In the above figure, $ABCD$ is a parallelogram, where $AB$ is produced to $E$ such that $OC = OB$.

Consider $\Delta OBE$ and $\Delta OCD$,

$\angle 1 = \angle 2$

[vertically opposite angles]

$\angle 3 = \angle 4$ [alternate angles]

$OB = OC$ [given]

$\therefore \quad \Delta OBE \cong \Delta OCD$

[by ASA Congruency rule]

$\Rightarrow \quad BE = CD$ [by CPCT]

Also, $AB = CD$

[since, $ABCD$ is a parallelogram]

$\therefore \quad AB = BE$

**46.** (b) A. $\sqrt{x} - 12 = \sqrt{4} - \sqrt{x}$

$2\sqrt{x} = \sqrt{4} + \sqrt{12}$

$2\sqrt{x} = 2 + 2\sqrt{3}$

$\sqrt{x} = 1 + \sqrt{3}$

$\therefore \quad x = (1 + \sqrt{3})^2 = 4 + 2\sqrt{3}$

B. $\sqrt{x} + \sqrt{x - \sqrt{1 - x}} = 1$

$\sqrt{x - \sqrt{1 - x}} = 1 - \sqrt{x}$ ...(i)

On squaring Eq. (i) both side, we get

$x - \sqrt{1 - x} = 1 + x - 2\sqrt{x}$

$\Rightarrow -\sqrt{1 - x} = 1 - 2\sqrt{x}$

Again squaring both sides, we get

$1 - x = 1 + 4x - 4\sqrt{x}$

$\Rightarrow 5x = 4\sqrt{x}$

$\Rightarrow \sqrt{x} = \frac{4}{5} \Rightarrow x = \frac{16}{25}$

C. $x = 3 + 3^{1/3} + 3^{2/3}$

$\Rightarrow x - 3 = 3^{1/3} + 3^{2/3}$

Cubing both sides, we get

$(x - 3)^3 = (3^{1/3} + 3^{2/3})^3$

$\Rightarrow x^3 - 9x^2 + 27x - 27$

$= 12 + 3(3)(x - 3)$

[since, $3^{1/3} + 3^{2/3} = x - 3$]

$\Rightarrow x^3 - 9x^2 + 18x - 12 = 0$

**47.** (b) I. True,

II. False; Area of parallelogram

= Base × Height

III. True,

Area of Parallelogram $PQRS$

= Area of Parallelogram $SPQR$

$\therefore PQ \times ST = SP \times UQ$

$20 \times 12 = PS \times 16$

$\Rightarrow \quad PS = \frac{20 \times 12}{16} = 15\,\text{cm}$

**48.** (a)

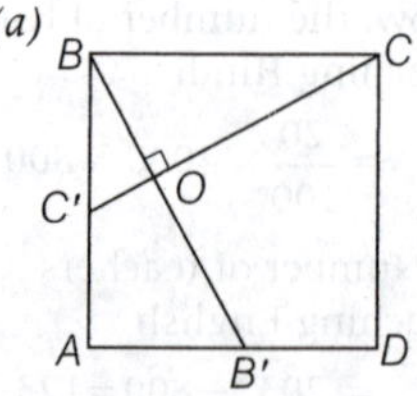

Consider $\Delta AB'B$ and $\Delta BC'C$,

$\angle BAB' = \angle CBC'$ [90°]

$AB = BC$

[side of square]

and $BB' = CC'$ [given]

$\therefore \quad \Delta AB'B \cong \Delta BC'C$

[by RHS Congruency rule]

**49.** (b) Volume of the water accumulated the reservoir

$18\text{ h} = (120 \times 75 \times 2.4)\text{ m}^3$

Let speed of water = $v$ km/h.

Then, width of cuboid $b$

$= \frac{20}{100} = \frac{1}{5}\text{ m}$

Height $= h = \frac{20}{100} = \frac{1}{5}\text{ m}$

Length of water cuboid formed in 18 h

$= 18\,v\text{ km} = 18 \times 1000\,v\text{ m}$

$= 18000\,v\text{ m}$

Volume of the water accumulated in reservoir in 18 h

$= 18000v \times \frac{1}{5} \times \frac{1}{5}$

$= 720\,v\text{ m}^3$

$\Rightarrow 720v = 120 \times 75 \times 2.4$

$\Rightarrow \quad v = \frac{120 \times 75 \times 24}{720 \times 10}$

$= 30\text{ km/h}$

**50.** (a) We have,

$x - y + (\sqrt{x} + \sqrt{y}) = 10$

On putting $x = 9$

$9 - y + (\sqrt{9} + \sqrt{y}) = 10$

$9 - y + 3 + \sqrt{y} = 10$

$y - \sqrt{y} - 2 = 0$

Let $\sqrt{y} = a$, then

$$a^2 - a - 2 = 0$$
$$(a-2)(a+1) = 0$$
$$a = -1, 2$$
$$\Rightarrow \sqrt{y} = -1, 2$$

If $\sqrt{y} = 2$

$\Rightarrow \quad y = 4$

[$\because \sqrt{y} = -1$ is not possible, so neglect it].

## Practice Set 2

**1.** (c) Let sides of two regular polygon be $x$ and $2x$.

Interior angle of first regular polygon

$$= \left(180° - \frac{360°}{n}\right)$$
$$120° = 180° - \frac{360°}{x}$$
$$\Rightarrow \frac{360°}{x} = 180° - 120$$
$$\Rightarrow \frac{360°}{x} = 60°$$
$$\Rightarrow x = \frac{360}{60} = 6$$

Now, measure of each interior angle of the second polygon

$$= 180° - \frac{360°}{2x}$$
$$= 180° - \frac{360°}{2\times 6}$$
$$= 180° - 30°$$
$$= 150°$$

**2.** (d) Here, $x = 2$, $y = -1$ is a solution of the equation

$$2x + 3y = k.$$
$$2\times 2 + 3(-1) = k$$
$$\Rightarrow 4 - 3 = k$$
$$\Rightarrow k = 1$$

**3.** (d) Given, $ABCD$ is a parallelogram.

$\therefore \angle A = \angle C = 55°$

Also, $AEFG$ is a parallelogram.

$\therefore \angle A = \angle F = 55°$

**4.** (b) In right $\Delta ABC$,

$$AB = \sqrt{(AC)^2 + (BC)^2}$$
$$= \sqrt{(12)^2 + (16)^2}$$
$$= \sqrt{144 + 256}$$
$$= \sqrt{400} = 20 \text{ cm}$$

Now, in $\Delta ABC$,

Let $a = 48$ cm, $b = 52$ cm and $c = 20$ cm

$$\text{Now,} \quad s = \frac{a+b+c}{2}$$
$$= \frac{48 + 52 + 20}{2}$$
$$= \frac{120}{2}$$
$$= 60$$

Area of $\Delta ABC$

$$= \sqrt{s(s-a)(s-b)(s-c)}$$
$$= \sqrt{60(60-48)(60-52)(60-20)}$$
$$= \sqrt{60\times 12\times 8\times 40}$$
$$= 480 \text{ cm}^2$$

and area of $\Delta ABD$

$$= \frac{1}{2}\times AD\times BD$$
$$= \frac{1}{2}\times 12\times 16$$
$$= 96 \text{ cm}^2$$

$\therefore$ Area of shaded region

= Area of $\Delta ABC$– Area of $\Delta ABD$

$= 480 - 96 = 384 \text{ cm}^2$

**5.** (a) Given, $\angle CBE = 130°$

$\angle ADC + \angle ABC = 180°$

[$\because ABCD$ is a cyclic Quadrilateral]

$\angle ADC = 180° - \angle ABC = \angle CBE$

$\angle ADC = 130°$

**6.** (a) Let the cost of 1 orange and 1 apple be $x$ and $y$ respectively.

I. $5x + 3y = 43$ ...(i)

II. $x =$ ₹ 5 ...(ii)

$$\therefore \quad 5\times 5 + 3y = 43$$
$$\Rightarrow 3y = 43 - 25$$
$$\Rightarrow y = \frac{18}{3}$$
$$\Rightarrow y = ₹\ 6$$

$\therefore$ Total cost of 4 oranges and 5 apples $= 4\times 5 + 5\times 6$

$$= 20 + 30$$
$$= 50$$

**7.** (c) Let the length and width be $a$ and $b$ of rectangle. New length after decrease $= \frac{1}{2}a$

Similarly, width after increase

$$= \frac{(100+50)}{100}b$$
$$= \frac{3}{2}b$$

Original area $= ab$

New area $= \frac{3}{4}ab$

$\therefore$ Decrease in area

$$= \frac{ab - \frac{3}{4}ab}{ab}\times 100 = 25\%$$

**8.** (d) (A)

$$x^{a^2b^{-1}c^{-1}} \cdot x^{a^{-1}b^2c^{-1}} \cdot x^{a^{-1}b^{-1}c^2}$$
$$= x^{a^2b^{-1}c^{-1} + a^{-1}b^2c^{-1} + a^{-1}b^{-1}c^2}$$
$$= x^{\frac{a^2}{bc} + \frac{b^2}{ac} + \frac{c^2}{ab}}$$
$$= x^{\frac{a^3+b^3+c^3}{abc}} = x^{\frac{3abc}{abc}} = x^3$$

[If $a + b + c = 0$, then $a^3 + b^3 + c^3 = 3abc$]

Thus, (A) is false and (R) is true.

**9.** (d) For figure

$\angle APB = \angle QPR = 40°$

[vertically opposite angles]

By using the theorem, that the angle subtended by an arc at the centre is double the remaining part of the circle.

$$\therefore \quad \angle AOB = 2\angle APB$$
$$= 2\times 40° = 80°$$

**10.** (a) Since, $ABCD$ is a parallelogram.

$\therefore \angle A + \angle B = 180°$

[co-interior angles]

$$\Rightarrow 75° + \angle DBA + 60° = 180°$$
$$\Rightarrow \angle DBA = 45°$$

In $\Delta$ ADB,

$$\angle A + \angle ADB + \angle DBA = 180°$$
$$\Rightarrow \angle ADB = 180° - 75° - 45°$$
$$= 60°$$

**11.** (d) $BP = BC$ [Given]

$\therefore \angle BCP = \angle BPC = y^\circ$

Now, $4x^\circ = 2y$ ...(i)

[exterior angle property]

Also, $\angle 2 = x^\circ$ ...(ii)

[Alternate interior angle]

$y^\circ = x^\circ + 48^\circ$ ...(iii)

[exterior angle property in $\Delta PCD$]

From Eqs. (i) and (iii),

$2x = x + 48^\circ \Rightarrow x = 48^\circ$

$\therefore \angle BDQ = 48^\circ + \angle 2$

$= 48^\circ + x = 96^\circ$

**12.** (b) A. $16^{3/4} = (\sqrt[4]{16})^3 = 2^3 = 8$

$= (8^{\frac{1}{3}})^3$

B. $81^{0.25} = 81^{1/4} = \sqrt[4]{81} = 3$

C. $\sqrt[3]{625^{0.75}} = \sqrt[3]{625^{\frac{3}{4}}} = 5$

**13.** (a) $\angle ADE$ and $\angle ADC$ are supplementry angles

Thus, $\angle ADC = 89^\circ$

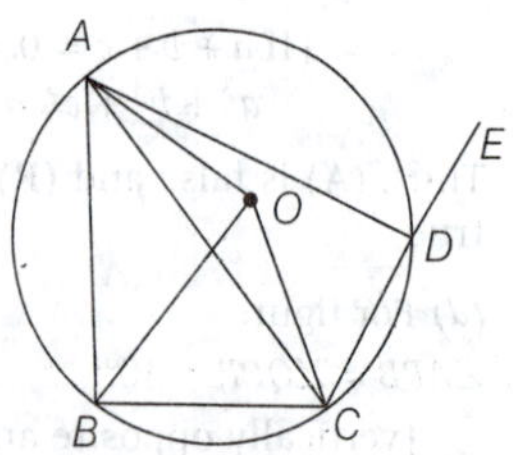


Similarly,

$\angle ABC = 180^\circ - \angle ADC$

$= 180^\circ - 85^\circ = 95^\circ$

In the circle,

$OA = OB = OC$

Thus, $\Delta AOB$ is an isosceles triangle

$\angle OAB = \angle OBA = 30^\circ$ [given]

Since, $\angle ABC = 95^\circ$

$\angle OBC = \angle ABC - \angle OBA$

$= 95^\circ - 30^\circ = 65^\circ$

Similarly, In $\Delta BOC$

$\angle OBC = \angle OCB = 65^\circ$

and

$\angle BOC = 180^\circ - \angle OBC - \angle OCB$

[by angle sum property]

$\angle BOC = 180^\circ - 65^\circ - 65^\circ$

$\angle BOC = 50^\circ$

$\Rightarrow \angle AOB = 180^\circ - 2\times 30^\circ = 120^\circ$

$\angle AOC = \angle AOB + \angle BOC$

$= 120^\circ + 50^\circ = 170^\circ$

As, $\Delta AOC$ is an isosceles triangle.

Thus, $\angle OAC = \dfrac{180^\circ - 170^\circ}{2}$

$= \dfrac{10^\circ}{2} = 5^\circ$

**14.** (b) $\angle CEB = \angle EFQ$

[corresponding angles]

$\Rightarrow 25^\circ + y = 75^\circ$

$\Rightarrow y = 50^\circ$

Also, $\angle FEB + \angle EFQ = 180^\circ$

[co-interior angle]

$(\angle FEG + \angle GEB) + 25^\circ + y = 180^\circ$

$\Rightarrow \angle FEG + 20^\circ + 25^\circ + 50^\circ = 180^\circ$

$\Rightarrow \angle FEG = 85^\circ$

In $\Delta EFG$,

$\angle FEG + \angle EFG + x = 180^\circ$

$\Rightarrow 85^\circ + 25^\circ + x = 180^\circ$

$\Rightarrow x = 70^\circ$

**15.** (b) Draw $HK$ parallel to $AB$,

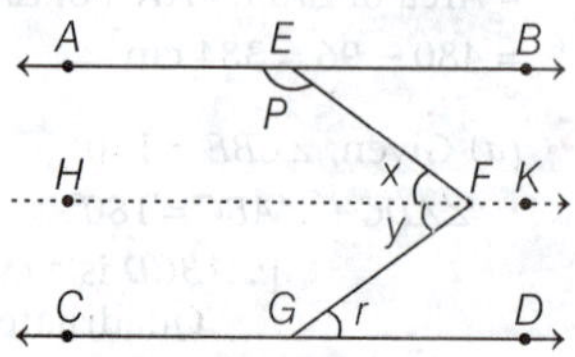


Let $\angle EFH$ be $x$ and

$\angle HFG$ be $y$ such that $x + y = q$

$p + x = 180^\circ$

[co-interior angles]

$y = r$

[alternate interior angle]

Adding both equations,

we get

$p + x + y = 180^\circ + r$

$\Rightarrow p + q = 180^\circ + r$

$[\because x + y = 2]$

$\Rightarrow p + q - r = 180^\circ$

**16.** (b) After plotting $\Delta ABC$, graphically, it clearly seen that $\Delta ABC$ is isosceles triangle

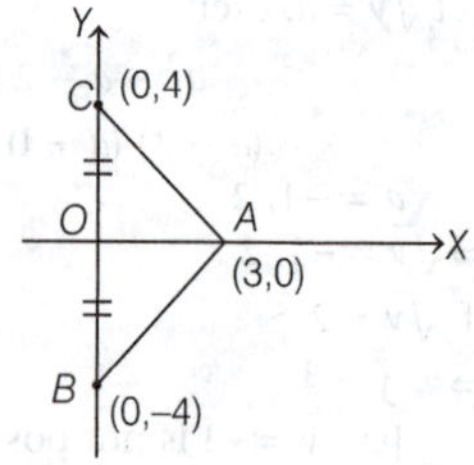


Area of $\Delta ABC = \dfrac{1}{2}\times AO \times BC$

$= \dfrac{1}{2}\times 3\times 8$

$= 12$ sq units

**17.** (a) $\sqrt{(x+y+z)(x+y-z) + (z^2 - x^2 - y^2) - 2xy}$

$= \sqrt{x^2 + y^2 + 2xy - z^2 + z^2 - x^2 - y^2 - 2xy} = 0$

**18.** (d) I. In $\Delta WRS$,

$\angle 2 = 180^\circ - \angle WRS - \angle RSW$

[by angle sum property]

$= 180^\circ - 90^\circ - 25^\circ$

$= 65^\circ$, which is correct.

II. $\angle 2 = \angle 3 = 65^\circ$,

[vertically opposite angles]

which is incorrect.

III. In an isosceles $\Delta WUV$,

$\angle 4 = \angle WVU$,

$\therefore \angle 4 = \dfrac{180^\circ - 65^\circ}{2}$

$= 57.5^\circ$, which is correct.

IV. Similarly, In an isosceles $\Delta VWR$ $\angle VRW = \dfrac{65^\circ}{2} = 32.5^\circ$

Now, $\angle 5 + 90^\circ + \angle VRW = 180^\circ$

[supplement]

$\angle 5 = 180^\circ - 90^\circ - 32.5^\circ$

$= 57.5^\circ$, which is incorrect.

**19.** (b)

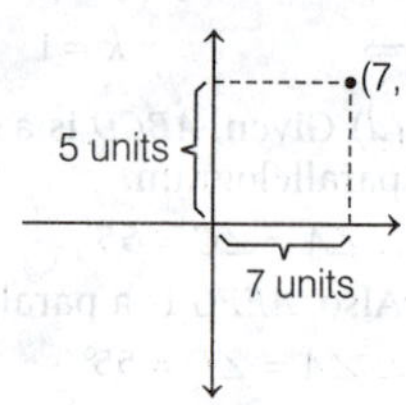


Other than this, since direction is not given, so points can be $(-7, 5)$, $(-7, -5)$, $(7, -5)$.

**20.** (*a*) Let $r$ be the radius of base of the hemispherical dome.

Since, circumference of base of the hemispherical dome

$= 17.6$ m

$\therefore \quad 2\pi r = 17.6 \Rightarrow r = 2.8$ m

Now, curved surface area of the hemispherical dome

$\Rightarrow 2\pi r^2 = 2 \times \frac{22}{7} \times (2.8)^2$

$= 49.28 \text{ m}^2$

Given, cost of painting

$100 \text{ cm}^2 = ₹\ 5$

$\Rightarrow$ Cost of painting

$= \frac{100}{100 \times 100} \text{m}^2 = 5$

$\Rightarrow$ Cost of paining 1 $\text{m}^2$ of dome $= ₹\ 5 \times 100 = ₹\ 500$

$\therefore$ Total cost of painting entire hemispherical dome

$= 500 \times 49.28 = ₹24640$

**21.** (*d*) $x = \frac{\sqrt{6}+\sqrt{5}}{\sqrt{6}-\sqrt{5}}$ and $y = 1$

Now, $\frac{x+y}{x-y} = \dfrac{\frac{\sqrt{6}+\sqrt{5}}{\sqrt{6}-\sqrt{5}} + 1}{\frac{\sqrt{6}+\sqrt{5}}{\sqrt{6}-\sqrt{5}} - 1}$

$= \frac{2\sqrt{6}}{2\sqrt{5}} = \frac{\sqrt{6}}{\sqrt{5}}$

**22.** (*a*) Since, alternate angles between parallel lines are equal

$\therefore \quad \angle x = 30^\circ$

**23.** (*c*) An equation is said to be homogenous if its each term had equal degree.

Thus, by definition option (c) is a homogeneous expression.

**24.** (*c*) Let $0.\bar{6} = x$

Then, $\quad x = 0.666 \ldots\ldots \quad \ldots$(i)

$10x = 6.666 \ldots\ldots \quad \ldots$(ii)

Subtracting Eq. (i) from Eq. (ii), we get

$9x = 6 \Rightarrow x = \frac{2}{3}$

Let $0.\bar{7} = y$,

then $y = 0.777, \ldots\ldots\ldots \quad \ldots$(iii)

$\Rightarrow 10y = 7.777 \quad \ldots$(iv)

Subtracting Eq. (iii) from Eq. (iv), we get

$9y = 7 \Rightarrow y = \frac{7}{9}$

Now, $x + y = \frac{2}{3} + \frac{7}{9}$

$= \frac{6+7}{9} = \frac{13}{9} = 1.\bar{4}$

**25.** (*a*) $A$ has coordinate $\equiv (3, 2)$

Point $Q$ has coordinate $\equiv (3, -2)$

{ordinate will change sign}

Now, after reflection of point $Q$ about $Y$-axis the ordinate will not vary but abscissa will change sign.

$\therefore$ Coordinates of final point $\equiv (-3, -2)$

**26.** (*c*) $x^3 + 6x^2 + 11x + 6$

$= x^3 + 5x^2 + x^2 + 5x + 6x + 6$

$= x^3 + 5x^2 + 6x + x^2 + 5x + 6$

$= x(x^2 + 5x + 6) + (x^2 + 5x + 6)$

$= x(x + 3)(x + 2) + 1(x + 3)(x + 2)$

$= (x + 3)(x + 2)(x + 1)$

$\therefore$ The polynomial is divisible by both $(x + 1)$ and $(x + 2)$.

**27.** (*b*)

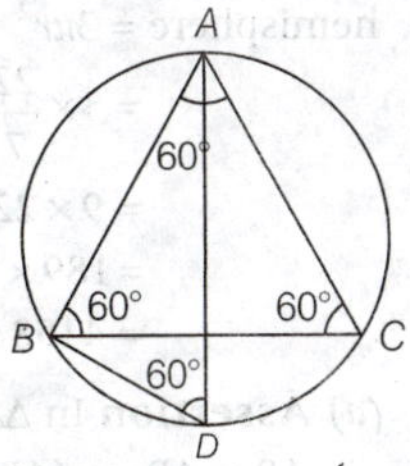


$\angle ADB = 60^\circ = \angle ACB$

[$\because$ angles in the same segment are equal]

**28.** (*b*) $\frac{\sqrt{5}+\sqrt{3}}{\sqrt{80}+\sqrt{48}-\sqrt{45}-\sqrt{27}}$

$= \frac{\sqrt{5}+\sqrt{3}}{4\sqrt{5}+4\sqrt{3}-3\sqrt{5}-3\sqrt{3}}$

$= \frac{(\sqrt{5}+\sqrt{3})}{(\sqrt{5}+\sqrt{3})} = 1$

**29.** (*b*) (3, 4) is a solution of $3kx + 5y = 2$

$\Rightarrow \quad 3k(3) + 5 \times 4 = 2$

$\Rightarrow \quad 9k = -18$

$\Rightarrow \quad k = -2$

**30.** (*d*) Points with abscissa positive are of the form (+,+) and (+,–).

They lie in I and IV quadrants respectively.

**31.** (*a*) In $\Delta KK'M$ and $\Delta LL'M$

$\angle KK'M = \angle LL'M = 90^\circ$

$KK' = LL'$ [given]

and $\angle K'KM = \angle L'LM$

Hence, $\Delta KK'M \cong \Delta LL'M$

[by ASA Congruency rule]

**32.** (*d*) $3b + 1 = 2 \Rightarrow 3b = 1 \quad \ldots$(i)

and $2a - 3 = 5$

$\Rightarrow \quad 2a = 8 \quad \ldots$(ii)

Subtracting Eq. (ii) from Eq. (i), we get

$3b - 2a = 1 - 8 \Rightarrow 3b - 2a = -7$

**33.** (*b*) Let the unit's place digit be $x$, and ten's place digit be $y$,

$\therefore$ Number $= 10y + x$

The new number of ten reversing the digits.

$= 10x + y$

$\therefore$ Difference

$= (10y + x) - (10x + y)$

$= 9y - 9x = 9(y - x)$

According to the question,

$9(y - x) = 27$

$\Rightarrow \quad y - x = 3$

$\Rightarrow \quad y - 3 = 3$

$\Rightarrow \quad y = 6$

$\therefore$ If one of the digit is 3, then other is 6.

**34.** (*b*) Let the base radius and the height of the cone be $r$ and $h$ respectively.

Let the slant height of the cone be $l$.

$\therefore \quad C = \pi rl = \pi r\sqrt{r^2 + h^2}$

and $V = \frac{1}{3}\pi r^2 h$

$\therefore 3\pi Vh^3 - C^2h^2 + 9V^2$

$$= 3\pi\left(\frac{1}{3}\pi r^2 h\right)h^3 - \pi^2 r^2 (r^2 + h^2) h^2 + 9\left(\frac{1}{3}\pi r^2 h\right)^2$$

$$= \pi^2 r^2 h^4 - \pi^2 r^4 h^2 - \pi^2 r^2 h^4 + \pi^2 r^4 h^2 = 0$$

**35.** (*d*) Arc $RS$ subtends 44° at the centre $O$, so it subtends half the angle at $Q$ i.e.

$$\angle RQT = 22^\circ$$

$$\Rightarrow \angle PRQ = 90^\circ$$

$$\therefore \angle TRQ = 90^\circ$$

Hence, $\angle RTS = 90^\circ - 22^\circ = 68^\circ$

**36.** (*a*) We have, $p - q = \frac{10}{9}$

and $pq = 5/3$

Now,

$$(p-q)^3 = p^3 - q^3 - 3pq(p-q)$$

$$\Rightarrow \left(\frac{10}{9}\right)^3 = p^3 - q^3 - 3\times\frac{5}{3}\times\frac{10}{9}$$

$$\Rightarrow p^3 - q^3 = \frac{1000}{729} + \frac{50}{9} = \frac{5050}{729}$$

**37.** (*b*) $25x^2 - 30x + k$ is a perfect square

Thus, $D - 0$

$$\Rightarrow b^2 - 4ac = 0$$

$$\Rightarrow (30)^2 - 4\times 25\times k = 0$$

$$\Rightarrow k = \frac{900}{100}$$

$$\therefore k = 9$$

Hence, $k = 9$

**38.** (*a*) Radius of conical cap

$$= \frac{1.5}{2} = 0.75\text{ cm}$$

Thickness of conical cap

$$= 0.2\text{ cm}$$

Volume of each conical cap

$$= \frac{1}{3}\pi r^2 h = \frac{\pi\times 0.75\times 0.75\times 0.2}{3}$$

Radius of new cone $= \frac{4.5}{2} = 2.25\text{ cm}$

Height of new cone = 5 cm

Volume of new cone

$$= \frac{\pi(2.25)^2\times 5}{3}$$

Number of conical cap

$$= \frac{\text{volume of new cone}}{\text{volume of each conical cap}}$$

$$= \frac{\pi\times 2.25\times 2.25\times 5\times 3}{\pi\times 0.75\times 0.75\times 0.2\times 3}$$

$$= \frac{225\times 225\times 5\times 10}{75\times 75\times 2}$$

$$= 3\times 3\times 5\times 5 = 225$$

**39.** (*d*)

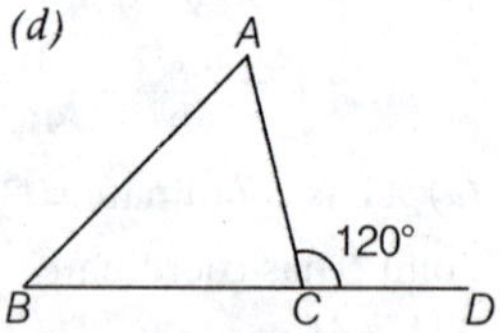


$$\angle BAC + \angle ABC = 120^\circ$$

[by exterior angle property]

$$\angle BAC + \frac{2}{3}\angle BAC$$

$$\frac{5}{3}\angle BAC = 120^\circ$$

$$\angle BAC = \frac{120^\circ\times 3}{5} = 72^\circ$$

**40.** (*b*) Volume of the hemisphere $= 19404\text{ cm}^3$

$$\Rightarrow \frac{2}{3}\pi r^3 = 19404$$

$$\Rightarrow r^3 = \frac{3\times 19404\times 7}{22\times 2}$$

$$\Rightarrow r^3 = (21)^3 \Rightarrow r = 21\text{ cm}$$

Total surface area of hemisphere $= 3\pi r^2$

$$= 3\times\frac{22}{7}\times 21\times 21$$

$$= 9\times 22\times 21$$

$$= 189\times 22$$

$$= 4158\text{ sq.cm}$$

**41.** (*a*) **Assertion** In $\Delta ABP$,

$$AB = AP \Rightarrow \angle APB = \angle ABP$$

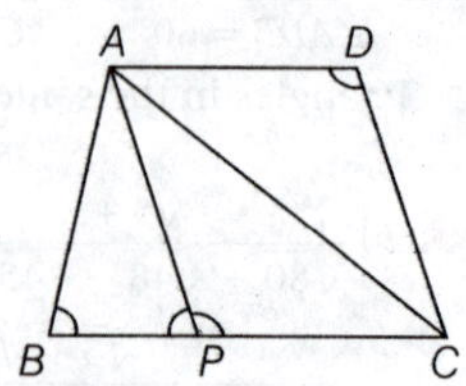


$APCD$ is a parallelogram

$$\angle APC = \angle ADC$$

$$\angle APC + \angle APB = 180^\circ$$

[linear pair of angle]

$$\angle ADC + \angle ABP = 180^\circ$$

Thus, $ABCD$ is a cyclic quadrilateral because the sum of either pair of opposite angles of a cyclic quadrilateral is 180°.

**42.** (*d*) Let the breadth be $x$.

In $\Delta ABD$,

Pythagoras theorem

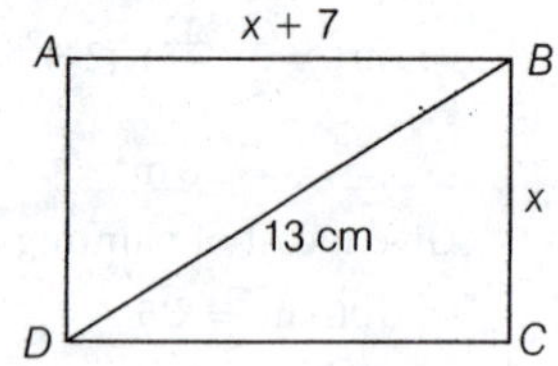


$$(x+7)^2 + x^2 = 169$$

$$2x^2 + 14x + 49 = 169$$

$$2x^2 + 14x - 120 = 0$$

$$x^2 + 7x - 60 = 0$$

$$(x+12)(x-5) = 0$$

$$x = 5$$

$\therefore$ Perimeter of rectangle

$$= 2\times(5+12) = 34$$

Now, length of equilateral triangle $= \frac{34}{3}$

$\therefore$ Area of equilateral triangle

$$= \frac{\sqrt{3}}{4}\times\left(\frac{34}{3}\right)^2$$

$$= \frac{17\times 17\times\sqrt{3}}{9} = 55.6\text{ cm}^2$$

and area of triangle

$$= \frac{1}{2}\times\text{Base}\times\text{Height}$$

Hence, both (A) and (R) are false

**43.** (*a*) $2^{-m}\times\frac{1}{2^m} = \frac{1}{4} \Rightarrow \frac{1}{(2^m)^2} = \frac{1}{4}$

$$\frac{1}{2^m} = \frac{1}{2}$$

$$\Rightarrow m = 1$$

Now, $\frac{1}{14}\left[(4^m)^{\frac{1}{2}} + \left(\frac{1}{5^m}\right)^{-1}\right]$

$$= \frac{1}{14}\left[(4)^{\frac{1}{2}} + \left(\frac{1}{5}\right)^{-1}\right]$$

$$= \frac{1}{14}(2+5) = \frac{1}{2}$$

**44.** (c) $BD = \sqrt{AD^2 + AB^2}$

$= \sqrt{(9)^2 + (40)^2} = 41$ cm

$\therefore$ For $\Delta DBC$,

$s = \dfrac{28+15+41}{2} = 42\,\text{cm}$

$\therefore$ ar $(\Delta DBC)$

$= \sqrt{s(s-a)(s-b)(s-c)}$

$= \sqrt{42 \times (42-28)(42-41)(42-15)}$

$= \sqrt{42 \times 14 \times 1 \times 27}$

$= 14 \times 3 \times 3 = 126\,\text{cm}^2$

$\text{ar}(\Delta ABD) = \frac{1}{2} \times 9 \times 40$

$= 180\,\text{cm}^2$

$\therefore$ Total area $= (126 + 180)\,\text{cm}^2$

$= 306\,\text{cm}^2$

**45.** (b) Coordinate of $P = (-5, 3)$

and $Q = (-5, m)$

According to the question,

$m + 3 = -5 - 5$

$\Rightarrow m + 3 = 10$

$\Rightarrow \quad m = -10 - 3 = -13$

**46.** (b) $\text{ar}(\Delta AFB) = \frac{1}{2}$ ar

[parallelogram $ABCD$]

{$\therefore$ Areas between same parallels and same base}

ar (parallelogram $ABCD$)

$= 2 \times \text{ar}(\Delta AFB)$

$= 2 \times \text{ar}(\Delta DCB)$ ...(i)

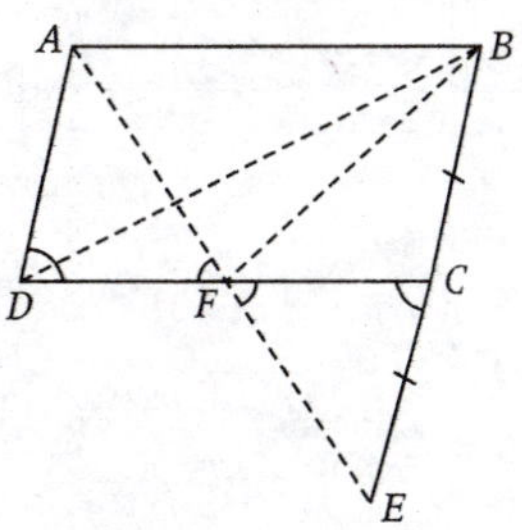


In $\Delta ADF$ and $\Delta ECF$,

$\angle AFD = \angle EFC$

[vertically opposite angles]

$\angle ADF = \angle ECF$

{alternate angles}

$BC = CE = AD$

$\therefore \Delta ADF \cong \Delta ECF$

{by AAS congruency}

$\therefore \quad DF = CF$

ar (parallelogram $ABCD$)

$= 2 \times \text{ar}(\Delta DCB)$

$= 2 \times 2 \times (\text{ar}(\Delta DFB))$

$= 2 \times 2 \times 3 = 12\,\text{cm}^2$

**47.** (a) Let $h$ cm be the height of the cone.

We have,

Diameter of spherical canon ball = 28 cm

Radius of spherical cannon ball = 14 cm

Diameter of the base of the cone = 35 cm

Radius of the base of the cone equal $= \frac{35}{2}$ cm

Volume of the cone = Volume of spherical cannon ball

$\frac{1}{3} \times \pi \times \left(\frac{35}{2}\right)^2 \times h = \frac{4}{3} \times \pi \times (14)^3$

$\Rightarrow \quad \left(\frac{35}{2}\right)^2 h = 4 \times (14)^3$

$\Rightarrow h = \left(4 \times 14 \times 14 \times 14 \times \frac{2}{35} \times \frac{2}{35}\right)\text{cm}$

$h = \left(4 \times 2 \times 2 \times 14 \times \frac{2}{5} \times \frac{2}{5}\right)$ cm

$= \frac{896}{25}$ cm $= 35.84$ cm

**48.** (d)

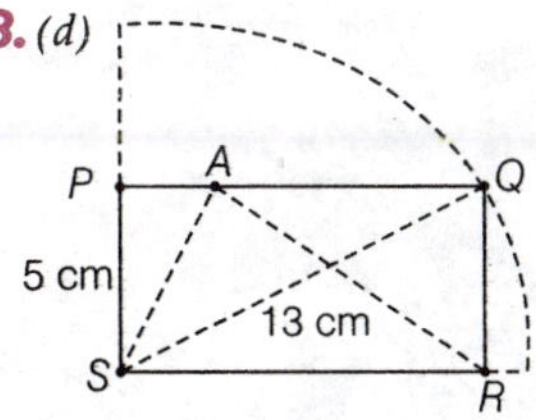


$\text{ar}(\Delta ARS) = \frac{1}{2}\text{ar}(PQRS)$ ...(i)

$QS^2 = PS^2 + PQ^2$

$\Rightarrow \quad PQ = \sqrt{QS^2 - PS^2}$

$= \sqrt{(13)^2 - (5)^2} = 12\,\text{cm}$

$\therefore \text{ar}(\Delta ARS) = \frac{1}{2} \times 12 \times 5$

$= 30\,\text{cm}^2$

**49.** (i) (a) We have, $x = 2\sqrt{5} + \sqrt{3}$ and $y = 2\sqrt{5} - \sqrt{3}$

$\therefore \quad xy = (2\sqrt{5} + \sqrt{3})(2\sqrt{5} - \sqrt{3})$

$= (4 \times 5 - 3) = 17$

$\therefore \quad x^2 + y^2 = (2\sqrt{5} + \sqrt{3})^2 + (2\sqrt{5} - \sqrt{3})^2$

$= 20 + 3 + 4\sqrt{15} + 20 + 3 - 4\sqrt{15}$

$= 46$

$\therefore x^4 + y^4 = (x^2 + y^2)^2 - 2x^2y^2$

$= (46)^2 - 2(17)^2 = 1538$

(ii) (c) We have, $x = \sqrt{3} + 3\sqrt{2}$ and $y = \sqrt{3} - 3\sqrt{2}$

$\therefore \quad xy = (\sqrt{3} + 3\sqrt{2})(\sqrt{3} - 3\sqrt{2})$

$= (\sqrt{3})^2 - (3\sqrt{2})^2$

$= 3 - 9 \times 2 = -15$

So, $x^2 + y^2 = (\sqrt{3} + 3\sqrt{2})^2 + (\sqrt{3} - 3\sqrt{2})^2$

$= 3 + 18 + 6\sqrt{6} + 3 + 18 - 6\sqrt{6} = 42$

$\therefore \quad x^4 + y^4 - 8x^2y^2$

$= (x^2 + y^2)^2 - 10(xy)^2$

$= (42)^2 - 10(-15)^2$

$= 1764 - 2250 = -486$

**50.** (b) Since, $M$ is the mid-point of $AB$.

$\therefore \quad AM = MB$

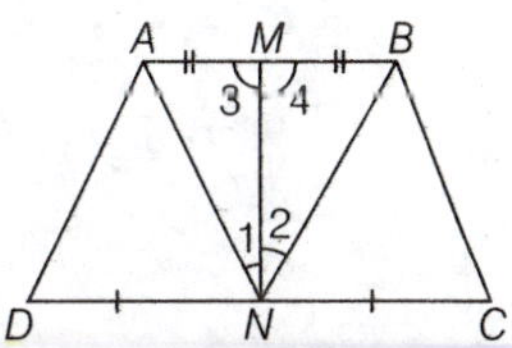


Now, in $\Delta AMN$ and $\Delta BMN$,

$AM = MB$

$\angle 3 = \angle 4$ {each 90°}

and $MN = MN$ {common side}

$\therefore \quad \Delta AMN \cong \Delta BMN$

{by SAS congruence rule}

$\angle 1 = \angle 2$ [by CPCT]

$\because \quad \angle 1 = \angle 2$

$\Rightarrow 90 - \angle 1 = 90 - \angle 2$

$\Rightarrow \quad \angle AND = \angle BNC$

In $\Delta ADN$ and $\Delta BCN$,

$AN = BN$

$\angle AND = \angle BNC$

and $DN = NC$

[$\because N$ is the mid-point of $CD$]

$\Delta ADN \cong \Delta BCN$

{by SAS congruence rule}

$AD = BC$ [by CPCT]